OF LAW AND THE WORLD

OF LAW AND THE WORLD

Critical Conversations on Power, History, and Political Economy

DAVID KENNEDY AND

MARTTI KOSKENNIEMI

Harvard University Press

Cambridge, Massachusetts London, England 2023

Printed in the United States of America

First printing

Publication of this book has been supported through the generous provisions of the Maurice and Lula Bradley Smith Memorial Fund.

Library of Congress Cataloging-in-Publication Data is available from loc.gov

ISBN 9780674290785 (cloth)

Contents

Preface

The seven texts that follow are the edited transcripts of conversations we had between August 2021 and February 2022 while the COVID-19 pandemic kept us homebound. We had met long before—at a diplomatic cocktail party in Geneva in the mid-1980s, where we found ourselves in a corner talking about Adorno and the intellectual disappointments of our chosen field. In the years since, we remained close friends, followed similar career paths and intellectual trajectories: some time as practicing lawyers, some time in and around intergovernmental institutions, and a lot of time in the academy as teachers and scholars. We often collaborated at conferences and in mentoring and lecturing. We both had the sense that we were pursuing similar themes and political projects in our scholarship, if in different ways. We were often linked as European and American "critical" voices in international law.

The pandemic gave us the opportunity to talk about those common themes and experiences. We were as intrigued by the overlaps as by the differences. What is or was "international law," how important or interesting does it seem today? What does it have to do with hegemony, with unequal patterns of ownership, authority, and status? We've both focused on the intellectual history and current practice of legal professionals in the North Atlantic. But what about everyone else? What happens when we bring all this to "political economy," a more salient frame for critical reflection now than when we began? There is a theme running through all of the discussions: What do we mean by "critical" or "heterodox" when thinking about law, power, or history?

Our different professional, intellectual, and personal experiences inflected our engagement with these shared themes. Martti was a career diplomat in the Finnish foreign service before entering Finnish university life.

David has taught at Harvard University his entire career, with breaks in a variety of professional settings. Though we often read the same critical literatures, the intellectual and political worlds in which we did so were miles apart.

Talking things through, like teaching, does clarify one's thoughts. It also opens questions that don't find answers, reframes ideas, and raises themes in different ways as conversations unfold. As in any good conversation, we returned to issues and examples, reshuffling what we had to say about them. We drew on our prior work along the way; full citations are provided in the list of works at the end of this book. Much of Conversation 2 was first published by Routledge in *Leading Works in International Law,* edited by Donna Lyons.

We have both been blessed with wonderful mentors, colleagues, students, friends, and family throughout our careers. The more we talked together, the more often we felt their influence and support. We are particularly grateful to Tiina Astola, Arnulf Becker, Dan Danielsen, Janet Halley, Karen Knop, Päivi Leino-Sandberg, Ralf Michaels, Vasuki Nesiah, Guy Priver, and Jonathan Zimmerman for their engagement with this project and comments on early drafts. Our thanks also to Ian Malcolm, our commissioning editor at Harvard University Press, who encouraged us to turn these conversations into a book. We would like to pay special tribute to Karen Knop who passed away suddenly and unexpectedly as we were finishing the manuscript. Karen was an altogether exceptional academic whose contributions had enriched our community for many years. Her comments on this manuscript were absolutely invaluable.

We make no overarching argument in these conversations. Rather, we share the thoughts that emerged as we talked with one another; we hope there will be something refreshing in the format. One conclusion that became clear is how tenuously we had scratched the surface of these issues in forty years of scholarly work. There remains so much to understand, and the objects for critical reflection are not standing still. We hope these conversations will stimulate your own critical thinking. We'd love to hear what you discover.

David and Martti, Cambridge and Helsinki, 2023

OF LAW AND THE WORLD

CONVERSATION ONE

What Is Critique?

David: I'm looking forward to these conversations, although it's hard to know where to begin thinking about law's many roles in the world. We're both thought of as "critical" voices in "international law"—perhaps we should start by talking a bit about those two terms.

For me, "critique" is less a method or school of thought than a posture of skeptical suspicion toward some object—like international law. If you have that kind of animus, you harness what you can find in the traditions you have been exposed to and have at it. That can be thrilling in itself—the intellectual and social pleasures of mobilizing your resources to unravel what seems a worthy opponent. Quite conventional modes of analysis can be as useful as self-consciously critical ones; legal traditions as helpful as weird things you find in other disciplines. So, normal-science doctrinal or historical analytics, perhaps with a bit of psychoanalysis or postmodern literary theory or economic policy argument or Marxist social theory dragged in from here or there.

My sense is that for people who start with a critical orientation, a lot depends on whom they encounter, in writing and in person. In my experience, critique has been as much a collective as an individual project—I had mentors and students and partners in crime all along the way, you among them.

How do you see the critical impulse arising and finding expression?

Martti: It's always been more of a sentiment or a posture than technique. But it does resonate with well-known twentieth-century literatures—Marxism, psychoanalysis, critical social theory, structuralism, poststructuralism, and so on. Those readings have invited us to be suspicious of the most common explanations or justifications for legal—or international legal—phenomena. Somehow these explanations miss the massive injustice of the world, or may even have been complicit. But what has prevented at least me from becoming a loyal adherent to any one of the critical literatures is that their critical power leads in different directions, they almost cancel each other out. While the older criticisms seek depth, and fundamental structures behind surface phenomena assumed to tell us what was *really* going on, newer ones rather focus on the surface, taking language and its phenomenological experience seriously. Or, if you wish, the older ones invite looking *behind* legal language and experience; the newer ones take that language or experience superseriously. I have both fallen into a *marxisant* interpretation of social forms as obstruction over "real relations"—but also celebrated a culture of formalism and taken legal language and cultural form very seriously.

I think the adoption of both an in-depth and a surface critique should be understood biographically, in view of what happened in social and legal thought in the 1970s and 1980s. The critical animus arose as a generational thing, a political thing, and an intellectual thing. My generational influences have to do with having come of age in northern Europe as a politically active person in those decades. Domestic politics appeared stale. But the world was burning—imperial wars, the East-West opposition, famine and revolution in Africa, cultural revolution in Europe—the 1960s generation began to penetrate public institutions. The prior generation's experience with the war had become distant. Together with student friends we read all kinds of new social and political theory, organized meetings, and used student unions and party organizations to demand the expansion of democracy in education. One felt that everything was political—stale, but also just a tipping point away from some real transformation.

David: And somehow the political and the intellectual flowed together, no?

Martti: Yes. We wanted to become intellectuals by reading Popper, Kuhn, Habermas, and the Frankfurt school, trying to find new ways of political engagement. At the law school in Turku, my hometown, hermeneutics was big. That was, in retrospect, a good thing because it highlighted the absence of philosophical and political ambition in Anglo-American analytical jurisprudence. But to be an intellectual, hermeneutics was there to attack—structuralism was a first response, then Foucault and Derrida and poststructuralism. These were analytically tougher than hermeneutics and did not endorse social-democratic politics. All this was good preparation for later engagement with international law, I now realize. Learning about the debates in critical legal studies in the United States gave these intuitions a powerful edge, and eventually led me from diplomacy to the university. The context of the US law school must have been radically different.

David: Formation is certainly key. Where one starts, who else is around. The literatures you mention were all in the air in American universities in the 1970s. I'd probably add those my high school teachers considered canonical—Weber, Freud, Sartre, French movies—well, and Bergman—and postwar theologians like Niebuhr, Tillich, Buber. My senior year, I somehow became fascinated by the structural linguistics of Benjamin Whorf and Edward Sapir. And by people like Marcuse, brought to our attention by the 1960s generation. So much had just happened in the late 1960s and early 1970s. By the time I got to college, it was easy to feel belated, needing to catch up. I don't think I was "critical" in any sense other than that of my milieu in college. But everyone I knew thought the war was a catastrophe—morally, politically, in every way—and showed the mendacity of the whole political class. And then there was Watergate—a gripping story that might just unravel the whole thing . . . but didn't.

It was only in graduate school—and particularly law school—that I encountered people—and ideas—that were *against* the established order in a more profound and interesting way. I had studied history and international relations in college, and I remember reading Kuhn's theory of "paradigm shifts" in scientific reason and the Left/progressive world systems and dependency ideas prevalent in international relations at the time. In law school came strands of European social theory making their way into American law in what was becoming "critical legal studies" as it reworked and extended heterogeneous legacies in American legal thought.

Like the high school material, these were all resources when I later tried to think differently myself—which I probably wouldn't have done, certainly not in so determined a way, had I not found mentors and playmates who were also trying to do that. Mentors really were crucial; it wasn't like the unfolding of ideas. The student paper that became my first international law article owed a great deal—certainly in tone and structure—to my first-year encounter with Roberto Unger.[1] *International Legal Structures*—like my critique of Henkin—was self-consciously modeled on Duncan

Kennedy's "Form and Substance in Private Law Adjudication," which Duncan gave me to read in the first weeks of law school.[2] I've ended up in a lifelong conversation with Duncan, whose ideas, provocations, and intellectual support are present in everything I've written.

Martti: You invoke heterogeneous literatures, to be sure, but joined by the message that things were more open-ended than people thought, there was room for experimentation. But to make use of the possibilities the political had to be closely aligned with the intellectual, as you said.

David: It didn't seem that way to me at first; critical ideas were fascinating, but their relationship with politics was elusive. Entering law school, I was a typical progressive student of my generation interested in international affairs. The world seemed terribly unjust. Becoming a lawyer promised a career doing something about it. And international law was the field with the right name, so I studied it. International law did purport to talk about—even adjudicate—big things I was interested in: Vietnam, nuclear weapons, the North's responsibilities for economic development in the South, American interventions in Latin America, the Iran hostage crisis, the energy crisis, and more.

The international law mavens I encountered wore their commitment to international law on their sleeves, each elaborating a theory about how it worked and why it was important. At the same time, they seemed to realize the legal materials were thin, contradictory, intellectually weak. They were good-hearted, cosmopolitan people; the field's weakness seemed to demand fealty that it might one day be strong.

Martti: I think much of international law in Europe is still like that, but go on.

David: They had a hard time ginning up persuasive arguments about the things they purported to consider. There were competent, but not particularly compelling, international legal arguments both for and against the legality of nuclear weapons or invading Vietnam or placing mines in Nicaraguan harbors or sharing wealth with the South or nationalizing natural resources or . . . the list went on. International lawyers seemed content with that—or lacked the cultural authority to insist that one or the other argument was the sounder one. They were ready to acknowledge that Iran raised a good point about American interventions that should mitigate or justify the seizure of hostages, just as the United States raised a good point about the broader context of threat it felt was posed by the Sandinistas' authority in Managua. Each international legal professional had his own, often idiosyncratic position on such things—as on the bindingness of international law and a host of other questions. But why listen to any of them in particular?

More than that, talking about any of these things in legal terms seemed to miss the point: Should arguments about the "legality" of American bombing have any weight in one's ethical assessment of the Vietnam War? And yet, people kept doing it. Leading international lawyers seemed more concerned with promoting the status of international legal argument itself than doing anything with it. It wasn't just the people. The doctrinal and theoretical materials seemed more like arguments *for* international law than efforts to engage the world. Which gave the whole field a "doth protest too much" feel.

For all that, international law seemed a reasonable place to take on the sensibilities of the post-Vietnam culture of rulership. The glory days of postwar "best and the brightest" were over; the certainties and moral self-confidence that would saturate the elite after 1989 or the recommitment to formalism, managerialism, and empirical social scientific expertise that followed were all impossible to imagine. And critiquing a weak discipline had its advantages. The only difficulty was explaining to anyone else why it was worth bothering about.

But, Martti, let me ask you more directly what you were *against*. The international law notables of the time became my target—Louis Henkin first, and then many others. Looking back, it was a strange choice. I found these men quite sympathetic—cosmopolitan gentlemen in an otherwise terribly parochial academy and profession. And, yet, disappointing. If I critiqued them, maybe I'd make them stronger—maybe they'd even thank me, bring me into their world.

Martti: What was I *against*? A surprisingly hard question. Like you, I had all the views that a progressive law student would have—and the right adversaries. But my encounter with international law was different from yours. I joined the foreign ministry in 1978, where many of my closest colleagues and superiors were left lawyers with an anticapitalist and development agenda. I was not against them; on the contrary, I admired their activism: pushing environmental issues, women's rights, legal items related to the New International Economic Order. But I did come to suspect that the tools they, too, worked with—international law, human rights, United Nations (UN) diplomacy more generally—were not up to the job. I also learned eventually that they were not representative of the wider diplomatic and legal world. The international law establishment—people I met at UN conferences, professors whose books I had begun to read—had no critical awareness. Nothing would ever change if it were up to them. Their self-image as authorities on justice and equality was sometimes outright revolting. But I did not credit this to their malevolence; I got along with everyone pretty well. It was just that international law went nowhere near to meeting their official expectations. (I later learned that maybe they did not actually have such expectations, and I reflected on that predicament at the end of the 1990s in "Between Commitment and Cynicism.")[3]

David: How such a weak field kept going—I struggled with that in a student paper that became "Theses about International Law Discourse."[4] I proposed that international law was failing as a practical project—becoming weaker as it became more complex and prevalent—because "it is not meaningful to speak of a particular solution to a legal problem as having been compelled by a line of reasoning. It is not true that some arguments, because of their content, are more convincing or persuasive than others."[5] What kept it going was a failure to see how contradictory and indeterminate it was. The 1970s had a kind of "last days of Pompeii" feel—the oil crisis, economic disarray—and I imagined international law would unravel as folks came to see its weaknesses. In my first historical article, "Primitive Legal Scholarship,"[6] I proposed a parallel: after the Reformation split the field, an entire legal worldview fell apart as the indeterminacy of its modes of reasoning became apparent. Maybe this too shall pass.

I was off base on both counts. International law kept going precisely because it was so open-ended. Awareness of all those contradictions didn't make it fade away. I had probably been too influenced by Thomas Kuhn's argument that a scientific consensus could suddenly shatter as awareness of its limitations rose to prominence.[7] And by Roberto Unger's apocalyptic invocation of the contradictions in 'liberalism.'[8] An early object lesson in the false starts that seem to go with intellectual work. There have been a lot of those!

Duncan Kennedy's structuralism pointed in a different direction—more Lévi-Strauss. Modes of cultural interpretation don't collapse around their contradictions but function by transforming contradictory alternatives—the "raw and the cooked"—into adjacent alternatives, which seemed to resolve the tension.[9] Learning to be a competent legal reasoner meant knitting conclusions out of a field of gaps, conflicts, and ambiguities. Perhaps resolving contradictions by elision, transformation, denial, or deferral was, as I put it in *International Legal Structures,* the "subtle secret of its success."[10] That didn't make it a good thing, but it explained something of how it worked. And explaining how it worked in this sense seemed a critical thing to do—as if it worked by not noticing these recurring antinomies and elisions. My short initial piece on Henkin was like that, as I recall, describing how his text seemed to work, to sound plausible—how it knit contradictory impulses together, deferred or promised resolution of tensions it couldn't resolve, things like that.

That international law worked precisely because elites understood and managed its weakness also made sense of some early reactions to my work—as if patting me on the head and saying, "Yes, yes, dear boy, it's contradictory. I mean, what did you expect?" And if you said, "Yeah, but it's an exercise of power and isn't grounded the way it claims," folks would say, "Well, are you surprised to find that law is an exercise of power? Perhaps it doesn't always work, but the goal to bring the world into the rule of law is a pretty noble project, don't you think? Join the team."

Martti: Sorry to interrupt, but I wanted to say that I do recognize that reaction, though I interpret it a little more charitably. So not only "Yes, dear boy, it is contradictory" but also genuine gratitude for having been given an explanation for something that colleagues *knew* but for which they had no explanation. The indeterminacy critique may sound flattering because it suggests that legal work is really hard, the materials never suffice, there is always choice, and, as you would say, responsibility involved for those acting through law. Things really get more interesting once the analysis moves forward to those actual choices, demonstrating that if they are not logical entailments from the law but from something like patterns of normal behavior among the legal class or the structural bias of an institution, then hostility may sometimes step in, though not necessarily.

Nor is there always hypocrisy. I think practitioners have a really complex, though often not very clearly articulated, sense of what we have called the "politics of international law." But it is often hard in discussions to address the substance of that complexity; there is a powerful conservatism in the field, an unwillingness to deal with a problem that nevertheless is part of any professional experience. I suppose hypocrisy or cynicism may be a part of this, but I would rather look for some other frame of explanation.

David: On my side of the Atlantic, they weren't grateful in that sense—they were confident they had always already known about the worm at the heart of being. They were more puzzled. What did I see that was new? I don't think Henkin probably liked my saying, "You fudge a lot of contradictions," but I don't think others found it surprising or particularly telling. They were worried about real problems; here I was fiddling with words.

I thought a structuralist map of the field's materials was like a secret decoder ring—everyone would want one. But no mainstream teacher seemed to. Their project was another one: adumbrating sophisticated arguments for their specific case-by-case good judgment. They weren't turning over cards from a structuralist deck, they were meditating on the just outcome for a particular situation. Here critical inquiry may have strengthened my professional capabilities, but at some loss to my participation in the habitus of professional practice.

So I'm less sure about their sense of responsibility. They were proud to be acting in the world—if only by making international legal arguments. But conjuring with contradictory materials to generate the experience of their authority was also a way of eliding responsibility. "It wasn't me, it was the law."

Still, we can start to see the entanglement of the field's internal structure and external impact. We've each sometimes pursued "internal" and "external" critique as separate paths—the materials are indeterminate, the world impact unfortunate—but the distinction confuses as much as it clarifies. We've also both argued that the internal structures of expert materials and practice have an impact, certainly on the authority of mandarin speakers which itself helps the haves come out ahead. More than that, a universalizing language that promises virtue while mud-wrestling contradictory objectives into reasoned analysis can have a legitimating, hegemonic effect.

I tried to figure out the embedded conservatism you describe by looking for blind spots and biases one regime at a time: human rights, European law, international economic law, comparative law, law and economic development. Again, a lot of false starts and shifts in strategy—each field opened to critical inquiry in a different way. Nevertheless, whatever their specific deformations, each purported to be about equality and turned out to be about hierarchy. In each case, for all the contradictory plasticity of materials, some kinds of problems and some voices were off the table and out of sight. By promising to "take everything into account," these elite practices consolidated their authority while keeping what they didn't consider offstage. Along the way, the reasoning and outcomes that emerged strengthened one ideological or material interest over others.

Martti: The external side of our critiques—as you call it—was always more tentative, more vulnerable, than the internal. Showing gaps and contradictions in the law, once you learned how to do it, became easy. So was the demonstration that, despite this, coherent patterns of decision arose everywhere in practice. Legal institutions operated in quite predictable ways. That was, after all, the very problem: the same people continued to win and lose over and over again. If that was not the outcome of legal reasoning (because it was contradictory and full of gaps), then it had to result from something else—a *structural bias*. But what did that consist of, and how did it work? This was a much harder nut to crack.

Showing that the system did not (internally) have a leg to stand on, was empty or self-contradicting, alone went nowhere to show that it is evil or that its consequences are unjust. External critique was needed. But we both hated it if critique offered itself as dogma, promising something like a true and righteous alternative to a false and evil mainstream. Things were more complex than that. Moreover, external critique rarely worked unless it could tap onto a corresponding suspicion or malaise in the interlocutor, a readiness to question existing biases. Even then, commitment to the system may override such initial suspicions, or be translated into mild reform rather than engagement with the frame.

Another thing I want to underline is the rhetorical and linguistic dimensions of our early criticisms. We were both influenced by the "linguistic turn." I was quite stunned at how powerful structuralist analysis was in law and how utterly ignorant the field itself was of it. Here was now a demonstration of how it was possible to argue almost anything in a legally "correct" way. *From Apology to Utopia* even proposed a "grammar" of international legal language to show this.[11] That then raised questions about why it was then *these* and not *those* outcomes that were preferred by the field. The field responded to such questions in bland platitudes about balancing and scope of discretion. Ad-hocracy and pragmatism. This was disappointing.

David: No kidding.

Martti: So, although both of us stayed away from conventional methodological debates, this did not mean that we weren't influenced by certain methodological writings. For me, the linguistic and rhetorical approaches were and remain indispensable. They totally destroyed the kind of midlevel play with concepts that one frequently encounters in the texts of official doctrine, as well as the naive realism that imagined *effectiveness* or *compliance* as the law's main problems. They opened the way for a younger generation to look beyond the habitual forms of abstraction in the field. But I suppose there are big variations between local legal cultures in this respect.

David: Absolutely. It felt great to find a grammar and structure to the scattered and contradictory materials and idiosyncratic analyses that constituted the field. If it was all organized around irresolvable antinomies, the ad-hocracy of the practice was no surprise. On the other hand, *not* finding a structure helped preserve the professional experience and cultural authority of "sound judgment." In that sense, the organizational key did have critical bite and you could feel the resistance. Mandarins don't want you to find the decoder ring.

I want to stress that in figuring this out, *cohort* was as crucial as intellectual heritage and mentoring. I was pushed, educated, and led by students and colleagues with lots of diverse critical projects. You and I didn't come up with this stuff—certainly not on our own. We were borrowing, being pushed, learning, experimenting. Remember how alive heterodox, critical, theoretical, leftist thinking was in those years across the humanities and social sciences?

Martti: That is true, I used to leave office at lunch hour to visit the Academic Bookstore at the center of Helsinki at a time when they still carried loads of new social science and humanities texts. But for law, I would have continued reading European hermeneutics had I not—through you—encountered critical legal work from the United States.

David: I arrived at Harvard as the critical legal studies movement was underway. It was a fascinating, intoxicating mix of political and intellectual discussion, controversy and engagement, if overwhelmingly focused on American law. There was a lot of conflict and ferment in the American legal academy in those years—people were getting fired for pursuing critical inquiries. Writing a lot, even before I was quite sure what I wanted to say, was also a strategy to keep my job. Moving among fields, diving into high theory were others. The result was pretty scattered.

There were so many new influences in law schools then. I encountered David Trubek in graduate school and found a link between critical theory and development studies. When Guenter Frankenberg arrived in Cambridge from Habermas's institute to figure out what "critical legal studies" was all about he started a life-long conversation with German critical legal thought. Lots of us were trying to figure out what German critical theory and French "theory," as we called it—poststructuralism, postmodernism—could offer. Students who cut their teeth on that at college brought it to legal studies—Nathaniel Berman probably the best example in our field. He was constantly challenging me to be more "pomo"—I remember visiting him in Paris and being taken around to hear all the French heavyweights.

There was a lot of cross-disciplinary borrowing, also in law. Jerry Frug and I worked together closely in those years—he on the city, me on the international. In the American academy, literature and cultural studies were hotbeds of theory. Jerry and I went to their events and I tried my hand at cultural criticism in the then fashionable style. I remember critical race theorist Pat Williams and I spending a couple of summer weeks together in New Hampshire studying with literary theorists Marge Garber and Barbara Johnson—even Derrida showed up—while I was writing "Spring Break" and she was writing *The Alchemy of Race and Rights.*[12]

Martti: Though Foucault and Derrida were big names in Europe, they did not translate into the kind of legal activism they spurred in the United States. I was nevertheless fortunate to come to legal theory in Finland where the influence of the philosopher G. H. von Wright had spurred a very lively, eclectic jurisprudential community. It may have been stalled politically by its unthinking commitment to Nordic social democracy and the welfare state, but in terms of intellectual analysis, it was, I think, the best Europe had to offer. I could not have produced my work without those readings from legal semiotics, systems theory, analytical hermeneutics, and versions of (Marxist and other) realism that were available at home. But only encountering US critical literature gave these readings a powerful edge.

David: At the same time, in the United States, feminist voices were bringing new critical tools to bear on the field, often starting by noting the absence of women in the worlds of diplomacy and international law, then asking how issues of concern to women were sidelined in the doctrinal materials and how insights from feminist theory—on the public/private split or the nature of patriarchal authority—could open lines of critical inquiry across the international law corpus. Feminist theory was as present as critical/French material—more urgent and conflicted, but very *present* in the academy, in the air. I remember Hilary Charlesworth, now a judge on the International Court of Justice, pressing me in class in the early 1980s. Clare Dalton and Mary Joe Frug were linking feminism with pomo theory—"postmodern legal feminism," they called it.[13] What Clare was doing with contracts I was trying with treaties. What Mary Joe was doing with legal doctrine I was trying to do with my experiences as a human rights advocate. In writing about the origins of the League of Nations, I foregrounded the role of women's movements, doubtless under their influence.[14] These were all parallel projects, which picked up steam with the next generation of students and colleagues—people like Karen Engle, Karen Knop, Kerry Rittich, Vasuki Nesiah, Ileana Porras, Annelise Riles, Helena Alviar, and many more.

I mention these people to stress the element of collaborative conversation in critique, at least as I've experienced it. In the 1990s, another generation of students brought an equally determined focus on the experiences of the third world with international law. Their target was less the North American international law canon than their own precursors—the earlier generations of third world intellectuals who became international legal scholars and institutional players.

For someone like Antony Anghie, the models and mentors—and opponents—were people like novelist V. S. Naipaul and the international lawyers Christopher Weeramantry, Muthucumaraswamy Sornarajah, or

B. S. Chimni, alongside T. O. Elias, Mohammed Bedjaoui, and the other leading legal figures of the decolonization generation. Tony insisted, like Hilary before him, that people like you and me come to terms with their critical priorities. Theirs was also a conflicted and intensely personal as well as theoretical space—lots of disagreements and alternate pathways among people like James Gathii, Makau Mutua, Balakrishnan Rajagopal, all of whom were students at Harvard, organized conferences, reading groups, debates.

And it went on like that. This kind of activity has an enormous impact—I know I tried both to read what they were reading and contribute to their projects. I've stopped naming names before the time the Berlin Wall fell—even mentioning these folks reminds me how many others there have been—right up to the present. I've really been privileged to be challenged and engaged by so many amazing students and colleagues.

Martti: You received those influences firsthand; reading about them in Finland, we kept wondering what to do with them. My partner, Tiina Astola, taught me always to ask "the woman question" in politics and at work; feminist legal scholarship was lively at the university, and some colleagues at the foreign ministry, including the head of the international law division, Holger Rotkirch, were committed activists. But the Nordic context prevented that from developing into a radical, oppositional voice. For good and bad, I suppose. Later on, perhaps inspired with what went on across the Atlantic, the situation changed; there is much less complacency now with the inherited gender politics of the welfare state. The same with development. *Law and society* and *reflexive law* were big in the jurisprudence department in the 1970s and 1980s but quite integrated into the social-democratic mainstream. The later focus on identity and colonialism has distanced academic work from what goes on in government. But it is hard to make generalizations. Europe is a varied terrain—Finland is not Poland, and neither is Spain nor France nor the United Kingdom. The struggles may be the same, but the arrangement of forces varies.

David: Indeed. And I know my experience at Harvard was hardly typical—worth mentioning, I think, because thinking critically really does take a village, as they say. At least in my experience, the pressures and challenges from all sides in those years got the pot boiling. As I recall, both feminists and third-worlders in those years seemed to find external questions more salient—it took some doing to interest them in the internal contradictions of North Atlantic legal thought. I think my engagement with them helped me figure out how the internal and external might be related. Kimberlé Crenshaw was at Harvard then as well, mentored by Derrick Bell and Duncan Kennedy as she helped build the network that became critical race theory. The early critical race work was also looking for links between the internal and external critiques of the dominant legal order.

This kind of challenge—and opportunity—continues. *Racial capitalism* has placed race at the center of international legal scholarship and revitalized a long tradition of Black and Pan-African thinking about international law. Feminist and third-worldist traditions have expanded and developed; they continue to press against the white male North Atlantic international law world. I'm also thinking of people bringing world systems analysis or contemporary Marxist modes of critique to bear—Susan Marks, Akbar Rasulov, and Tor Krever, among others in our field.

As the problems motivating critique shift to technocracy and the power of scientific and expert knowledge, Sheila Jasanoff and her colleagues have drawn international law folks into the science and technology studies tradition, just as those animated by the inequalities visible after the 2008–2009 economic crisis brought various notions of "political economy" back to the field. So, there's a lot going on, and it's much broader than what you and I have been doing.

In the end, the critical project is a set of relationships: there's an impulse, there's an object that feels worthy of critical energy, and then there are mentors and intellectual legacies offering tools of engagement and colleagues, interlocutors, fellow travelers who speed one along.

Martti: No doubt the names you mention have formed an exceptionally inspiring community for critical work. There were others, too, such as Anne Orford from Melbourne on Gunter Frankenberg from Frankfurt. But no matter where you originally start—international or domestic law; international relations; some branch of history, politics, or social science—the group of people who began to think of themselves as new approaches and, with your help, organized under that label in the early 1990s has grown into the most important center for critical legal reflection on the global "situation." Though, of course, differences and tensions remain. It is one thing if you are educated in the United States or if you come to the field as a Francophone student from, say, North Africa. Even though strong heterodoxies exist in both places, they are hard to join together. Mohammed Bedjaoui or Georges Abi-Saab are well known as anticolonial critics but may not feel sympathy toward poststructuralist lawyers from Harvard or Helsinki. There is some good recent work—I am thinking of Anthea Roberts—on the many lives of international law: how it is one thing in Australia and another in France, both yet different from, say, Russia or China.[15] If the mainstream in those places is wildly different, then so must heterodoxy be.

You reference the complex ways in which feminist and postcolonial agendas have become part of the core critical vocabulary—though in different ways in different places. In many locations, people doing classical public international law are barely beginning to adopt such vocabularies—even as they may possess long traditions of Marxist or otherwise leftist legal study. But conservatism appears in many forms and throws a long shadow over legal training in Europe. Critical strands that used to exist within early twentieth-century French or German public law, for instance, have left almost no mark in those countries' present-day internationalist mainstream.

I suppose that TWAIL—third world approaches to international law—has had most success penetrating the internationalist curriculum. Being in some ways *for* the decolonized camp has become an acceptable, even expected posture in many places. But materials produced under that label are very eclectic. Again, I suppose there is a generational issue. You and I were once reading Adorno and Horkheimer, but I am uncertain if today's TWAIL activists still do, especially if not educated in the West. The linguistic turn was a big thing in the 1970s and 1980s—but a neo-Marxist would hardly be impressed.

David: "Identity" has become a starting point for critique in a way it wasn't when we began. International law was itself *against identity,* where identity was national, but to critique international law was not at all to be *for* national identity. The idea was to get away from that choice, so empowering for both national and international elites. We now see "cosmopolitan" as an identity, but the "citizen of the world" self-conception was built as an escape from identity. The tragedies of the postcolonial state were so visible that it made the early generation of anticolonial international lawyers seem as much part of the problem as of the way forward. We could see why they had insisted on national sovereignty, but if it had been an emancipatory project, it came to seem an unfortunate step backward. At best, a necessary "stage" in development—how confident we were in the direction of progress!

It turned out that identity had a lot more to offer—and the critique of identity required a lot more than relegating it to the past. But I still see a divide between critique rooted in the consolidation and representation of an identity and critique rooted precisely in the undoing of that kind of rigidity. There, I'm on the identity against identity side of things, if we can think in those terms. Perhaps that's what folks bringing "queer" thinking to international law have in mind now.

Martti: I know. For any invocation of identity, one tends to look for the contrasting identity, trying to push the point that it can be both liberating and constraining.

David: Still, the initial critical impulse is usually rooted in identity, if by that we mean life experience. We've talked about our identities in that way. I have often met students from peripheral places or identity positions who became lawyers as an answer to their marginality, only to find their marginality confirmed rather than overcome. That can certainly ignite a critical impulse. Perhaps you're from east or central Europe and think the European Union (EU) is the answer; you go to Brussels to work and, yikes, maybe not. Or you come from an elite stratum in a third world nation and think human rights or development will give you an establishment seat at the global table—until your early professional experiences suggest otherwise. To make sense of that experience, you start looking around for new intellectual resources.

Let me raise a different question: What about audience? Critical analysis is a performative thing, and audience is one way to ask about the effect one seeks. I did start by writing *up* to mentors—both those with critical projects and those in the international law field. But I was never going to convince the leading figures that they were part of the problem. That does happen, but the result is usually a more sophisticated version of what they were doing before. We can both think of fields that absorb critical energy like a sponge. The World Bank website is a good example: they have an army of internal researchers who domesticate critical reflections on the development experience. The human rights movement is another. My little list of possible "dark sides" has been taught all over the place to aspiring human rights advocates as issues for which they may someday need a response.

I think my work got stronger after I gave that up and wrote *out* instead, building an audience among younger people who had come to international affairs and law with their own critical energy and were interested to see how someone else raised questions or opened avenues for critical understanding. But also writing to figure things out for myself—perhaps with the fantasy that someday someone will look back and say, "Well, at least someone saw what was happening." I was just dreaming, but one does when one writes.

And for you, Martti? There's an aspect to your work—the comprehensive weightiness of the tomes, quite unlike my own—that is its own performance.

Martti: I think I oscillated between the sense that from now on nothing can go as usual—and that, oh well, this kind of academic work is unlikely to have much effect. Perhaps by bombarding the establishment with thick tomes . . . But I was—still am—really interested in giving a clear expression to the importance of law for the way the world has become and to the capacity of legal analysis to illuminate the working of social and political institutions. My reluctance to produce policy proposals or explain critical positions by naming large structural causalities arises from an interest to speak to people who recognize the fragments I bring them as part of the injustice of the world but lack faith in any clear existing remedy. Or perhaps, like me, they feel that available remedies are "part of the problem." The audiences have always been students and colleagues with an already critical suspicion but nowhere to take it. It turns out there are lots of such people.

David: Surprisingly so.

Martti: As you know, I ended up writing *From Apology to Utopia* as a diplomat; no doubt I was thinking of my left colleagues as an audience. The idea was to try to show to them—and later also students—that having that suspicion was fine, that there was an explanation for why international law was so disappointing, and how it might be employed with less danger of bad faith. It did not have a ready-made set of solutions to world problems; on the contrary, it was often an aspect of them. But it could still be used for good purposes. I did not write against them; rather, more to impress them and invite them to think about it in a new way. In addition, I chose a rather 'philosophical' style for *From Apology to Utopia* because that's how my readings up to then had suggested critical intellectual work had to be carried out. Turns out it wasn't such bad choice. But I still like my later, more informal narrations better.

None of this has ever been very well thought out, I admit. But I had sympathy with many colleagues who were doing UN legal work and wanted to develop intellectual tools to assist that work in a critical direction. I did not have much of a sense about the strength of the structural biases and path dependencies. Also, my earliest assignments were with the UN Environment Programme, where there were lots of younger lawyers trying to think through this new field. It was a dynamic moment. Unlike elsewhere in the UN, I sensed that some sort of transformation was under way and believed that the kinds of critiques I was employing might be helpful in articulating its necessity and future direction.

David: I agree that, somewhat paradoxically, a key objective is to show how important law—and international law—really is in the reproduction of an unjust world. International lawyers—and they are not alone—often imagine law as a weak force, struggling to restrain or channel forces much larger than themselves. And legal expertise is often organized to highlight powers outside or prior to itself: the politicians legislated, the facts demand, the sovereign acted, the economy requires. It turns out that all these apparently external things rest on legal foundations that could be put together in various ways.

How do you see the relationship between critical analytics and good professional practice? I know your time in the foreign ministry has informed your writing. For me the privilege of being in professional circles—in Brussels, at the UN High Commissioner for Refugees (UNHCR), at Davos; but also at the faculty lunch table—has been crucial in understanding how the establishment authorizes and reproduces itself.

What do you think?

Martti: When we met for the first time at that diplomatic reception in Geneva in the middle of the 1980s, we realized we were both trying to find out whether the critical tradition, Horkheimer and Adorno, and so on, had anything to say for international law. I was reading *Dialectic of Enlightenment*,[16] a tremendously complicated book but one that discussed the weaknesses of enlightenment "reason" in a way that resonated with my own disillusionment with international legal institutions. Was there a way to salvage that reason somehow? And what if there wasn't? I had earlier had my infatuation with Freud and was thinking about that type of deep-structural analysis as the way to penetrate the obvious problems in "legal reason." But although those intellectual influences offered an attitude and a posture that was important, sure, it did not offer any clear way to operate with international law.

I think I have always preserved some sense that legal reason is somehow necessary and hopeful. And that what colleagues in the foreign ministry did in the 1980s was part of it. The immediately available forms of that reason were far from satisfactory, however. The formal analysis of relations between concepts and principles, the normal science of European law, was intellectually crude and abstracted from the problems of the world. (I am surprised over and over again at how much of that type of analysis still remains). But the problem-solving view of many US lawyers seemed to me no better; it took what other people thought were the important problems and relied on policy formulations that were no less problematic than legal concepts. But one could always think of these as styles of argument that were actually persuasive to different audiences. So why not engage in them? Legal practice did not display any strong relationship to reason, but one could distinguish more or less powerful cultural forms of it. And, paradoxically, the best critical moves also offered the most persuasive technical arguments. There was always a temptation to just go with the flow. Some of that may be visible in the fragmentation report I produced with the International Law Commission (ILC) in 2006—though that was, in part, a collective work.[17] But in the end, the deradicalization of critical techniques in this way was disappointing.

David: One can slide from critique to "being an ever better" professional, no question. So many of the tools are the same—a lot depends on the animus and formation a person brings to it. There is a Kantian *What Is Enlightenment?* dimension to both critical and professional practice: thinking things through, getting to the bottom of things, steering clear of unexamined beliefs, questioning assumptions—all bolted to a more modern pragmatism and the pluralism of notionally being open to all ideas.

Martti: Much critical work has to do with trying to manage the relationship between the rational and the irrational. (Or, does "manage" sound like one has already failed?) I have always wanted to find out how the subconscious operates in legal-bureaucratic practices—though without appearing like some New Age sage. I have wanted to stay close to the professional concerns of colleagues. This means often writing in such a way that what you have sometimes called an "abyss" opens in front of the reader and leaves them to decide what to do with it—engage, deny, look elsewhere, postpone. I am really reluctant—incompetent—to offer policy proposals or therapies. In some sense, even trying these is weirdly self-defeating. The traditional story suggests that the irrational should be put in a box in some way, so that the rational self can manage it properly. But surely that has been a failure; I think our work can provide a glimpse to what Jameson might call the "political unconscious," but it cannot provide much therapeutic advice.[18] For that I see no other remedy than just working with the materials without committing finally to any of the knowledge systems they emanate from, maybe playing them against each other.

David: Ah yes, the irrational, the unconscious, the sort of half-conscious—a great target, neither internal nor external in the way we've been using the terms. Are the habits of desire and aversion *outside* professional reason, part of the context, if in the head and heart? Or superinternal, alongside the grammar that organizes the overt material? Both? Something entirely different?

The literatures we were reading were all over the map. It was an eclectic and opportunistic search for ideas that might be useful—or just intriguing. I remember reading the Frankfurt school/critical theory literature on the "external" side and the structuralist/postmodernist literature on the "internal" side. They didn't play that well together. I wrote an article about how they complemented and contradicted one another, suggesting how you could draw on various strands of each.[19]

Before we leave this, I did want to say something about the word *deconstruction,* so much a part of our conversations then. The word has crept into the world, often to describe people like us or what we do. But mostly it just seems to mean having a negative attitude about something and pulling it apart in a pragmatic, normal science, way.

Martti: I know, *deconstruction*—a bogeyman of a word, isn't it? It is indeed something else than mere pragmatic disassembly and reassembly. What I took from it—aside from the hermeneutic of suspicion—was thinking of texts as prior to speech and analyzing them by identifying binary oppositions where one pole seems initially preferable to the other, and then showing that the preferred side was utterly dependent on the suppressed side. Like in the opposition of objective/subjective, reason/passion, or identity/community, even when we officially prioritize the former, it is actually ruled and conditioned by the latter. But then we learned, in moving from structuralism to *post-*, that the re-created binary could equally be deconstructed so that finally all texts would attain an interpretive fluidity that opened the grammar for legal argument and competence.

I know, this may not be Derrida, whose interests were metaphysical instead of methodological. But I could not avoid the temptation of using this manner of reading legal texts; it produced a welcome challenge to the search for bureaucratic consensus or translating that into a struggle over values and preferences. Deconstruction demonstrated very clearly how apparently rational legal arrangements can be destabilized by pointing to the passionate impulses underlying them; how something like *rule* or *right* can only exist and be affirmed against the background of a rather unthinking commitment to some project or preference. Such destabilization would then open possibilities for (legal) imagination and action.

David: There were—might still be—people who take Derrida or "deconstruction" to have proved that all texts are always indeterminate or some such thing. Often to have proved something they feel they already knew. I didn't take him that way. The real-life fluidity of a text depends on how rigid the people are who are doing the reading. You can whack away with your deconstructive mallet, and they just keep thinking their interpretation sound. That's that—one reason things are so sustainably reproduced, whatever the criticism. I came to think of deconstruction as an experience rather than a textual property or reading practice: the text's structural features made it susceptible to a reader suddenly finding it open where it had seemed closed.

Who knows what Derrida thought, but for me, deconstruction was also a hypothesis about how texts are put together which noted some strange but recurring features. First of all, *the ubiquity of oppositions*—as in the structuralisms we were familiar with—coupled with the hypothesis that often—always?—each element or pole contained something of its opposite, just as you said. And that the terms were in hierarchy—like presence and absence. So, for international law, *sovereignty* is sovereignty in a community and international *community* is a community of sovereigns. And yet, sovereignty has a kind of priority. Community seems artificial, sovereignty organic. Or, law is something made, politics something prior, something real, and so forth.

Three quick points emerged for me. First, legal argument often seems to work by *not noticing* the residual element of the thing decided *against* in the thing that was decided *for*. Highlighting that element can be a strategy for undermining or reinterpreting the apparent choice. Second, specific doctrinal or theoretical positions which may differ only marginally along a continuum can be interpreted—advocated or denounced—as expressing one or the other extreme. A subjective test of *opinio juris* would turn custom into treaty—that kind of thing. This gives legal argument both its all-or-nothing feel in debating marginal adjustments and its capacity to reframe the meaning of outcomes *both* as choices and, alternatively, as compromises. Third, the deconstruction hypothesis illuminates the unsayable: either pole in an absolute form. In sources of law doctrine, neither "God gave it to me" nor "I have the power to take it and so I will" establish valid norms. You have to temper your justice claims with their pedigree in sovereign consent or shared civilization and your authority claims in the recognized perquisites of your sovereignty.

Derrida made a great deal out of what he called the "dangerousness" of the shadow presence of the excluded term. I read this both as a danger to the stability of the text, its availability to be reopened, and as a psychological vulnerability in the practice of interpretation. A hypothesis, if you will, about the phenomenology of inhabiting such a textual universe, which was suggestive to me about the mindset of the legal elites of the time. It was not just that they knew you could make arguments either way and nonetheless felt making arguments one way or the other was a mark of professional pride or sophistication. They were also unsettled to be so disenchanted. The lurking danger of unraveling helped me understand the field's insistence on itself. And the obtuseness about irrational or unconscious matters—there was impassioned advocacy and pragmatic understanding of its limits, but no investigation of this doubled professional self. Or of the institutional or geographic distribution of piety and pragmatism which accompanied it. Take the UNHCR or Médecins Sans Frontières—pious with donors in headquarters and pragmatically savvy, even cynical, in the field.

Martti: You speak of deconstruction as a phenomenology, I learned it in the 1970s and 1980s as a form of textual critique. Either way, it opens up to an analysis of social relations: the mutual dependency of master and slave, or North and South, public and private, sovereignty and property. Although, in practice, everything happens between the opposite poles; if you do not have a clear view of the poles, you do not see the instability of that medium position either. For example, "sustainable development" may operate a compromise between "development" and "environment" for some time; but it remains unstable, a momentary truce, until either pole believes it now has the strength to overcome its opposite. I always read your *A World of Struggle* in this way: experts with projects struggling against countervailing projects—but meeting each other in some center of vagueness.[20] A lot takes place as boundary work where jurisdictional disputes are decided, though always only in a temporary manner.

Isn't legal education a kind of training to think of hierarchies as unstable? How else can lawyers learn to argue both sides of a dispute? And when they then have to take a position, they always end up in a rhetorical place that is really no place at all, the place of "reasonable solution," or "proportionality," of the "equitable principle." On the one hand, there is a fixed structure of concepts tied into a system; on the other, a smorgasbord of materials capable of being arranged in whatever ways. The conclusion emerges like a rabbit from a hat; it is right because . . . it is right. That's how modern legal discourse operates, that's how poetry operates, and that's why the *performative* aspect of being a good lawyer is so important, to make this all seem like the work of reason.

David: There we were, traveling very parallel tracks. In the American legal establishment of the mid-twentieth century, however, nobody was a formalist. Critical people often come to law thinking law's problem is formalism and dogmatism. Formalism has returned, but it wasn't the problem then. Everybody was a pragmatic, postrealist person who used legal materials *overtly* in a mode that you found only behind the scenes in UN practice. It always takes some work to bring students—particularly from Europe, I think—through the critique of formalism to the critique of antiformalism.

For the American antiformal jurist of the postwar era, a case could best be resolved through *sound judgment,* a loosely pragmatic and ethical mode of assessment rooted in an elite sensibility which bespoke cultivated experience that was a source of great pride. Good legal work took heterogeneous elements into account and required one to sort through a welter of contradictory considerations—legal, sociological, economic, ethical, and more—to come to a workable, if modest and tentative, solution. Oscar Schachter—who had had a kind of late Marxist training—went so far as to claim that a "method of contradictions" was at the core of professional wisdom. He lauded Dag Hammarskjöld for understanding the antinomies in the UN Charter and demonstrating that *diplomacy is operation within contradiction*. That was the sensibility of the "best and the brightest" and the leading edge of liberal thought about good government and reasonable elite practice.

All of which made structuralism useful for understanding elite reason. Elites were going around in circles, thinking they were superrealistic, pragmatic, fresh thinkers. Even the various theories of international law on offer at the time—naturalism, positivism, neonaturalism, neopositivism, and so on—seemed in a dialogue that rotated among closely related and opposed positions.

But let's turn to your historical work. I know we will talk more about this in a future conversation, but you've just finished a second massive work tracing the legal imagination about international affairs across centuries. Can you speak to this work as a critical practice?

Martti: Well, not all historical work is critical. The majority isn't. For instance, the kind of history that wants to present a discipline—say, *international law*—as a tradition maturing over time into its present fullness is not. Nor are the contrasting histories for which law is either a rational set of responses to needs of "globalization" or a passive legitimator of hegemony. Critical history would reject both such ways of believing that present law is somehow necessary—has the kinds of institutions, rules, or problems that it has—because they could not be any other way, because some social or cultural law has made it that way. Instead it presents law's truths as a result of conflict and focuses on law's role as constructive of the positions from within conflict is waged. It is not linear but kaleidoscopic; actions at a microlevel depend on but are not determined by macrolevel structures.

The Gentle Civilizer of Nations aimed to bring "modern international law" down from its metaphysical heights.[21] It invited readers to think of it as a project of a limited group of certain well-positioned late nineteenth-century Europeans. It did not represent any law of progress but simply the wisdom and stupidity of a handful of individuals, their experiences and desires, their ideas on themes such as war and commerce and government and race. There had been other ideas on those themes, but they did not converge as modern international law. I tried to provincialize the field in the way that Dipesh Chakrabarty has suggested, to describe something Europeans regard as obvious and timeless as actually quite specific and time bound, rather like wearing a tie.[22] This, I thought, might allow comparing modern international law with other ideas and projects that other people have had—or now have. *The Gentle Civilizer of Nations* questioned the competence of those men to speak *for the universe as a whole.*

David: I'm with you on that. You know the old saying, "The past is a foreign country." There's no question that historical inquiry can give you a perspective on today's "eternal verities." You can teach the history of international law against its present forms. Moreover, if people shifted the goalposts before, there's no reason it couldn't be tried now. They were, after all, just a bunch of people doing things—and we're a bunch of people too.

I've always found Michel Foucault's little essay opposing *genealogy*—for him a Nietzschean term—to the "search for origins" useful in marking the ambition of critical rather than conventional historical narrative.[23] For me, writing history critically has also meant telling a story that unsettles something in the target field's historical understanding. Foucault's essay suggests a bunch of ways to do this. So, recapturing accidents and moments of rupture can unsettle a field's sense of continuous (progressive) development or logical unfolding. Identifying the victories and defeats beneath current arrangements can clarify the distributive winner/loser quality of what is inhabited as universal progress.

Martti: Exactly.

David: I'm sure we'll talk more about this in our conversation about history, but just as an example, my "Primitive Legal Scholarship" aimed to contest the historical narrative of the Carnegie Endowment for International Peace's Classics of International Law series in which international law developed progressively from Suarez through Grotius into the twentieth century. Rather, I claimed, there were huge ruptures between the legal minds of large historical periods—the world of Vitoria and Grotius, of nineteenth-century "traditional" international law, of its twentieth-century "modern" version. The piece also aimed to reflect modern international law in the distant mirror of its pretraditional forebears, contrasting a world before the intellectual synthesis of the late nineteenth century with the world that emerged from its dissolution, and to explore the role of contradiction or opposition in the disintegration of a world view, for which the Reformation offered an excellent case study.

I agree that historical inquiry can provincialize what claims to be universal—for you, the men of 1873, and for me, the postwar UnitedStatesean international law tradition as the American establishment came to terms with its hegemony. Whether that mode of reasoning or its global influence *benefits* the United States is, of course, a different question. Again, a distinction I'm sure we'll come back to.

Sometimes you have to construct a tradition to critique it, and dramatize the *local* to place the purportedly *universal* within it. You made your little cohort of guys the *local* of European liberal international law cosmopolitanism. With Terry Fisher, I assembled *The Canon of American Legal Thought* to argue that there was such a thing as "legal thought"—to make something that seemed like reason itself be visible as a particular tradition—and to sketch a specifically UnitedStatesean tradition.[24] Only with that in mind could I make sense of the "Americanization" of postwar international law.

On the other hand, though, critical work sometimes aims to universalize what claims to be particular. Duncan Kennedy's "Three Globalizations of Law and Legal Thought" is a good example.[25] He argues that national legal elites repeatedly identified the specificity of their national legal culture in parallel terms—Mexican legal thought is *social,* about interdependence and solidarity, but then so is . . . one national tradition after another. He presents this as evidence for the globalization of a mode of legal thought—dressed up everywhere as something distinctively local.

Martti: Can I just take up something of what you just said about your very useful *Canon of American Legal Thought*—namely, that what you were doing was to contextualize legal thinking as a response to specific American questions and histories? Some people would say such an approach incapacitates you from making generalizations. If every legal thinking exists in a box, is time bound and culturally specific, then there is nothing more to be said about it. I know that neither one of us thinks in those terms. But I'd like to hear your view on that, as well as the connected issue of speaking in terms of *traditions*. So much of what we've learned and, I think, endorsed in our writing is that traditions are figments of imagination, constructed out of the wish to show the weight of something in view of the needs of the present. Are legal traditions "real"? And how do they relate to the contrasting desires to contextualize and to say something about the *longue durée*?

David: I suppose traditions can be both invented and real—self-dramatizations and identifications that have effects on the self and others. The Carnegie Foundation thought interwar international law would benefit from being understood as the inheritor of a tradition: a universal intellectual conversation that stretched from Vitoria right through to the League of Nations. They published those volumes to have an effect: to reframe what your "men of 1873" were doing in a universal *longue durée*. If that's what you're against, critical reflection will mean unsettling this claim: there wasn't a continuous tradition; it wasn't universal; the interwar period was sui generis, and so on. Claiming you think you're in a tradition, but you invented it; you think you invented that, but it repeats familiar moves; or you think that's universal, but it's parochial—that kind of thing. James Brown Scott was right to see a continuity in language across centuries; he was wrong to think it universal, and so forth. You've made claims of all these types.

Martti: Which suggests that good historical work proceeds both from the specific to the general and the other way around.

David: Indeed. Let me raise a somewhat different approach which may speak to your recent work *To the Uttermost Parts of the Earth*.[26] We have been speaking about critical narratives which aimed either to unsettle or to provincialize claims of the international law tradition—it was neither continuous nor progressive, and it was parochial rather than universal.

Lots of friends and fellow travelers have written critically about the international law tradition to situate it in a *political project* rather than a national or regional tradition. Not in the provincial world of European legal thought, for example, but in the European political project of colonialism. Or in the projects of American "empire," "neoliberalism," or "capitalism." We will surely come back to this in our conversation about hegemony and difference.

But, at a minimum, that kind of story identifies quite different continuities. For example, in "Primitive Legal Scholarship" I aimed to show that people in the "international law tradition" approached a problem they all identified as central to their tradition—"legal relations among equal sovereigns"—in radically different ways in the sixteenth to seventeenth, eighteenth to nineteenth, and twentieth centuries. You do something similar in *To the Uttermost Parts of the Earth,* allowing legal words like *jus gentium* to identify continuity in the "legal imagination" as it grapples with various matters across time. The existence of a legal advisory profession and the considerations of "situations we would now think of as international" offer a continuous thread across centuries in the book.

TWAIL scholars, starting with Tony Anghie, aimed to disrupt this frame by positing—interpreting—a different continuity.[27] He argued that if they were preoccupied with "relations among sovereign equals," it was only within Europe. Their larger preoccupation was understanding and facilitating European domination everywhere else, where sovereignty was a lack or a problem or a future rather than a magisterial political reality to be stabilized. You may be saying something similar about *dominium* and *imperium*—twin preoccupations, both conceptual and practical, over centuries of legal work. Placing these two at the center of the story makes the conventional international law story's focus on intersovereign relations alone a partial one.

I think it is important to distinguish Tony's argument from the claim that international law was an (important) tool for colonial projects. It may have been that too, just as American legal thought may have been a tool for constructing an American empire beneficial to some interests we might identify as American. But his claim that international legal doctrines and ideas were "forged in the colonial encounter" is about the internal preoccupations of the established European thinkers rather than their impact or influence. That said, his story posed the question, How significant *was* international law as an imperial tool or legitimation practice? You don't ask that question if you're still thinking in conventional terms about relations among sovereign equals.

I read your *To the Uttermost Parts of the Earth* as doing something similar. It poses a question: If international law was about the entanglement of commerce and sovereign power, partners in the imagination of legal actors, how significant was international law in the political economy of the world or in the emergence of various global capitalisms, from mercantile to industrial to financial, and so on? Again, two topics to which we'll return—but you wouldn't think about it this way if you imagine international law to have always been preoccupied with the worlds of diplomacy, statecraft, and war.

Martti: I'm glad you put it in those terms. I have often wondered about the character and power of the postcolonial position that seems to oscillate between the understanding of international law as terribly powerful and as terribly weak. The black legend that indicts international law as a key instrument of colonialism, imperialism, capitalism, or racism seems to me the exact reverse of the liberal progress narrative. Each depends on a separation of the law from "political power"—in the one case, law as a passive instrument, and in the other, as truth to power. Both overlook law's role in framing the thinking and acting where relations of power occur—the way in which legal words such as *empire, sovereignty, property,* or *contract* structure the conditions of struggle. Anghie's great contribution was to focus on the consolidation of a conceptual world that would frame the world of possibilities for subsequent generations. That's where its critical power lies.

To the Uttermost Parts of the Earth took the vocabularies of *sovereignty* and *property* and described how they then framed the relationships and hierarchies that arose in Europe and conditioned European expansion between the sixteenth and nineteenth centuries.

David: When we talk about law and 'political economy' I want to come back to exactly that.

Martti: Well, just to foreshadow, I began with the view of *people*—kings, royal counsel, noblemen, lawyers, theologians, professors, and polemicists of many stripes—with projects, on purpose refraining from postulating some historical law or a tradition guiding their hand and accounting for what they accomplished or failed to accomplish. This was not a history of a "discipline" or a tradition; it was about how certain legal words helped to justify, consolidate and critique the formation of hierarchical relationships from Europe to 'the uttermost parts of the earth'.

David: You said there was also a role—the 'legal adviser'—that could be located in all these situations, that carried the words along, developed them.

Martti: Yes. Legal advice was the confessional practice of law as faith. But I also wanted to construct a narrative that was not just about people and projects confronting each other by accident, as it were—ad hoc relationships of power and subordination. I wanted to provide readers who think in terms of large words, such as *imperialism, capitalism, nationalism, colonialism, religion,* and so on (as I also do), as well as complex ideas about politics and law, with fragments from the past that also speak to such words, but ambiguously. Sovereignty and property link to such large narratives in complex ways. I wanted to invite the readers to think about their own frames critically, without expressly adjudicating on them myself.

Of course, I was not neutral. I do think that some such large frames are more accurate than others, though not necessarily the same frame everywhere. But for reasons of style and persuasiveness, I wanted to leave space for the reader to think. Are the struggles over the meaning of sovereignty and property part of a history of colonialism or capitalism or of "order among states"? Of the law of nations, or of political economy? To some extent all of them, I think, as they penetrate each other. My effort was to describe them as a set of narratives about human pursuits and struggles, fear and ambition, good and bad choices. Whatever frame the reader might use to understand these moments, this was the kind of material it should cover.

David: That makes sense to me. They were operating *within* a world of sovereigns and property, and you follow the work that constitutes those frames. Let's talk a bit about the effects of legal "framing," as you called it, of law in the "conceptual foundations."

We know that legal doctrines and institutions directly distribute material and ideological stakes. That's a key reason people use them! Consolidating victories, legitimating power, excluding rivals, absolutely. Indeed, the idea that international law *legitimates* has become a go-to explanation for both its positive normative significance and its malevolence. We know that colonialism and slavery—like capitalism or global warming or war—are built on legal foundations. With different legal arrangements you would have different colonialisms, different slaveries, different capitalisms. Figuring out just how can be an appealing critical project. I tried to connect the humanitarian world to unsatisfying outcomes in *The Dark Sides of Virtue,* through interpretive reflections on my experience as a human rights advocate, in the European Communities' efforts to engage east and central Europe after 1989, in UNHCR's effort to establish a "right to asylum," and in the professional effort to constrain the incidence and instruments of war with international legal norms.[28]

But I suspect that in colonialism or capitalism or slavery or racism, international law is a relatively small part of the story, even taking its legitimation effects into account. Some doctrines, some actors, some arguments. But also, as you point out, some "conceptual foundations." In *The Gentle Civilizer of Nations* you suggest that the *legal vernacular* has some connection with the humanitarian promises and practices of colonialism. It didn't cause colonialism; perhaps it made colonialism worse. But perhaps also in some ways better. At a minimum, it expressed a colonial mentality, and we can read it as a kind of witness to colonialism.

Martti: And you can say the same about its relations to the other large words—capitalism, nationalism, racism, neoliberalism, and so on.

David: The world-making impact of this kind of conceptual framing is hard to establish but difficult to ignore. It may seem, for example, that if one interprets the world through the lens of *sovereignty,* European states have it while others don't, and you're on your way to domination. But there are lots of ways to get to domination by *recognizing* the sovereignty of the victim—treaties of cession, perhaps most obviously. What about *dominium* and *imperium* as conceptual foundations or language for professional imagining and acting? Can you say more about international law as a conceptual foundation? As a professional vocabulary with blind spots and biases? As a way of framing the world that establishes and disestablishes various powers?

You may have had a similar experience. When students hear I have a "critical approach" to international law, I think they expect me to dwell on international law's role supporting colonialism or slavery or war. They're not expecting a tour of international law's framing work—you have to be a sovereign to play, the international is public and cosmopolitan, the national private and cultural, and so forth—all of whose effects are more difficult to identify, more multiple, and, I suspect, more pervasive.

Martti: I agree that law's framing role is way too underappreciated, not only among students. But how, exactly, does a legal vernacular such as the one in *The Gentle Civilizer of Nations* operate as a frame? Obviously it does not *determine* anything in a causal fashion. So I linked it to a certain "sensibility" that reigned among a European elite at the time for which it gave an expression and which it also helped to uphold. In *To the Uttermost Parts of the Earth* I studied it by concentrating on the effects of the idioms of *sovereignty* and *property*. I drew attention, for example, to the late medieval moment, when a group of European lawyers began to imagine the king as not just a particularly powerful member of the nobility, a *suzerain*, ruling over his immediate vassals, but instead a *sovereign* whose authority extended over everyone in a territory. From there on, a whole discourse emerged on drawing the boundary of sovereign power in this way and that. It became a platform of struggle; did it lie with a person, a "nation," or a "state"? Did non-Europeans also possess it? The stakes were high. Another example from the end of the book: in the mid-nineteenth century, two vocabularies competed for understanding the law outside the state—those of "international society" and "civilization." The former focused on the "social question" and the latter on an idea of European cultural supremacy—and became, eventually, the ruling idiom (though "international society" never quite vanished from the scene). And, of course, there are loads of contemporary examples: Is "development" better framed as basic rights or an economic prosperity question? Should the government of the deep seabed be seen in terms of management or protection of marine resources? Is the development of an international communications and technology law about security or expanding access? The consolidation of a frame does not make struggle go away, of course, but does create a structural bias and limits the available outcomes.

This focus on framing leads some people to point their finger at us, inquiring about empirical evidence, statistics, causal hypotheses, and demonstrations. A first response, as we noted earlier, is that critique is not about problem solving, not least because the problems that the world offers us are often not the most important problems—they are problems for those who rule and often directed at strengthening that rule. But instrumental views also ignore the way that they themselves presuppose all kinds of framing maneuvers and decisions on meaning. When lawyers ask about "compliance," they naively suggest that it is obvious what there is to comply with. For critique, it is much more important to see how law gets interpreted in such a way that *this* instead of *that* action is the right way to comply. To focus on instrumental aspects is to assume that the question of what the law is an "instrument" for has already been resolved. But that is always a matter of political contestation, of reading the law—not a single rule but the legal system as a whole. And instrumental generalizations from policy are no less indeterminate than generalizations from rules.

David: On problem solving we *are* on the same page. It is so easy to focus on solving the problem rather than the process by which *this* became the problem to solve and *that* became the context for its solution. *These* became the responsible actors, *those* the tools of engagement.

Problem solving also frames the world, placing a corset of "what can be done by the available authorities in meaningful political time" around the analysis. At least in American social science, empiricism then further tightens the strings, shrinking *what we know* about problems and solutions to the barest minimum of demonstrable conventional—or "counterintuitive"—wisdom. As a result, a general commitment to international solution mongering leads to an underestimation both of the dark sides of the available solutions and of the wider range of things to try.

Critical reflections can sometimes reframe the situation to shift what seems the problem. A classic example: reframing "global warming" as something intensely local and distributional rather than universal and amenable only to "global" solutions for which there is no workable machinery.

You know, folks seem to remember the more concrete criticisms in *The Dark Sides of Virtue* and "The International Human Rights Movement: Part of the Problem?"[29]

Martti: Yes, it's wonderful, it's very didactic.

David: But the more elusive framing elements I found in those situations are harder to apply in other contexts. Thinking of east and central Europe as "behind" the West as you design a structure for accession to EU membership, that kind of thing. My objective was both to offer a *checklist for pragmatists* and to challenge pragmatic problem solving by unpacking these background conceptions. More broadly, there seemed to be a recurring tension between a pragmatism that lost track of ethical commitment and morally self-confident advocacy that lost sight of its dark potential. Here

I was thinking about Max Weber's essay "Politics as a Vocation," reinterpreting humanitarian activism as "political" in Weber's sense: demanding passion, an ethic of responsibility, and a sense of proportion. International problem solving encourages something else—a commitment to international problem solving *itself* and a flight from responsibility into normative and technocratic expertise. So we end up with an institutional structure that thinks it's about the world but turns out very importantly, to be . . .

Martti: About itself.

David: Exactly—that seemed characteristic of a lot of international institutional life. To serve the institution is to serve the world or even to reform the institution is to reform the world.

Martti: As you have often said, international institutions appear often more interested in their own endless reforms than in effects on the ground. That does fit with my experience with various UN bodies. Was any person anywhere outside the UN system affected by anything done by the ILC as I sat there in 2002–2006? Did these draft conventions, guidelines, reports, have any effect? Whose life was improved by the ILC exercise on environmental liability that began in the 1980s and ended up in the Draft Principles on Allocation of Loss in the Case of Transboundary Damage in 2006? Or the Draft Articles on Transboundary Aquifers in 2008? Posing such questions may be unfair, but it is characteristic that they were not asked in the UN system, or anyway, not pursued in a serious way. This is not to attack those who prepare such instruments, only to draw attention to the way institutions become self-absorbed so that still, after all these years, their principal concern lies with the production of texts with minimal attention to their effects on people's lives.

David: And not just texts like that—all kinds of professional work oriented to strengthening or reforming the profession, the language, the institutions themselves. Work on the self as if it were work on the world, that kind of thing.

Martti: Institutions tend to enchant those who work in them. How to fight it? Is it possible to become an insider with an external mindset, a critical mole? To alienate yourself from colleagues in this way—is that tenable? These questions are not normally treated within legal education. And yet, somehow paradoxically, excelling in what one does often requires the ability to think outside the box. So perhaps it has its more immediate reward. Anyway, I have come to think the mindset of institutional actors more important than institutional design.[30] That's why I find talk about global constitutionalism, for instance, often so uninteresting. I do not think process can save us. I am much more interested in how people *relate to* process and to each other through it. Maybe this is what you have meant when you have written about responsibility. Maybe it is simply raising the enchanted/disenchanted problem in another register.

David: Well, I've always preferred thinking *against* the box to thinking outside it! And you can do that anywhere.

Before we leave the discussion of effects, conceptual frames worth mentioning are the notion that equality and exchange are the normal patterns in international diplomatic and commercial relations rather than inequality and domination, and that global governance concerns the global public interest rather than distribution, winners and losers. Everyone involved *also* realizes that governance is a distributional enterprise. Lobbyists at the global level are as adept as any in Washington at identifying costs and benefits, winners and losers. But the background idea that diplomacy is among equals and trade is about bargains, exchange and the realization of universal "gains from trade" rather than their distribution is part of the enchantment.

Martti: The terms in which inequality gets spoken suggest that everyone is busily trying to correct it; no institution can afford not appearing to be in the "eradication of inequality" business. And yet, the Old World keeps getting reproduced every day. Why? I think Susan Marks made the relevant point already years ago.[31] Standard rights work pays too much attention to the victims and not enough to the perpetrators. Poverty does not fall upon people from the sky. It is the result of the choice of policies that benefit someone. I really like her question, "What if *exploitation* were a legal term"? The point is to bring out the structural nature of victimhood, of poverty as a result of structural dependency—one's loss is another's gain.

David: Yes, although I think Susan has been misunderstood on that point, because when you say "Don't focus on the victims focus on the perpetrator" people go straight to "Yes, we do need to prosecute those people." But what she is talking about is the social or structural governing conditions under which this kind of victimhood is allowed or encouraged. And for which there may not be an individual perpetrator. So she is, at least as I read her, embroidering what has been individualized into a broader economy.

Martti: We may need to take up the issue of individualization later, and maybe say a few words about criminal law in an international context. Both are related to the neoliberal reframing of world problems in the 1990s and 2000s. Victims and perpetrators are individuals—so let's have individual rights and individual criminal responsibility! Of course, Susan's point was to focus on structural relationships. You cannot individualize the fact that while 80 percent of Europeans, and I suppose a similar number of Americans, are double or triple vaccinated against COVID-19, the number for Brazilians is 5 percent, or for the Sierra Leoneans 2 percent. "Oops, how did that happen?" It could be said that the developed North has established a pattern of solving its problems by externalizing them to the South.

A few years ago, people thought "fragmentation" was the great globalization problem. How does trade relate to environment, security to human rights, investment to development? How to deal with conflict of regimes and incompatible governance objectives? But lawyers kept talking to each other, coordinating and streamlining, and suddenly there was no longer any problem. And yet, the solutions were rarely thought in terms of distribution of values or presented to political decision-makers. "Fragmentation" became "diversity." The system reframed itself.

It was a rare feat for South Africa and India to succeed in influencing the global intellectual property regime in the context of the HIV crisis. But what can Pakistan do if an Australian mining company seeks to enforce a contested investment arbitration award of US$6 billion that corresponds almost exactly to the latest International Monetary Fund loan it had received to relieve its economic crisis?[32] All of this is structural, of course—a pattern repeating itself in time.

David: I think I have said something similar in criticizing the routine identification of "global problems" by people in the global governance business. Our problem solving would look different if we bracketed the identification of *global* and the easy assumption that problems—like the gains from governance or trade—are *common* to all. But *nothing is "common to all mankind."* Calling something common or universal or global is a claim, not a fact.

Back to "global warming." We know the effects, like the causes, will be local and very unequally distributed. Somehow these *distribution* questions take second place to the effort to find a "global solution"—distribution is for implementation or the allocation of responsibility. And it seems natural that a global problem will require a global solution which kicks the ball up to the global problem-solving arena—the last place an effective solution might be devised—while allowing everybody to hold their problem-solving fire until a global solution can be crafted. So it's the frame that's off, creating a disconnect between increasingly Cassandran predictions and lamentations and feeble "realistic" responses.

Martti: Perhaps the *global* can be seen as a new placeholder for the succession of other false universals such as Christianity, civilization, and development—each marking a line between those who have "achieved" it and those who have not, with a definite trajectory marked for the latter.

David: I think we've covered what we meant to today. I'm sure we'll return to lots of these themes in subsequent conversations—probably revising or contradicting what we've said here. But shall we stop here for now?

Martti: Good idea.

For all works by David Kennedy and Martti Koskenniemi, only short citations are given in the notes. Full citations can be found in the "Authors' Works Cited" section.

Notes

1. Kennedy, "Theses."
2. Kennedy, *International Legal Structures;* Kennedy, review of Louis Henkin, *How Nations Behave;* Duncan Kennedy, "Form and Substance in Private Law Adjudication," 89 *Harvard Law Review* 1685 (1976).
3. Koskenniemi, "Between Commitment and Cynicism."

4. Kennedy, "Theses."

5. Kennedy, "Theses," 357.

6. Kennedy, "Primitive Legal Scholarship."

7. Thomas S. Kuhn, *The Structure of Scientific Revolutions* (Chicago: University of Chicago Press, [1962] 2012).

8. Robert Mangabeira Unger, *Knowledge and Politics* (New York: Free Press, 1975).

9. Claude Lévi-Strauss, *The Savage Mind* (Chicago: University of Chicago Press, 1966).

10. Kennedy, *International Legal Structures,* 294.

11. Koskenniemi, *From Apology to Utopia.*

12. Kennedy, "Spring Break"; Patricia J. Williams, *The Alchemy of Race and Rights: Diary of a Law Professor* (Cambridge, MA: Harvard University Press, 1992).

13. Clare Dalton, "An Essay in the Deconstruction of Contract Doctrine," 94 *Yale Law Journal* 997 (1985); Mary Joe Frug, *Postmodern Legal Feminism* (Abingdon, UK: Routledge, 1992).

14. Kennedy, "The Move to Institutions."

15. Anthea Roberts, *Is International Law International?* (New York: Oxford University Press, 2017).

16. Max Horkheimer and Theodor W. Adorno, *Dialectic of Enlightenment,* trans. John Cumming (London: Verso, [1972] 1997).

17. Study Group of the International Law Commission, *Fragmentation of International Law: Difficulties Arising from the Diversification and Expansion of International Law: Report of the Study Group of the International Law Commission,* finalized by Martti Koskenniemi (Helsinki: Erik Castrén Institute of International Law, 2007).

18. Fredric Jameson, *The Political Unconscious: Narrative as a Socially Symbolic Act* (Ithaca, NY: Cornell University Press, [1981] 1982).

19. Kennedy, "Critical Theory, Structuralism and Contemporary Legal Scholarship."

20. Kennedy, *A World of Struggle.*

21. Koskenniemi, *The Gentle Civilizer of Nations.*

22. Dipesh Chakrabarty, *Provincializing Europe: Postcolonial Thought and Historical Difference* (Princeton, NJ: Princeton University Press, [2000] 2008).

23. Michel Foucault, "Nietzsche, Genealogy, History," in *Aesthetics, Method and Epistemology* 369 (James D. Faubion, ed., Robert Hurley et al., trans., New York: New Press, 1988).

24. Kennedy and Fisher, eds., *The Canon of American Legal Thought.*

25. Duncan Kennedy, "Three Globalizations of Law and Legal Thought: 1850–2000," in *The New Law and Economic Development: A Critical Appraisal* 19 (David M. Trubek and Alvaro Santos, eds., Cambridge: Cambridge University Press, 2006).

26. Koskenniemi, *To the Uttermost Parts of the Earth.*

27. Antony Anghie, *Imperialism, Sovereignty and the Making of International Law* (Cambridge: Cambridge University Press, 2005).

28. Kennedy, *The Dark Sides of Virtue.*

29. Kennedy, *The Dark Sides of Virtue;* Kennedy, "The International Human Rights Movement."

30. Koskenniemi, "Constitutionalism as Mindset."

31. Susan Marks, ed., *International Law on the Left* (Cambridge: Cambridge University Press, 2008).

32. See Tethyan Copper Co v. Islamic Republic of Pakistan, ICSID Case No. ARB/12/1 (2019).

CONVERSATION TWO

What Is International Law?

David: This time, let's step back from critical method to think a bit about the *object* of critique. After all, a precursor for critique is identifying the thing you're against—a thing that seems worthy, important, and yet inadequate—even venal. For both of us, at the start, "international law" was that thing. You've remained more closely focused on international law than I, while I've drifted across a range of fields where law touches "global affairs." But let's start with international law and see where the conversation takes us.

It has certainly been a shape-shifter. Each of us has written about international law as a body of texts, a pattern of doctrines and a set of institutions, but also as a profession, an academic field, an ideological and political project, a domain of professional expertise, a style of analysis or mode of thought. And probably that's just the beginning of the list. The way one identifies the target is linked to the critical projects one pursues; let's see if we can talk about that connection.

Perhaps we could start by comparing the international law you depict in three of your books? Each identifies a different international law target and pursues a different critical strategy. Here's a first oversimplification—see what you think.

In your first book, *From Apology to Utopia,*[1] "international law" is a textual tradition among leading European authors that's embodied in scholarly works and in the arguments put forward in cases and advocacy projects. You critique the texts as contradictory, indecisive, and, as the title suggests, caught somehow—perhaps philosophically or sociologically or phenomenologically—between "apology" and "utopia." Between ratifying what is and promising what isn't, but nothing in between, and you suggest that consequently there's nothing there that should be normatively compelling. The *who* and *why* and *what results* sides of the story are less apparent.

Then, in *The Gentle Civilizer of Nations,*[2] you associate "international law" with a very small group of European men and give their project a birth and death date, commencing with the founding of the Institut de Droit International in 1873 and flagging in the late twentieth century. Their arguments may also have been caught between ratifying what is and foreshadowing what might be, but that's not your critical focus. Rather, your critical project seems to be associating international law with the culturally specific political and ideological projects these men pursued quite successfully for almost a century, whatever the quality of their argument.

And then you introduce your latest book, *To the Uttermost Parts of the Earth,* by warning us, "This is not a history of international law. Instead, it's a history of the legal imagination as it operates in relationship to the use of power in contexts that we would today call international."[3] Here the critical project is more about world making, if I got it right—people in Europe using a legal vocabulary that imagines a larger world and then figures out the ambit of authority and ownership, sovereignty and property, political power and commerce for that world over centuries. Presumably the legal vocabulary enabled and constrained the kind of world they made—and we inherit. It is not a unified profession, in the sense of *The Gentle Civilizer of Nations*—all kinds of people play. And the legal elements include things we put in other compartments; you place property, for example, up there with sovereignty. Your focus is patterns of power rather than textual patterns of contradiction.

If I'm on the right track, can you help flesh this out, comparing the three "international laws" and the critical projects of the three books? I ask this because there are obvious parallels in my own work. From my first book, *International Legal Structures,*[4] which focused on the argumentative patterns in leading doctrines and cases, through historical work on the disciplines of international public law, international economic law, comparative law in the specific UnitedStatesean conditions of American ascendancy after World War II, to my more recent *A World of Struggle,*[5] with its broader focus on the dispersion of legal knowledge practices in global power.

One difference in our approach may be our relationship to international law. I think I've operated more transversally, trying to open various adjacent fields to critique rather than going deep, as you have. All these other fields seem as important for world making—more, perhaps—than 'international law' in the traditional sense. But let's start with your depth project if I can call it that. International law per se—what's the *se*?

Martti: Texts, ideas, practices, histories, institutions. Of course, the law can be examined from a number of angles. I have always found it odd—a little disappointing, to be honest—that international lawyers, especially in Europe, have fixated so closely on thinking of it as a doctrinal or a philosophical practice, ignoring until very recently its sociological, historical, or systemic aspects. Mostly, the field has operated in rather formalist terms, deriving conclusions from concepts and linking concepts together in purportedly larger principles representing objectives that international law is supposed to have. Even academic lawyers have had great difficulty in extracting themselves from the perspective of the players of the game to examine the nature of the game itself. I suppose this is at least in part a result of their ideological attachment to it, their sense that international law is more than just a technique, that it is true and valuable in itself and that the more international law there is in the world the better. Perhaps we can come back to that point later on.

Anyway, you are right that those three books do conceive of their object in different ways—just as your *International Legal Structures* has a very different object than the humanitarian practices you studied in *The Dark Sides of Virtue* or the experts in struggle depicted in *A World of Struggle*.[6]

From Apology to Utopia examined international law as an intellectual discipline that had to do with solving intellectual, even philosophical problems: What follows from state sovereignty? How does some fact turn into "customary international law?" How should one construct the meaning of a treaty text? This was the international law I saw portrayed in textbooks and I tried to show that, well, if you want to understand it that way, it has a number of really basic difficulties. To the extent that it succeeds in what it is doing, this cannot be owing to its rational power. *The Gentle Civilizer of Nations*, on the other hand . . .

David: Wait, before you go on, let's see if we can pin that down a bit. So, for *From Apology to Utopia*, the field is its texts and also in some way a philosophical intellectual project. The texts are somehow caught up in a philosophical problem—or maybe they promise a resolution to a question they then can't provide, something like that? That sounds like people doing philosophy and failing. I think you've been read that way sometimes—"Martti shows that international law is bad philosophy"—but . . . well, we never thought *that* was the project. We're bringing peace and justice to world affairs or trying to solve problems as best we can.

In *From Apology to Utopia* you leave the people, their project, and the question of international law's power somewhat suspended. I read the book as a classic "structuralist" analysis that brackets the *who* and *when* and *where* deliberately, asking of the texts themselves whether the problems *they* pose can be or have been resolved in the terms they use. So, for example, the texts promise to provide compellingly reasoned conclusions but turn out to be contradictory or indeterminate. Or the texts promise precisely not to be either apologizing or offering utopian promises but rather to bring normative limits to bear on practical activities. Promises that are broken. As a result, you treat your analytic findings as a kind of failure—as if international law *had* promised it could do something it can't. It's a kind of "naked emperor" critique, which is important if it *is* the emperor walking down the street and if people had thought he was clothed. Then the import would be to dethrone the guy. Isn't that what you were trying to do there?

Martti: Yes, that's right. But it began as an experiment at first. I noticed that most of the literatures suggested that the basic concepts of international law came together as a coherent whole and that this coherent whole represented a certain type of philosophy. This underlying philosophy would then provide good answers to legal problems. I just found it odd that if you took those concepts really seriously, this was not at all the case. The conceptual world of international law was, if you looked closely, full of gaps, contradictions, and answers that begged the question. That's what I proceeded to show. The emperor was naked, as you put it.

There was no underlying "system" that could have supported the field's everyday practices—almost whatever could be argued though it. If the law still gave an *impression* of coherence, it had to come from elsewhere than its conceptual world. Something like ideology must be at work. I first believed that this would utterly undermine those practices. If they did not—indeed could not—be justified by the principles of justification they invoked, you could no longer continue doing that, could you?

But it was not that simple. Not only did the practices continue as they had but I also learned that many practitioners knew very well that there was no such "coherent system." They still felt that things worked reasonably well most of the time, though they did not have an explanation for why they did. Some thanked me for having given an explanation to an intuition they had always had: international law is not the practice of some theory. It did not depend on any underlying philosophy. Things worked because they reflected shared assumptions about the acceptable or the decent way to work with legal materials.

There was no philosophical project, only a mixed bag of assumptions, propositions, and techniques that could be employed this way or that. All of that was ruled by a sort of practitioners' consensus, or as I then began to put it, a "politics" by another name. This was certainly provocative (because the texts promised a *departure* from politics) and I have later come to think the claim of law as politics as having its own problems. But, anyway, the conclusion of that first book really was that if you want to take international law seriously, you shouldn't imagine it as an intellectual discipline, an offshoot of some philosophy, a project for "perpetual peace."

David: So no one thought the material coherent—or the emperor clothed. That still leaves the question whether he actually *is* the emperor in the first place. I guess I'm wondering about the power question—what's the authority of this practice? How and to whom and for what do these texts "apologize" and with what effects? For whom do they make utopian promises or predictions and what happens as a result?

I put it this way because folks often read my *International Legal Structures* in a similar way. We talked about that reaction last time: "Kennedy shows that doctrines about the 'sources of law,' for example, are imprisoned between equally impossible extremes, either ratifying rather than restraining sovereign power or imagining a community that isn't there as the origins of normative authority." The result is a "meaningless" or "impossible" dialogue. I remember Pål Wrange using my text in a video art installation in Sweden: two televisions facing one another, repeating a quote he found in that book—something like "International law is an interminable, impossible dialogue." Thereafter, he went on to a successful diplomatic career as an international lawyer.

I remember a senior American colleague of mine—Abe Chayes—gleefully telling me, "No one will be able to write about sources of law again!" He said that because he had long been a realist skeptic of what he saw as European international law doctrine. As a leading American practitioner, he was *désabusé* in the extreme; of course, it was all a mirage, a construction of delicate indeterminacies. But he also thought it worked and was worthwhile—why, he asked, would I want to "deconstruct something we haven't even managed to construct yet?"

I tried to take both his doubts and his fealty seriously; contradictory materials *could and did* reach apparent and effective resolutions precisely by practices of deferral, elision, repetition, and so on. The emperor's authority somehow transcended his nakedness. Indeed, somehow his nakedness was part of what kept him on top, was what generated the fealty that kept him there. People keep doing international law, texts keep being generated which are received as competent performances that resolve problems, persuade people, legitimate or delegitimate action, and so on. It was a thin, intellectually weak, philosophically fragile thing, but international law in 1985 nevertheless kept on keeping on—as a professional practice and sociopolitical enterprise. I ended the book with something like "Interminable argument is the subtle secret of its success." Perhaps this is one way to think about the different emphases of your *From Apology to Utopia* and my *International Legal Structures*.

This also seemed characteristic of international law as a social-theoretical enterprise. It was an odd period, but for three quarters of a century, the major figures in the international law field all felt they needed to offer a *theory*—an explanation of how law arose and operated in international affairs. The theories were pretty idiosyncratic, the differences pretty narrow, but they seemed to be terribly meaningful to their proponents. I'm sure you remember all these strange sociological accounts of normativity, all of which were "realist" and "antiformal" in some way, mixing shared values and past practice in various ways. Part of what struck me at the time was the parallel between these theory debates and the doctrinal arguments people made about the norms themselves. Both the "theory" world and the "practice" world rotated around the same conundrums.

Nothing seemed to hinge on what theory you liked best—I always thought it was more a series of alternative arguments you could make, and students needed to learn to make—to respond to skeptics who might ask (as my grandmother once asked me), "But David, do they really have international law?"

Martti: Yes. It was astonishing that the authority of those texts seemed independent of their lack of persuasiveness in view of the standards they themselves set up. Perhaps they could be better seen as assemblances of good legal style, or taxonomies of professional argument from which it could be possible to choose in view of the "practice" that always loomed as a future promise for aspiring students. But you are speaking as if that world were wholly in the past. And, well, I guess for us it is. Neither one of us is any longer interested in showing the mere analytical weakness of the field's constitutive texts. But a lot of the public international law world in Europe, and in institutions originating in the European projects that I sought to describe in *The Gentle Civilizer of Nations,* still lives by them. From this perspective the United States is the outlier, your "American practitioner" the exotic alien.

David: True, which sharpens the question of what those texts and that practice *do* in the world. Are they "a good thing or a bad thing," as my grandmother would also always ask me? I'm sure we'll get to that—and there have doubtless been upsides and downsides for various people and interests. But international law seems more interesting as a power project in the world than as a philosophy exam that misses the mark, no? How do you see the "philosophical project" now? You've said the practitioners you encountered—like my colleague—did intuit the difficulties you described.

Martti: That's right. I only treated it as a philosophy project because that's how those texts presented it. But there was always a professional understanding, or a consensus, that they should not be taken overly seriously as such.

David: The image of a "professional consensus" holding the thing together foreshadows what we both explored more directly later on, along with the suggestion that the consensus was in some sense in bad faith, in the sense of using materials that claimed—and claiming about their materials—attributes they knew were not there. As young scholars, it probably made sense to focus on the texts people told us were classics to see if they made sense on close reading. Still, I think we were both pretty unspecific in these early books about who was using these materials and how they experienced them.

That silence on the sociological and phenomenological dimensions of international law was part of what motivated me to write up my experiences *using* human rights norms in "Spring Break" and "Autumn Weekends."[7] In the early years of the human rights movement, I went to Uruguay to bring universal norms to bear on behalf of a few prisoners whom my colleagues and I interpreted as prisoners of conscience. Later I went to Portugal to participate in advocacy for East Timorese independence on behalf of similar normative material. I wanted to explore how these texts—or these arguments—were embodied in professional styles, how it felt *to be* a speaker of international argument. Sometimes it felt great, empowering—or at least shielding from irrelevance. But often it felt pretty tentative, like a game we were all playing, knew we were playing, and might suddenly stop playing. I felt—and hoped my readers could feel—the kind of rising nausea one gets when impersonating a naked emperor.

Martti: "Spring Break" became a huge hit and remains so for good reason. It declared a wholly different, almost unheard-of way to treat an international legal problem from the perspective of a practitioner participant. It was methodologically liberating by bringing in what feminist literatures had long insisted, that one should set aside the mock objectivity that constrained legal writing. The personal was political, and the other way around. It had psychological depth and it was a gripping read. But I read "Autumn Weekends" more as a pastiche, a riff on the academic fixations of international lawyers, a little like David Lodge's *Small World,* important in trying to show people what had always been there to see but few had taken note of.

David: I can see that—I also think "Spring Break" the more innovative. My idea in "Autumn Weekends" was to explore a parallel professional practice in those activist/academic confabs as the advocacy platform narrated itself into existence, people finding themselves spoken by roles, and so on. But I suppose that's why the "four seasons" I'd imagined never materialized—I'd taken that angle as far as I could at that point.

Before we go on to your second book, one difference of emphasis is worth mentioning. The way you put it a moment ago makes sense to me: the materials can't resolve the problems they pose, so something else must be going on. Internal structure can't deliver, so something external to the materials must be doing the work. That *something* could range from unstated assumptions and professional sensibilities through more self-conscious ideological positions and material interests all the way to the forces of historical context. Of course, this does happen. And I understand your hesitance about using the word *political* to describe these diverse elements—it suggests something conscious, contestable and pursued in a conventional vocabulary of "interest" or "ideology." There I'm in agreement as well.

Nevertheless, I've tried to push against this internal/external division, initially by focusing on the ways the materials themselves, despite their contradictions, *do* manage to come to resolutions whose sociological and phenomenological impact can be assessed. The inability to resolve contradictions spawned an interminable practice of *trying to*. It took a lot of creativity to knit together each day what one knew could come to be unraveled that night, and the effort was a form of rulership. In this sense, the internal was also external—generative of an authoritative professional practice. "Spring Break" and "Autumn Weekends" tried to give that sociological shape.

At the same time, the supposedly external worlds—political interests or ideologies—were also articulative practices, performances more than material forces. Someone needed to figure out what was in the interests of "labor" or "the United States," to claim to represent that interest or ideology, and to make an argument which would or wouldn't be effective/persuasive. Those arguments also seemed to be built from a rather unstable and contradictory batch of materials. Supposedly material interests and structural necessities—like ideological commitments—couldn't be the driveshaft of legal argument without being brought into that space, whether overtly or within the mind of the interpreter. The external was already inside, if I can put it that way, or was running on parallel tracks.

This, of course, raised the question, Who is doing that, and why? Perhaps that takes us to your *Gentle Civilizer of Nations* and the men of 1873 you identify as the embodiment of international law: guys with a project and a professional vocabulary for pursuing it in the world. I guess, first, how to relate these men to your first book: Were the gentle civilizers of 1873 doing apology to utopia?

Martti: Well, the most important aspect of the relationship between *From Apology to Utopia* and my account of the men of 1873 in *The Gentle Civilizer of Nations* was that I no longer imagined the field in philosophical terms. Instead of intellectual operations, I now saw the field as a craft—you taught me, among many other things, to use the expression "people (here, *men*) with projects." So that's how I depicted international law in that later work. If the field was not ruled by logic but by a "practitioners' consensus," what, then, was that consensus?

Here I suggested that modern international law began with a group of late nineteenth-century Victorian or French Third Republic liberals with two projects. First of all, they wanted to introduce liberal legislation across Europe. They set up the Institut de Droit International to coordinate their humanitarian activities and their lobbying with European governments—not with great success, it has to be said. On the other hand, they were interested in civilizing what they called the "Orient"—that is to say, the conduct of European colonization. The book was partly a historical, partly sociological, even biographical study of the activities and opinions of a group of European elite lawyers.

I used the expression "sensibility" to canvass the professional consensus among late Victorian jurists; it was liberal-tolerant at home, authoritarian in the colonies. It was critical of sovereignty, expansive-civilizational abroad, and utterly Eurocentric. It was oriented toward courts and international institutions, and it had its more or less "formalistic" and "realistic" strands that competed with each other until the 1960s or so. So in that sense, apology and utopia all the way down. But I would now set the field's lack of argumentative power aside in an effort to construct its coherence on the sharing of a professional sensibility—almost like an aesthetic—that had by the 1960s expended much of its innovative force; it would now encounter challenges and aspirations of a new generation to which it could no longer effectively respond. Though it did, of course, continue. But that is another story.

David: I like the way you expanded their professional "expertise," if I can call it that, to include legal theories or methods, ideological predilections, and so on, as they pursued their projects.

Can you say something about the link between identifying "international law" with these guys and your critical impulse in the book? I recall your saying you found them sympathetic figures and could feel some nostalgia for their project. Was your critique that they were playing with an incoherent/contradictory set of materials? Or that they were alternating between apologizing and utopianizing? Or that they were in bad faith? Or was it that they were part of a larger malevolent European project, both ideological and material, of imperialism dressed up as universalism, humanitarianism—as law, after all?

Martti: You mentioned earlier your effort, in *International Legal Structures,* to find closure in these texts from their "sociological and phenomenological impact." *The Gentle Civilizer of Nations* employed the wide and informal notion of "sensibility" as the ground on which international lawyers could seek resolution to their problems. This would be nothing logically compelling, but still, something—a world-view, a culture, an aesthetic—around which consensus could form among reasonable professionals.

I worry a little about the bad faith argument of the sort that may be associated with the argument in *From Apology to Utopia.* The "sensibility" that united most of the protagonists in *The Gentle Civilizer of Nations* was alert to the injustices of the world. Of course, some of the lawyers were in denial or had the kind of cynical consciousness that bad faith connotes. But I wanted to avoid suggesting the law's complicity in the world's wrongs should be laid on *their* shoulders as individuals—in a way no more than the devastations of the First World War should be attributed to those who went into it with enthusiasm in 1914. I actually had sympathy with many of them—having to work with such fragile tools in such unpromising conditions. It was hard to share their opinions, but those were common among middle-class professionals from the North Atlantic at the time.

I was more interested in casting them in mildly tragic terms; many of their projects—the push to arbitration just before the First World War, the mandates system of the League of Nations, its codification efforts and its collective security system—never really worked in a satisfactory way. I wanted to sketch them as sincere, but not very savvy about the surrounding world. They dealt with hard problems with more or less wisdom and stupidity, just like we do. I wanted to direct my critique, above all, against the system, the structures of authority and subordination in the law, and only secondarily their lack of effort in trying to understand it. I wanted to invite readers—often international lawyers—to be able to identify with them.

David: I wouldn't snuggle up to them quite so readily—they were aiming to rule in the name of virtue, thought they had the ticket for that, and seemed to feel no responsibility for how it worked out, for the *dark sides,* to coin a phrase. Still, I meant "bad faith" in a narrower sense—more that at some level they knew things about themselves, their vocabulary, that they were denying than that they were disingenuous or consciously deceitful. I understand what you mean, though—decent, reasonable professionals, weak tools, unsuccessful projects, and, in that, representative of a ruling elite, or at least one division in the European establishment.

I made a similar study of the intertwined academic and professional projects of people in the postwar United States who were thinking legally about global matters.[8] Their professional vocabulary and style—"sensibility," if you prefer—characterized the postwar American establishment, many of whose projects were successful; often, sadly, all too successful. In the postwar American ascendency, legal hegemony was an effect of multiple professional fields: international economic law, comparative law, law and development, European law, and, of course, the extraterritorial impact of national public and private law and professional practice. International law was low on the list.

Professionals dealt with law and international matters from within their subject specialty, foregrounding national regulatory regimes and private law arrangements: international tax, international aspects of antitrust, international business regulation, the law of armed conflict, and so on. Even in academic curricula, international law competed with other efforts to synthesize the treatment of law in global affairs—transnational law, international economic law, the foreign relations law of the United States—each of which foregrounded different questions and materials than what was usually termed "public international law."

Martti: Those were hegemonic moves, weren't they? I mean refusal to participate in a game whose rules had been created and were constantly tweaked in favor of other actors and interests. A new playground would be offered by such alternative legal vocabularies.[9]

David: Yes—they were each aiming for a comprehensive picture which could become dominant. A confusion of contending totalizations still characterizes the American scene. When my faculty made International Law a required first-year course some years back, no one could say what it should cover. Or everyone said something different. Ultimately, three general models were proposed, which instructors could modify as they wished. After a few years, the offerings were so disparate that the course was abolished, replaced by the general requirement to take at least one course which dealt with global matters, something more than one hundred courses in the curriculum were said to do. So one, two, three, many hegemonic contenders—each of whom could *also* pose as partial, useful perspectives, functional specialties.

For all that, I thought international law could provide an entry point, a baseline for comparison with adjacent professional worlds that would illuminate the larger sensibility of the postwar legal elite. For example, public international lawyers imagined the world and the law quite differently than did international economic lawyers, and yet these two professional sensibilities seemed to work in tandem. I wrote an article comparing the postwar Hans Kelsen with the international economic law scholar John Jackson to illustrate how this could be done.[10] There was a kind of partnership and division of labor between their visions which enhanced the rulership of each. The hegemony of that shared sensibility was my target: the "fields" were just a way to take aim.

Martti: Interesting what you say about the open-endedness of the "international law" idiom at Harvard. It was a totally different world in Europe, where "public international law" was part of the standard curriculum of the law faculty and textbooks across the continent organized it around the theme of "order among sovereigns." That's how I encountered it in law school in the 1970s, in the foreign ministry right thereafter, and still at the International Law Commission in 2002–2006, although by then, cracks had begun to appear in that image, dealt with more or less anxiously under the "fragmentation" theme.

David: That "public international law" had almost disappeared from the curriculum by the time I got to law school in the mid-1970s. With the result that amid so many diverse contending ideas about law *in the world,* you needed to give the field a shape to become an international law specialist or critic. Construct the field to critique it—as we discussed last time. I thought it reasonable to start by imagining international law as it seemed to imagine itself—as its texts imagined themselves, perhaps I should say. And that meant resurrecting the traditional disciplinary world you found all around. Still, one could easily find the standard doctrines, well-known cases and institutions, a few debates that preoccupied scholars: How does international law bind? That kind of thing. The library had a special international law collection with those impressive Carnegie volumes identifying the "classics." And there was a professional association and a leading journal whose board of editors provided a quick list of leading scholars and practitioners.

That experience helped me formulate a template for building the object for critique. I'd start with an identifiable *set of people and texts* that seemed exemplary of a broader conversation. The people had *roles* in the world that gave them the opportunity to develop and practice a *disciplinary style* of argument and engagement with others. They often shared *worldviews*—ideas about how the world was put together, where they stood, how power functioned, the objective and limits of their professional work. And a sense for their field's *classic problems* and *differences of opinion,* issues which divided the profession and were thought to need attention.

There were *projects* they claimed to be pursuing: sometimes humanitarian and progressive projects; sometimes problem solving; sometimes ordering and rationalizing a complex world in a particular direction: stabilize conditions for trade, prevent a relapse to war, promote intercultural understanding, and so forth. There were projects one might suspect they were also pursuing, whether consciously or somewhat consciously: intramural disciplinary projects, national projects, personal psychological projects, and so on. And there were projects one could, with the hindsight of history, see that their work supported: often cultural, political, or economic projects of empire, as these were men of the North Atlantic in a period of their hegemony.

You could imagine a critical engagement at each point. Why these men and texts—who could and couldn't play? Did the materials support the promises they made? Were the players in good faith about that? What was missing from their worldview? Which problems did they find easy to address, and which did they simply not see? Were their ostensible projects swamped by their unstated projects? Did their work on the self overshadow their work on the world? How did their work in the world distribute wealth and authority or cultural status?

Martti: I started in a world that seemed much more settled, where there was no difficulty at all to identify what "international law" stood for, what were its constitutive texts, leading authorities, principal critics. While at law school, I took those more or less for granted. Knowing those texts and those names, having a "feel" about how they came together and what they might stand for seemed to offer a road to a career in which one might make a difference. It was only when taking up legal work with the foreign ministry that I began to wonder about the field's limits and the lack of persuasive force of its constitutive texts.

I was especially struck by the contrast between that textual world and the very strong political commitment to the field among the practitioners, their good-natured camaraderie, their astonishing ability not to notice how what they declared as common interests and universal values invariably ended supporting the interest and routines of the institutions where they worked. It was the suppleness of the materials, and the contrast with the very predictable way they ended up being used, and the very formalism of those uses, that I wanted to examine in *From Apology to Utopia.*

David: But I want to get to your third book, *To the Uttermost Parts of the Earth,* which is a different kind of inquiry. There your critical project is not framed by the people and their continuity as a group, nor by the materials and their self-definition as international law, nor by a single intellectual puzzle, like, How do you get order among sovereign states? But rather, by the two ideas of *legal imagining* and *the use of power.*

Here's that sentence I cited earlier: "[This is] a history of the legal imagination as it operates in relationship to the use of power in contexts we would today call international." The book treats "the legal imagination" as a somewhat stable practice as people thought about exercising power. We'll talk more about power in a later conversation, but can you say a bit about how you identified a stable object of analysis across the centuries as a path for critical inquiry?

I ask because we've both tried to break up international law's self-understanding as a continuous and progressive effort to solve the enduring problem of order among sovereigns. My first historical piece, "Primitive Legal Scholarship,"[11] argued that the so-called founders of international law in the fifteenth and sixteenth centuries imagined the world and their role in a profoundly different way than their nineteenth- or twentieth-century "successors." In *To the Uttermost Parts of the Earth* you identify lots of ruptures, breaks—"incidents and accidents" as Paul Simon might say—which initiated new ways to be a ruling legal expert. How did you work the *continuities* across those ruptures—the continuities of "law" or "legal imagination," as well as "power" and "situations we would now call international"?

Martti: You ask me about the stability of the notion of international law, or "law of nations," in *To the Uttermost Parts of the Earth*. Here I treat it neither as an intellectual discipline nor a professional project. Instead I fixate on the persistence of the legal idiom, received from Roman law across five centuries of efforts to articulate relations of power in what we would now identify as the "international" world. The stable element here is language, plus a set of background assumptions and institutional priorities accompanying it. I was interested in producing a *longue durée* description of what people have been able to do with this idiom—especially how they have been able to justify, stabilize, and critique those types of historical authority that we have come to call "sovereignty" and "property."

I postulated a thing—"legal imagination"—that then labored with this vocabulary for half a millennium, defining and redefining the meanings that it communicated to audiences across the world. I was less interested in the intellectual or moral aspects of this process than I was in the way it translated real-world relations of hegemony and subordination into the extremely resilient and quite persuasive idioms of sovereignty and property. What did it mean for kings to claim "sovereignty" in their relations with domestic nobility and outside powers? How did it fare in its ubiquitous conflicts with claims about "property" made at home and in foreign lands? What other kinds of language did the legal imagination encounter as it moved about in the world?

I think you, David, have somewhere used the expression "power through articulation," which I find very useful to think about the way in which people of ambition use legal language to justify or critique exercises of authority. *To the Uttermost Parts of the Earth* is about the way concepts such as *sovereignty, property*, or indeed *law of nations* have been used to articulate claims for authority and social hierarchies at home and abroad. I do find it problematic that all my protagonists were European men; we need to come back to that later in these conversations. But my point here is that by focusing on "power through articulation" it was both possible to stay close to the actual practices of the disciplines I studied—especially their linguistic aspects—and nonetheless develop a critical perspective on them.

David: We should say more about how "articulative power" might be thought to function—perhaps in a later conversation. I intended *A World of Struggle* as a take on that.

Martti: I wanted to write without commitment to the methodological choices that appeared available for that kind of historical-conceptual study. I think we are both quite elusive about method—despite our effort last time to talk about it more directly. In the end I was surprised that in my latter two books, there was no discussion of formal method at all. *The Gentle Civilizer of Nations* referenced something I called a "sensibility" and the newer book focused on "imagination" and law as "bricolage," both introduced without a heavy apparatus of footnotes. I always felt that debates on method depart too far from the substance of my interest. It is not that I think one should not be aware of conversations on method. I do think it is necessary to know their point. But I find that they often detract from the critical impulse, direct attention in the wrong place.

Neither have you engaged—at least more recently—in deep methodological debates. There was this early text of yours that attacked legal hermeneutics, the interpretative turn.[12] That was what most US lawyers were doing at the time. But you have not followed up on that line. Why? My hunch is that you, too, think that they somehow work against the critical impulse. Instead, your trajectory has been from the formal analysis of *International Legal Structures* and the jurisprudential critique of the theory of interpretation to law as a sociological phenomenon, a structuring frame for the practices of rulership. Can you say something more about that trajectory?

David: You're right that I have left method questions in the background, informing my angle on things but not entering the text as actors. I feel the same way about the big names of social theory who hover around the edges. But let me bring one in here. Do you recall that great Woody Allen scene—a guy is mansplaining Marshall McLuhan to his girlfriend while waiting to buy movie tickets, and the guy behind them says, "Wait, I have Marshall McLuhan right here . . ."?

Anyway, let me bring Lévi-Strauss into the conversation somewhat that way. In *To the Uttermost Parts of the Earth* you use his term "bricolage" to describe the hodgepodge practice of legal professionals drawing on various materials lying about that seem useful.[13] There's something important there: people are working in a field and drawing on materials to bolster their projects rather than unfolding the materials in accordance with their own logic.

There's a second component to Lévi-Straussian "bricolage" which seems more dormant in *To the Uttermost Parts of the Earth,* but perhaps you meant to flag it by using the word. As I recall it, he claimed that although materials were picked up in an ad hoc manner, they were "structured" by repeated oppositions and patterns of resolution—the "raw" and the "cooked," and so on. These relationships, modes of their transformation and interaction, structure the cultural practice that is undertaken in an apparently ad hoc way. That is what makes the structure a kind of grammar, opening the world to sensible interpretation by competent participants in the culture. The poststructuralist or postmodern authors who influenced both of us took this further: the oppositions were also hierarchies, each term contained a shadow of the other, and so on.

Does that kind of structure lie beneath—or animate—the practices of legal imagining you trace in *To the Uttermost Parts of the Earth*? Not just ad hoc hodgepodging but a kind of grammar for competent imagining? Perhaps "apology and utopia" remain the "raw and cooked" of the practice—but I had the sense you felt "imperium and dominium" or "public and private, sovereignty and property, political and commercial" were doing that work.

Martti: I do think bricolage is structured. The antinomy of apology/utopia remains pervasive, and helps in analyzing any single legal speech act, though at different moments with varying force. But here I wanted to focus on another binary to which I gave the name "sovereignty/property." It appeared also in the public/private distinction that controlled how authority could be imagined through much of the period. But one fear I had was that people would think that I was trying to establish some sort of a world-historical structure for the development of what Hegel might have called a European "spirit" realizing itself through the transformations of legal language that could then be either celebrated or perhaps condemned. As I wrote there, although structural aspects of the world usually addressed by large notions such as *imperialism, capitalism,* or *nationalism* help us understand the past, they also gloss over its contradictory and discontinuous elements. Such words do throw important light on the past, but also leave things hidden.

Instead I wanted to take law seriously as a framing element for struggles over authority and resources. Imperialism, capitalism, and nationalism have each also a definite legal articulation: "empire," for example, looks back on Roman law and the term *imperium*, and that can then be put to work either to buttress or question some particular claim to authority. There is no capitalism without the ideas of contract and property, and no nationalism without states and citizens. Historians inclined to use large frames of explanation tend to see law as epiphenomenal, like Grewe's view of the law of nations as an offshoot of imperial policy.[14] I wanted to avoid such instrumentalism and instead focus on legal language as providing the conditions of possibility for relations of hegemony and subordination to emerge and consolidate.

David: Could you link that to your critical intention in the book? Or, perhaps, who were you writing against in identifying these themes across the *longue durée*?

Martti: The anti-instrumentalist point is one. I wanted to highlight law's constitutive, structuring character as against what I think of as naive views about the world consisting of single identities (empires, states, populations, rulers), conscious of what they desire and employing the law to fulfill those desires. The world of bricolage is messier, the intellectual, social, and psychological structures divided against themselves. Highlighting discontinuity is another. I wanted to write against the idea of a "tradition of international law," pointing instead to the many different contexts in which people have used the legal idiom—such as, for example, sixteenth-century practices of confession in Castile. Law was not one thing but many different things. A third point was to focus on law as power instead of truth or reason. The legal language did not, as it were, look backward on stable meanings that it would carry from the past to the present; instead, it was oriented forward to authority and subordination. It was not conversation but assertion.

David: Super. You had asked about my trajectory in moving from international law out toward the practice of "expertise" in *A World of Struggle*. I intended that book as a sociological interpretation of knowledge practices among people exercising power through articulation—from diplomats and development economists to human rights advocates, soldiers, and statesmen. I offered law as a possible model, exploring whether other expertise, like development economics, followed analogous patterns. I also stressed the continuities between the world's sophisticated players and outsiders or laymen, including my grandmother arguing with a shopkeeper in some foreign port. I imagined them all as "experts" making claims on a shared terrain, coming at one another with little backpacks of authorities and obligations and pictures of the world they could draw on to urge others in some direction.

At least across the examples I analyzed, there were common structural elements. A pattern of invoking extreme positions to characterize small differences on a continuum between contradictory poles; a kind of sophistication about the indeterminate status of the materials they used and the arguments they made; shared commonsense pictures of the world and of their situation with characteristic blind spots and biases; that kind of thing. The book makes the case that sophisticated players are in a kind of collective flight from responsibility into expert knowledge they inhabit with a doubled consciousness, at once ethically confident and pragmatic or both believing and not believing their own assertions.

I also intended the book as a methodological experiment. How far could one go in bracketing reliance on both agency and structure—the actor and the system—when developing a sociological account of global rulership? I proposed to take accounts of agency (I am the sovereign) and structure (the world system / capitalist system / postwar order / international system is like this) as *assertions* rather than facts: not *preexisting* the knowledge work of rulership but arising out of it as such assertions generated acquiescence: Yes, you are the sovereign, that is how the system is, we should do what that suggests. My critical objective there was to reframe these "facts" as malleable constructions, effects of authority. I've been working on a new book going at this in the opposite direction: how might we put "structure" back in the story without overlooking the uncertain performativity of rulership.

Martti: Although we've written our works pretty independently from each other, their problem settings and ambitions are still very close. You say you want to bracket structure and agency and deal with assertions. That's pretty much what I am doing as well; I focus on language that puts out claims, ideas, suppositions in dynamic contexts where things are at stake. How does language do this? How do specific articulations become authoritative and frame the range of our vision? What makes their authority erode in the face of competing vocabularies and assertions? How does language open the way for rulership? So instead of postulating large and stable structures such as *imperialism* or *nationalism* or *capitalism* I am interested in how linguistic maneuvers formalize so as to create, among other effects, the impression of the presence of such structures.

Your point about the need to account for both rupture and continuity is important. Focusing on language, it is possible to say that there is continuity when two people at the distance of two centuries say "law of nations" or "I am sovereign." But then the meaning of these two idioms ("law of nations" and "sovereign") is dependent on their context of utterance, however we decide to think about the "context." As you know, there is this debate about context and the *longue durée* among some legal historians today. I have found it hard to be enthusiastic about that conversation because obviously both are so important. Let me put it this way—both have an important role in *critical* studies of law: context explains law as part of political contestation, *longue durée* explains law's fixedness, the way it stabilizes hierarchical patterns. Each obviously conditions the other.

David: I share your lack of enthusiasm for those debates about historical context. Historical writing is a knowledge practice that constructs and asserts things like "the context" for a reason. How we imagine the context is an effect of successful historical performances and lasts until someone tells the story differently. I don't mean that anything can be constructed as context or *longue durée*, but certainly far more than folks typically imagine when they see context as outside interpretation, background to it. For example, I can imagine framing the sixteenth century as part of the present context—or the reverse. But let's leave that for a future discussion of historical work in international law.

Before we stop for the day, let's try to say a bit about what we take away as *critical* reflections on international law, properly so called. I meant my little list of critical takes on "human rights" as a list of hypotheses, cautions, qualifications on the common assumption that more human rights could only be a good thing. I wrote the list to encourage a more pragmatic weighing of costs and benefits by folks who might be overly enchanted by their vernacular—and then I wrote *The Dark Sides of Virtue* to illustrate the linked dangers of pragmatism and idolatry in humanitarian advocacy and policy.

International law is also often seen as an unqualified good, associated with order and justice and peace, with global problem solving and universally shared values—good for everyone. A list of possible downsides opens the way for a more nuanced assessment. You can certainly go too far—we've both seen critical projects which replace "It's all good" with "It's all bad." In the article I contributed to the collection you did with Annabel Brett on international legal history, I offered a corrective to this tendency in some work on international law and colonialism.[15] The key, I think, is developing a more sensitive Geiger counter for the impact on diversely situated people and projects.

Martti: It is also hard to evaluate because the causalities of international law—at least in its "European" variant of sovereign states acting in a world of universal rules and institutions—are so hard to detect. In some ways, it accounts for everything about the way the world is. So that if you think the world is unjust, it requires an enormous ideological push to think it is so *despite* international law. Surely a better analysis is that it is unjust because international law *made it so*.

But then, in the International Law Commission, for example, there was no interest to measure the effect of its texts in any sustained or systematic way. They were just thrown out there, hoping some good might result somehow. Much of the work of the commission, like the whole United Nations (UN) system, gave the impression of everyone busily orienting themselves to the most pressing global problems, suggesting that things were still under control. In truth, at least on the international law side, there was little sense of how the practices related to the world. It is hard for a suspicious mind not to break down the ideological effect of all that into specific critical points about obscuring, enabling, legitimizing, and so forth.

David: I think it is terribly difficult for international law aficionados to see it contributing to war, domination, inequality, injustice, global warming. The crazy irrelevance of a body like the International Law Commission reinforces that difficulty: How could something so marginal be blamed for anything? Surely the problem arises rather from the unreliable people who use—or don't use—the lovely doctrines they're busy writing down.

One way to get away from this is to think distributionally. Few things in life are good for everyone—who benefits and who loses? Some people certainly do benefit from human rights advocacy. With international law, there are doubtless many who benefit from an overvalued project credited with universal virtues—its mandarins, of course, but probably others, some of them hegemons and some not. And some people would certainly benefit were international law, say, to facilitate environmental despoilation and global warming or legitimate an unjust status quo. But others wouldn't. When international legal norms are effective in shaping the use of force, they clearly benefit some at the expense of others. That's why people keep trotting them out.

Neither of us has been anything like as comprehensive in identifying international law's possible dark sides as I was in "The International Human Rights Movement: Part of the Problem?"[16] But there are some critical observations we've each returned to over time. We've mentioned some of them already.

As an intellectual project—you called it *philosophical*—international law poses questions which the field's materials have a hard time answering. The "international law" embodied in the materials makes promises it doesn't keep—or keeps only by elision and deferral and repetition. It promises to "civilize" state behavior without being utopian or apologetic, but slides toward both. It claims to offer coherent and persuasive normative arguments but, on inspection, the arguments turn out to be flimsy.

All this might be good or bad for various players. For some it might be very useful to have a pile of indeterminate materials a professional class can call on to make (plausible or persuasive or effective) assertions about who should do what. To be masters of such a practice could be good for the profession. It might engender practices of denial or sophisticated splitting between pious claims making and cynical acknowledgment which might feel virtuous and realistic, even inevitable.

Martti: But those kinds of critiques still remain quite abstract; I mean, they do not resemble the specificity of the way you laid out the dark sides of human rights in that essay. It is still hard to map out the distributional consequences following from them.

David: I think we've tried to go further by showing that this practice is *interested* in the sense that it strengthens the solidity of existing arrangements by recasting them in universal normative terms; that's a possible effect of apologizing for things as they are and recasting them as precursors for a utopian future. Presenting itself as a continual work in progress, the field absorbs the energy of critique; if you feel the world is unjust, join us as we bend the arc toward justice. We need everyone's help—the established order is the path to its reform.

Martti: So that's a point about its general conservatism, the way it rules out larger or systemic change.

David: Along the way, there is a kind of world-making function as people get hooked on the idea that real states are—and should be—like we imagine states in Europe to be or to have been. That's the kind of "framing" effect we've touched on before. If you want to be part of the global conversation, you need to present yourself as European states imagine(d) themselves. That's how you get all those diplomats running around calling one another "Your Excellency"—more so the further they are from the North Atlantic. And doing so even when everybody knows at some level that most states and most governments are nothing like that and that relations in the real world are overwhelmingly between unequals rather than equals. Of course, again, many benefit from status quo reinforcement—including all those diplomats.

And then, we've both said that international law articulates a partial historical reality as *the* global reality: universalizing the western European experience and then the experience of American hegemony. International law carries a particular piece of the larger ideological project of Western hegemony: presenting an image of a virtuous and openly ordered global society as the dominant characteristics of the actual world situation. They help make it seem reasonable to imagine that both trade and diplomacy are about equality and negotiation, not domination.

Although international law is often contrasted with a political science realism of ruthless interstate power struggles, international law has always been an alchemy of progressive virtue and hard-boiled realism—that is your "apology to utopia," after all. In the American tradition, I think it was Myres McDougal who most famously pitched this parallel play as a virtue: the emerging American Cold War order as a project of ruthless force and magisterial ethical commitment, for both of which law was indispensable. But we could describe the same thing in less laudatory terms—as the ruthless brutality of statecraft as civilization, which is pretty much how Philip Allott narrates the tale for all his idealism about its potential.[17]

And then, lots of things that we don't like in the world turn out to be—or to have—legal structures in which "international law," however you define it, has some role. So war and poverty and inequality and global warming and environmental despoliation are also legal regimes, like colonialism or neoliberalism or slavery. Studying the legal structure of such things takes us to the role of law—legal professionals, languages, institutions—in the world, as you propose we do in *To the Uttermost Parts of the Earth:* "legal imaginings" and the exercise of power.

That's just a first list. If my human rights experience is any guide, we'd find the critical literature filled with many more were we aiming for a comprehensive guide. What would you add?

Martti: That's a really useful list. I think your *Dark Sides of Virtue,* where the list of potential human rights difficulties appears, has great impact among readers; people in the human rights camp have certainly become much more sophisticated about the need for strategic thinking. Perhaps one can sum up international law's dark sides by noting its simultaneous excessive abstraction and narrowness. Abstraction in the sense of inflated expectations about effects of legal and humanitarian activism—that if only existing international institutions were imagined as analogous to the domestic welfare state, then they can be used for precisely the purposes for which such a state would ideally operate. To be sure, everyone accepts that the analogy is only partial. But many believe that the state is the problem and that the more *international* the level where something is decided the better, and that if it is *legal,* then it must be humanitarian too.

David: That's so odd, isn't it—it cries out for a psychosocial explanation. Maybe the desire not to be where the rubber meets the road, or maybe something more slave-moralistic—to be that "gentle civilizing" murmur left in the corridor.

Martti: Over and over again, one sees the political energy of students (again, I am thinking mostly of European students) expended by their support of international against the local, legal against the political. As if a war would be okay if it is approved by the UN Security Council. As if an International Criminal Court could attain more than the indictment of a handful of African leaders.[18] As if international law were not saturated by conflicting interests and projects, applied by institutions where the word of some will always be louder than that of others. People are enchanted by the flourish of the practices of international rule—more conferences, reports, resolutions, rarely prepared to assess their effects on the ground. It is odd that in the widespread critiques of the wrongs of globalization—the trade regime, the investment regime, the financial regime—the implication of *law* is so rarely noticed and targeted: strict enforcement of contracts and private rights against regulatory policies of local communities. The "rule of law" is not an unmitigated good; what it means and whose claim it will support is a matter of contestation.

And narrowness: to make a clam of international law is to activate a body with limited jurisdiction, authority and resources. No doubt, this may sometimes be useful. But it will also redefine and temper that claim, situate it with parallel and countervailing claims and produce an outcome that is often impossible to implement against recalcitrant actors. And it will consolidate the authority of the system of decision-making of which this process is a part. This not because there is a "power politics" out there that opposes international law's good ideas—to the contrary, the structures of decision-making and implementation *are what international law is, precisely*. It is only the assumption that international law always supports the preferences *that I have,* while the preferences of my adversary reflect an egoistic interest or political bias, that often makes it too hard to see this.

David: International law is a kind of reassuring tonic—drinking it, you can confidently rule in the name of the universal. And it's not you who are ruling—it's the law.

Martti: One of the ways in which both of us have tried to deal with the problem has been to widen the perspective of legal activism; instead of thinking in terms of international law and multilateral diplomacy, you, for instance, have pointed to the triad *family, market, state* as three worlds within which influential background assumptions about governance are formed. If you really want to change the world, then it may be necessary to engage in all such frames. But I find much resistance against this.

David: It was Fran Olsen and Duncan Kennedy who first put me on to that triad.[19]

Martti: For example, I have recently argued that the right of property can be historically framed as an "international human right" to subordinate it to the very widespread jurisprudence from domestic and international institutions according to which rights can be *limited* and *balanced* and *reconceived* in a number of different ways.[20] This would mean to argue something as a human right not to support but to *weaken* it and open it to all kinds of countervailing considerations regularly thrown against human rights. But I found that activists resent it; for them, human rights have a sacredness that property should not enjoy.

This reaction—however we feel about it—represents the resentment that activists feel with respect to strategic considerations; you often draw activists' attention to them nevertheless. What would you say to critics arguing that they represent a sort of economic thinking—I mean, drawing upon something like rational choice often associated with law and economics? Is working in a strategic mode to capitulate to the adversary?

David: People think strategically in lots of ways; cost-benefit economics is one—quite powerful—way, I think. I'm all for bringing economic tools into the critical enterprise. I think the activist resistance is less to specific tools than to the desacralization that goes with evaluating "good law" or good activism strategically. I remember talking with a wonderful activist working to eliminate the death penalty in the Caribbean. I asked what he saw as the costs of success—who would lose if the death penalty were to be abolished. Somehow my question didn't compute—it was all win. But would life without parole become more common—also for people who would not have gotten the death penalty? What did he think? He just wasn't thinking about costs or downsides—he was focused on virtue. And then there's the question of who is an "activist"—the people promoting the death penalty were also pretty active and had lots of legal arguments and powers and entitlements.

Martti: So I take it that you would not accept that the kind of nominalism and stress on costs and benefits that has been part of your critical vocabulary (mine, too, though I suppose less so) would collapse it into law and economics or into some variant of what many people would associate with "neoliberalism."

David: Heavens, no! That "law and economics" was so narrow, improvising on a theme from microeconomics—almost without noticing that those economic models depended on a fantasy about the legal underpinnings of market activity, something shared with the professional sensibility we might call "neoliberalism." Economics has a lot more to offer!

Can I go back to your men of 1873 in *The Gentle Civilizer of Nations* for a moment? You do treat them nostalgically, and you're right that their world is gone. In a world saturated with law and legal articulations, "international law" as they understood it is a bit player. Nevertheless, across the global stage people now make claims in legal vocabularies and institutions that would not be foreign to them. Few people claim to be doing things because they have the guns to do it or because they have a spiritual belief in doing it. Rather, they claim a *right* or an entitlement, a cognizable reason that can be traced through the red thread of law, even if—or precisely *because*—the legal vocabulary generates reasons all sides can claim as theirs. And although their ideological promise hasn't been realized in the form that they imagined, their dreams—of law as humanitarian promise, of North Atlantic hegemony as benign—remain part of the basic imaginary of global rulership.

Martti: Right. As odd as it may seem, there is a sense in which everybody is a Victorian today.

David: Might your image of the 1873 project be a bit too static? After all, it is striking how much *innovation* went into making law so ubiquitous and the legality of transnational interaction so plausible. It took a century of intellectual work and many shifts in the professional image of both law and global society. Foregrounding that innovation is suggestive for efforts today to rethink the world's legal foundations.

You know the story. Even the international law "positivism" of legal validity assessed by judges analyzing practice—which we think of as traditional—was a twentieth-century invention, doubling down on things loosely remembered from classical legal thought as responses to Austin's earlier challenge to the possibility of law among sovereigns. That positivism was already something of an innovative break with the 1873 sensibility. It didn't last; adjudicators found they needed a law of principles and purposes, and then a more sociological turn to facts and realities as potent origins for normative argument. In the second half of the last century law could be found in social life—in whatever turned out to be enforced as norms, interpreted as norms, persuasive as norms, in a rough-and-tumble policy process thought to be underwritten by shared values.

Martti: Well, that sociological turn was already in place with French late nineteenth-century jurists and during the interwar period someone like Georges Scelle made his career as a gentle civilizer and a reader of Durkheim.[21] But do go on.

David: For sure and that's when the judges on the interwar Permanent Court of International Justice trained, after all. Those ideas really took off in twentieth-century international law as people tried to develop horizontal analogues internationally for the vertical legal orders within states. Everything had to happen interactively—there was no sovereign up there as lawgiver. Soon you had international rules, national laws and corporate norms, hard law and soft, policies and principles, formal rules and informal practices, even explicitly nonbinding arrangements could have legal consequences. Thinking this way, it made more sense to focus on modes of interaction than norms, on processes and procedures for handling claims or defining actors, sorting out their overlapping powers and jurisdictions.

Along the way came a more *functional, problem-solving* family of legal ideas. By late in the century, the regulatory, administrative, and dispute settlement functions for global life had been redefined as activities which might be done anywhere. Cities do it, states do it, corporations do it, nongovernmental organizations do it—even rock stars do it. And maybe law is more symbol than substance, more thought than institution: a shared consciousness which could be shocked, a measuring rod for legitimacy, the expression of a universal civilization. It became possible to speak openly of international law as an *ideology*.

Perhaps all this innovation looked like progressive development on my side of the Atlantic and like the end of an era on yours. But this intellectual and practical innovation didn't come as a resigned retreat from positivist rectitude or as a rejection of international legality. It came as people enthusiastically expanded law's role and potential in global economic and political affairs. And expand it they did. Each set of ideas suggested finding law in new places, using it in new ways, applying it to new domains. The result was an enormous legal dispersion. We can now see that the less decisive, determinative, or univocal law seemed the more prevalent it became.

Remember how, twenty years ago, North Atlantic elites celebrated law's global ubiquity as a great achievement—the emergence of a global order, an international system, a network of networks, a normative transnational legal process, a regime of universal values which could bring economic prosperity and underwrite democratic justice for people everywhere. Today that all seems long ago and you're right that we are a long way from 1873—but I'm not sure the project failed. Its resilience is pretty impressive—along with the intensity of intellectual innovation necessary to keep it going.

Martti: Yes. I agree that something of the dream of a single world, governed by a global constitution with courts and public institutions exercising jurisdiction over states, still animates many people. Talk about a "rule-based international order" is very common among European lawyers and politicians. But maybe there is reason to distinguish between the capture of that early vision by a public, international-law-governed world—the UN and the multilateral treaty system as incipient forms of world government, peaking in courts of international jurisdiction—and a much broader commitment to law and legalism that also was shared by the late nineteenth-century legal activists. Already at the time, they were keen on expanding liberal constitutional principles, as well as family and criminal legislation across Europe and eventually the rest of the world. They supported freedom of establishment, free trade, individual rights. These are ideas that in the 1990s became shared common sense across the North Atlantic world.

But the gentle civilizers were innovating in the 1920s and 1930s too. The League of Nations provided a platform and an example for functionalism, a more informal, less rule-oriented legal thinking. In their writings people like Kelsen, Ehrlich, and Ross were pushing in opposing directions; and let's not forget Schmitt and the German realist attack on the false universalism of the League. These had great influence at the universities, but almost none in the legal institutional world—until your Americans entered the international scene in the 1950s and 1960s.

It is good to remember that in the global economy today, everything is underwritten, organized, made possible, and articulated by legal rules, principles, vocabularies, and institutions. That's sure to be a prominent theme when we get to law and *political economy*. It is impossible to operate in the world without constantly claiming legal entitlements and denying them from others. These are not entitlements written in treaties or debated at the UN; they emerge from and regulate relations between all kinds of private, public, and semipublic actors, international and domestic.

This is why today, every ruler, company director, and activist needs a lawyer on their side to tell them how to attain what they want with the least cost.

David: A *strategic* role, for sure.

Martti: There is no interest that cannot be translated into a right of its holder. The result is that all social conflict has become rights conflict. The right to security of some against the right to freedom of others, as we have seen in the recent COVID-19 debates. Economic and social rights against property rights, collective rights against rights of individual members of those collectivities. There is no nonregulated space; every prohibition is also permission of everything not expressly prohibited. As a result, all contestation becomes legal work: balance those rights in this, and not that, way; draw the boundary of this rule here, and not there; read the principle in this, and not that, way.

David: That's why I've tried to take the focus off adjudication, much as the texts it throws off are useful in figuring out how the mindset functions. And I'd rather call these "entitlements conflicts" to bring all the other Hohfeldian positions into play—duties, privileges to injure without recourse, the whole lot.

Martti: Of course, this also opens avenues for critical legal work. With imagination, technical skill, and good luck it is sometimes possible to read a rule or balance the rights differently. But often the fact that interests are articulated as *law* makes it harder to change the institutional bias than if they were a matter of bargaining. Rights or prosecutions may therefore not always be the right way to go; better results might be attained by financial transfers, negotiating with industry representatives or lobbying with governments. But even in such cases, the participants may reference points about jurisdiction or standards of best practice that turn the focus away from the substance of the claim to the form in which it has been made. Better bring in the lawyers, in any case.

David: One question we'll surely also come back to is what to *do* with these critical reflections. Of course, there is the pleasure in feeling one has seen just how things have gone so far off the rails. The pleasures of critique itself. Another aspiration, I think, is to make it easier for people to ask foundational questions—what I think of as 1648 questions—in part by seeing how often they have been asked before and how much intellectual innovation has gone on.

Something about contemporary legal consciousness and professional practice discourages that kind of thinking, but many who now study international law yearn for foundational reimagination. You've illuminated many moments in which people shifted foundational pillars. So, you know, sovereign rights are distributed among all kinds of actors, and then there's the singular sovereignty of the state, or one country could own another until they couldn't, or countries could be diverse in their religious practices and get along with each other, or owning things here could mean owning them somewhere far away, regardless of whatever local political authorities may have thought about it.

Rethinking on this scale is so unusual now. Proposals to shift the foundational maps of sovereignty—Brexit or Catalonian independence or Pan-African union—might have been examples. Or not; we can see that Brexit has meant only an interminable negotiation over the details of interaction.

I'm not suggesting we reorient to problem solving—and I'm anyway not very good at coming up with policy proposals to reform things. In my experience, as soon as you say, "I have a policy proposal," someone will say, "It won't work," and then that's the end of it. And there are lots of well-known alternatives already on the table.

Of course, sometimes a policy proposal can function as a utopian heuristic—something that could be done tomorrow, would clearly address a felt wrong, but is wholly unrealistic in real political time. Or could signal a new direction of travel—Roberto Unger has aimed to identify reforms that might be possible in real political time and point to the ways they might be part of an apparently unreachable foundational change.[22] And then there are proposals that begin with the kind of distributional assessment common for lobbyists and sometimes enabled by critique: once you've identified the groups in conflict, the winners and losers, one can more easily carry a brief for one or the other.

Martti: Attention to the omnipresence of law may indeed have a conservative effect. "Everything is tried already or is being tried right now. All you can do is to take part or not take part." We have tried to avoid that effect in a number of ways. Pointing to the looseness, for example: "You can always argue the other way." We have used history to encourage rethinking. "Look here, sovereign power or rights of property have been imagined in all these different ways, they have no essential or necessary content." But loosening the sense of truth or necessity of something is not the same as proposing a solution. Internal critiques can go only so far.

You are right that neither of us has felt it imperative to come up with policy proposals. As you say, these are always the weakest part of a research, the ones easiest to attack because the data can always be interpreted in different ways. Moreover, thinking of academic work as problem solution is profoundly conservative; it takes for granted what hegemonic institutions project as relevant "problems," their understandings and priorities. I like to stress to students that instead of looking for the right policy, they should map the field of proposed or possible policies and inquire into the assumptions that make any one of them seem better than the others. They should *understand* decision-making, not pretend to be decision-makers. Of course, once they enter the job market, there is time for proposing policies.

But I believe we both think that the world's most significant problems lie elsewhere than in the efficient management of tasks that powerful institutions identify as such. Instead what we suggest is that some of the world's worst problems—massive global and domestic inequality, for example—have to do precisely with those institutions: how they are composed and set their priorities. What we have aimed at has been to loosen the sense that those institutions and their priorities are somehow necessary or true. That would be part of the effort you mention to make palpable the sense of choice and responsibility in the exercise of power, whether or not it takes place by reference to law or any other system of expertise.

David: We've gotten started, although doubtless just scratched the surface of "law in global affairs." Let's stop here—we'll develop a lot of these themes in our next conversations.

Martti: Perfect.

Notes

1. Koskenniemi, *From Apology to Utopia.*
2. Koskenniemi, *The Gentle Civilizer of Nations.*

3. Koskenniemi, *To the Uttermost Parts of the Earth,* 1.

4. Kennedy, *International Legal Structures.*

5. Kennedy, *A World of Struggle.*

6. Kennedy, *The Dark Sides of Virtue.*

7. Kennedy, "Spring Break"; Kennedy, "Autumn Weekends." See also Kennedy, *The Rights of Spring.*

8. See, for example, Kennedy, "Turning to Market Democracy"; Kennedy, "A New World Order"; Kennedy, "Receiving the International"; Kennedy, "New Approaches to Comparative Law"; Kennedy, "The Disciplines of International Law and Policy"; Kennedy, "When Renewal Repeats"; Kennedy, "The Methods and Politics of Comparative Law"; Kennedy, "The Twentieth-Century Discipline of International Law in the United States"; Kennedy, "Tom Franck and the Manhattan School"; and Kennedy, "The 'Rule of Law.'"

9. Koskenniemi, "Hegemonic Regimes."

10. Kennedy, "The International Style."

11. Kennedy, "Primitive Legal Scholarship."

12. Kennedy, "The Turn to Interpretation."

13. Claude Lévi-Strauss, *The Savage Mind* (Chicago: University of Chicago Press, 1966); see also Kennedy, "Critical Theory."

14. Wilhelm G. Grewe, *The Epochs of International Law,* trans. Michael Byers (Berlin: Walter de Gruyter, 2000).

15. Kennedy, "The Context for Context."

16. Kennedy, "The International Human Rights Movement."

17. Myres S. McDougal, "Law and Power," 46 *American Journal of International Law* 102 (1952); Philip Allott, *Eunomia: New Order for a New World* (Oxford: Oxford University Press, 2001).

18. Koskenniemi, "Between Impunity and Show Trials."

19. Frances E. Olsen, "The Family and the Market: A Study of Ideology and Legal Reform," 96 *Harvard Law Review* 1497 (1983).

20. Koskenniemi, "Rights and the Bourgeois Revolution."

21. Georges Scelle, *Précis de droit des gens: Principes et systématique,* 2 vols. (Paris: Sirey, 1932–1936).

22. See, for example, Roberto Mangabeira Unger, *Politics,* vol. 3, *Plasticity into Power: Comparative-Historical Studies on the Institutional Conditions of Economic and Military Success* (London: Verso, [1987] 2004); and Roberto Mangabeira Unger, *Politics,* vol. 1, *False Necessity: Anti-necessitarian Social Theory in the Service of Radical Democracy* (London: Verso, [1987] 2004).

CONVERSATION THREE

International Law and Power

Martti: In an earlier conversation we noted that even as we're being critical of public international law as it's usually imagined, we still think of law as a useful object of analysis, perhaps even more important than is usually believed in framing the way power operates in the world. For example, you titled your most recent book *A World of Struggle: How Power, Law and Expertise Shape Global Political Economy*, and my latest work is titled *To the Uttermost Parts of the Earth: Legal Imagination and International Power 1300–1870*.[1] However, in our postrealist era, it has become really hard to separate power from the practices in which we engage and the structures—intellectual and other—within which they are formed. Can you explain how you see power, and especially how legal power operates in the world?

David: I think a common starting point would be the desirability of seeing power as a legal thing, immanent in law in some way. This already places us a bit outside conventional discussions which laud international law's *usefulness* for power located elsewhere, and power as a thing that can be possessed and then used, through law or otherwise. I think you may use the word this way in *To the Uttermost Parts of the Earth*, where you speak of the legal imagination and the "uses of power." Certainly, people external to law who are pursuing projects try to mobilize legal resources—language, institutions, professionals. But part of the reason they do is that those legal materials—the legal imaginings themselves—are also acts of power, world-making imaginings and world-affecting assertions.

When international law's own power is discussed, the images are often quite gentle—as in that wonderful quote you picked up for the title of *The Gentle Civilizer of Nations*[2]—the law comes to *real power* softly, civilizing it, restraining it as it expresses it or implements it. The real *it* remains outside the legal field, *behind* those who express or implement it. Back there it can serve as a kind of universal causal explanation, a phlogiston to explain outcomes. If you picture power that way, it is easy to imagine it as a one-way street, outside the interactive social relations through which it becomes effective.

These images have all been resisted by lots of social theorists aiming to locate power *in* social relations rather than as something that animates social relationships or causes them to take a particular direction. I think we are both in that tradition.

What that means for law—and, again, this seems common ground—is that *power* is a description of an effective legal arrangement. That could mean, in classic realist terms, a successfully enforced entitlement or authority. Law also has ideological effects, framing the way people understand themselves and others, both by consolidating one, rather than another, of contending ideological positions and by expressing or reinforcing background ideas that don't rise to conscious contestation.

We might replace the statement "He has power" with a prediction that his (legal) authority will be effective in one of these ways. In this sense, the power is the effectiveness of legal arrangements in action, not something behind or prior to them. And it is a two-way street—or multiple-lane intersection—where people assert and yield or resist or reinterpret. I associate this idea with Hans Kelsen both philosophically and sociologically: there's nothing behind the legal order but the effectiveness of the legal order.[3] A bit of a koan, but that's the idea: it is law all the way down. This idea that power as a socially effective legal arrangement, nothing more, places law at the center of the inquiry, *as* power or constitutive of power. *So that's the first idea: power is a legal thing.*

Martti: I agree, of course. But how interesting that you would reference Kelsen in that connection! Kelsen was one of the people I had in mind when, in *The Gentle Civilizer of Nations* I wrote about the power of the "culture of formalism." Formalism has a bad reputation, not least with lawyers who think of themselves as "critical"—wrongly, to my mind. I always found Kelsen's critique of Jellinek's idea that "statehood" has two sides—a sociological and a legal side—quite powerful. According to Kelsen, the sociological side is completely dependent on—or embedded in—the legal. For a sociologist or international relations analyst to be able to identify some group of people or a piece of territory as a "state," this can only be done by internalizing the—quite complex—legal vocabulary of statehood.[4] So it is not the case that there are states in the world that then "use" law as an instrument of their power, because a "state" is a legal construction. Power operates in the way law constructs some set of facts as a state while excluding such construction with respect to other facts.

David: Exactly—which makes Kelsen a kind of legal sociologist. I was taught that Kelsen was a *formalist* and a *positivist,* stigmatized terms in those days, but what he had in mind—just as you say—was quite different from what folks associate with these words: legal interpretation through long deductive chains from authoritative acts of power, a legal system that is internally coherent and systematic, and so forth. More significant was precisely his criticism of the idea that something stands *behind* law. He has a wonderful passage ridiculing the idea that power is about guns and electric chairs—"dead things," he calls them—and he equates the *power/state behind the law* idea with the notion that dryads and nymphs inhabit trees—or a deity stands behind human affairs. But then he has a second move that takes him back to the sociological—what stands behind law is law *if you think so* and if the law is *effective.*

Where to go from here? I think we've both tackled the puzzle of law's power in different ways at different moments of our career, probably without making the law-as-power or power-as-law in society analytic very clear.

Martti: Concern about power underlies all of your writing, doesn't it? So, let's talk a little about the ways you have thought about power. In your first large work, *International Legal Structures,*[5] you were interested in how power operated through the discourse of international law, arguing that on their face those texts and doctrines seemed like a complex effort to refer power *outside* the law—most often into some further process or decision-making moment. I suppose that was a way to demonstrate the difficulty or perhaps impossibility to capture power within the formal structures of law and to push readers to look more carefully into where the real moment of decision was located.

But then your second work, *The Dark Sides of Virtue*,[6] left the terrain of discourse analysis on the side and instead focused on institutional practices. It was a more sociological work that examined the fields of human rights law, refugee law, and European law as sites of power—sites that seemed quite unaware of the way power and hierarchy operated within them. But it also contained one of your most widely read texts, the astonishingly autobiographical "Spring Break." In that essay you seemed no longer that interested in the workings of the language or formal structure of international law—or, indeed, international law itself—but wanted to pursue further into the context of the modern world of international lawyering as a sociological and even psychological terrain. How do you view that transition now?

David: *International Legal Structures* focused on the structure—the *grammar,* in the terms we've been using—of doctrines and arguments about doctrines. I think I took it for granted that international law was an important—powerful—thing without asking why or how. People studied it, practiced it, made these doctrines and arguments—must be important. And yet the materials were so contradictory, arguments had patterns that turned around irresolvable issues over and over—what kept it going? How could it nevertheless be significant—or, I suppose, powerful? The book argued that people making use of the material were adept at turning contradiction into some kind of resolution in various ways—shifting ground from the validity of norms to the process for their interpretation, from procedural concerns to substantive choices and back again, transforming one irresolvable choice after another into a position that seemed stable, at least for a time. I guess I could say, if law was the exercise of power, its form was preoccupied with restating its own puzzles. Which could be good or bad, I suppose. But if you thought legal materials carried clarity or wisdom—or that their deployment was driven by practical considerations, you were missing something. So a description of ambivalent power or the authority of uncertainty, something like that.

The autobiographical essay you mentioned came next and was more sociological. I wanted to explore the way people embodied law's narrative forms—how did "speaking as a lawyer" work when heading off to another country to speak "on behalf" of people framed as "victims" of human rights abuses? Who were the interlocutors, how were roles distributed between "lawyers" and others, or among lawyers? I was exploring the narrative power of law, I guess—how people and institutions *became* the actors and structures imagined by the legal materials. The other essays collected in *The Dark Sides of Virtue* came at this in various contexts. How did the narratives of "asylum" and "refugee" law affect the projects of good-hearted people working at the United Nations High Commissioner for Refugees (UNHCR)? How did the narratives of European law shape the projects of folks in Brussels dealing with east and central Europe? Or the legal narratives about war affect the practice of war—an essay I later expanded into a book.

One last thought on *The Dark Sides of Virtue*. I divided it in two parts: narratives in the key of virtue and in the key of practical policy. Whether you think of law as a tool (the action is in policy) or as a virtue (the making real of values) you'll miss the effects of the vocabulary or professional practice on the *shape* of each. Moreover, people shuttled between them, as if each could correct for the limitations of the other. Too realist, turn to values; too sanctimonious, be practical. Useful, certainly, but also an offloading of responsibility which obscured awareness of the limitations of each. So it was a study of the *irresponsible* power of these expert practices. This back-and-forth operated much like the shifts among concern about law's authority, procedure, and substance in *International Legal Structures*—a kind of apology or reinforcement for the authority of both.

Martti: Right. And now there is *A World of Struggle*, in which you have moved even further away from formal legal analysis and take on the operations of expert power in global governance. But you do still propose that the structures of political economy that seem to run a globalized world are much more embedded with legal entitlements and vulnerabilities than we conventionally tend to think. This then develops into a fresh analysis of legal power as framing the global world in which experts struggle and articulate their claims against each other and the public in general. Can you say something about whether this book is simply an extension of the argument in those prior texts or more a wholly different direction in your work?

David: I thought of myself extending rather than moving away from legal analysis; my question was whether other expert practices, adjacent to law, had similar patterns. I aimed for more systematic analysis of rhetorical power—or what I called "power by articulation"—whose dark sides, if you will, were deeply rooted in expert knowledge practice as well as in the particular limitations of the various settings I looked at: development policy, human rights, war, and so on. In all these settings people were deploying knowledge as power: How did that knowledge shape itself as power, and could we say something more general about expert power in the world, offer a protocol for analyzing other fields of expert practice? Would a more general picture of common expert patterns help us understand the hegemony of expert or technocratic power in the world? I thought it might. The image of performative articulation, of effective assertion, if you like, was central to my sense of power in that book.

Perhaps we can focus today on questions we've heard about our work in these various styles. Here are a couple I've run into; perhaps you have too.

- *Structuralism and the power question.* Particularly our early work reading texts in the structuralist mode, bracketing the context of their production to focus on their internal mechanics, can seem to bracket the question of power altogether or consign it to the context. Moreover, we both stressed the contradictory, open-ended, *indeterminate* structure of the legal materials we analyzed: How could they be both indeterminate and powerful? Doesn't that hive off the power question to blind spots or biases—and intentions—that come from elsewhere? We touched on that in our "critical method" discussion—disagreed a bit, as I recall.
- *Intellectual history and the power question.* We've both focused on leading figures and ideas in the North Atlantic international law traditions in periods of European or American efforts to universalize their vision and project their dominance outward in the world. What's the relationship between these intellectual traditions and those projects of world domination? Instrumental to or constitutive of colonialism? Something else? We will talk about international law's ideas about "the others" another time. Can we focus here on that in the key of *power*?
- *Performative power.* We've both focused on the world-making effects of what you call "legal imaginings" or I have labeled "expert knowledge

practices." How does this work, exactly? Is this what people mean by "hegemony?" By "legitimation?"

Martti: Okay, let's do it.

David: We both started by reading legal texts under the influence of a structuralist mandate to focus *internally* on the ways the texts fit together, their rhetorical operations and the unstated elements which seemed necessary for their sense making. This approach self-consciously bracketed both questions of their origin in social relations and of their effects in the world.

But that wasn't the whole story. The title of your first book—*From Apology to Utopia*[7]—suggests both a philosophical tension internal to the materials and a way they function in the world, either apologizing for things as they are or promising what could only be a utopia. You seem to say that international legal materials are stranded between these functions—and so are those who utilize them. And those are their *effects* in the world—or, maybe, that is its effect, to be that thing that oscillates, promising and moderating each, something like that.

Perhaps you could say more about the *usefulness,* if I can call it that, or, perhaps better, the *effect* of an ambiguous, contradictory professional vocabulary.

I'm thinking, for example, about the strange plasticity of the war/not war distinction in discussions of the Russia/Ukraine conflict. The vocabulary was "useful" to war makers and resisters on both sides, but it also framed their roles, their image of what war is and what they were doing. Making and unmaking the distinction, knowing it could unravel at any moment: that was a professional practice of both *communicating* and *waging* struggle.

How do you think about the use/effect of the knowledge practices you critiqued in *From Apology to Utopia?* Was that a book about power?

Martti: I think we both were quite annoyed by the assumption that international law was somehow innocent of the way the world was, that it was the "truth" that lawyers spoke to power. It was important to see law's truth as the kind of power/knowledge that Foucault had taught us to look for in human relationships. In law, those relationships were expressed and authoritatively reaffirmed in legal language. People are expected to yield. I came to law from a 1980s linguistic turn sensibility. Power operated within and was made visible in speech, and *From Apology to Utopia* aimed at explicating the grammar of international legal speech: How did it express relationships of power by turning them into authority/truth in a competent way? I used Chomsky's generative grammar, trying to think about the "competence" of the lawyer analogously to the competence of the native language speaker.[8] (By the way, I still think this as a powerful way to teach students what it is that happens to them as they learn law—they become "competent law speakers.")

David: Agreed—they can feel cognitively empowered.

Martti: Yep. That early work studied the formation of competent sentences in international law, and then tried to show how such sentences generated the feeling of closure or legal "truth" so that the human relationship expressed in them—right and duty, for example, or some other hierarchy—would have the sense of "validity" or unavoidability. Or—to take the example I began with—how does something get argued as a "state"? By learning this grammar lawyers would be able to produce an interminable number of sentences, even ones never produced before, and with them authoritatively lay down or reaffirm human relationships of superiority and subordination. *From Apology to Utopia* aimed to analyze relationships of power by formal, quasi-logical demonstrations.

That then led me to indeterminacy and structural bias. First, I showed—again, by a quasi-logical technique—that the relationships between legal concepts, and thus the power relationships addressed by them, generated by the competent use of grammar, were indeterminate, that they did not generate any real sense of truth or closure. They could always be "flipped." Competent lawyers did this all the time. Instead, to the extent that people *believed* in those inferences and relationships, this was an effect of a "structural bias." It followed from some extra-linguistic component in their world, for example background assumptions commonly held by people in *those* kinds of positions. Last time I said it relied upon ideology. The critical point was to conclude that legal language was power and not truth. It possessed no firm meaning, communicated no self-evident conclusions. The sense of closure or truth did not follow from any necessity embedded in legal concepts or methodologies.

David: Or truth as power? Legal argument that *might* be unraveled often does generate the effect of closure. That closure sometimes does come from another place in the expert's mind—we could call that ideology, or something more (psycho)social—but then the guy is speaking the truth of *that,* whether openly or consciously or not. Saying that's what's going on is, in turn, our interpretation.

Martti: Let me give an example. In 2010 the question of Kosovo's statehood came to the International Court of Justice. By reference to facts on the ground, in the aftermath of the Yugoslavian succession wars, it was quite possible to argue that Kosovo both "fulfilled the criteria" of statehood and did not. Legal precedent could be used to arrive at both solutions. But this was a time of Western predominance, and the West argued that it was a thing separate from Serbia—to the great annoyance of not only Serbia but also its ally, Russia—and that's the way the court decided. But of course, entities like Abkhazia or Luhansk, Northern Cyprus or Taiwan have not been so decided, never mind that in many ways the "facts" of statehood have been at least as well established there as in Kosovo.

David: Certainly; the rules or criteria are plastic enough to be mobilized on both—or many—sides. I've also heard you refer to indeterminacy as a *thesis*. What do you have in mind?

Martti: There's been a lot of attention on the indeterminacy thesis, and while some have expressed doubts about it, I often heard practicing colleagues say that it's a useful description of what they knew. "Of course," they would comment, "competent lawyers should be able to justify their client's case; indeterminacy makes that possible. And the judge will then choose." Despite the obviousness of this, international lawyers have a hard time coping with indeterminacy, because they feel that the law itself is not only "true" but also "good," and that it does stand outside and speaks enlightenment to power. Which, of course, is incompatible with indeterminacy.

According to the indeterminacy thesis, legal concepts or methods cannot constrain because they always logically allow one to say both *X* and the contrary to *X*. For every principle there is a counterprinciple, for every rule an exception. This was what made legal argument possible. It was not about semantics: even when rules are clear, the legal system of which they are a part offers counterrules or interpretative principles that allow deciding differently. On the other hand, however, everybody knows that legal institutions operate in predictable ways. If the *language* is indeterminate, the *world* is not. Indeed, you and I agree that that's the problem—it's too determinate, we know already beforehand who will win and who will lose. If institutions are not constrained by law's formal structure, they are constrained by *structural bias.* It is not law as language that constrains but something else, perhaps a "gentle civilizing" project or an institutional teleology embedded in it. This is where law's ideological power becomes visible, its distributive power, its power to shape and consolidate (but also critique) human relationships.

David: It's complicated. That image of an "indeterminacy thesis" seems so compulsory: there are two arguments, so law "can't constrain," so it must be something else . . . power? The power of "structural bias," which we'll need to unpack. This seems to let law off the hook—it's just a bundle of propositions among which you can choose. I did want to look at those other languages that get looped in—that was the *World of Struggle* project. But I don't want to turn the potential indeterminacy of the legal materials into a *necessity.*

There are lots of gaps, ambiguities, and propositions pointing in opposite directions in legal materials. And the legal fields we explored turned around central antinomies which could not be "resolved." They were opposing objectives or commitments of international law as a whole—apology and utopia, community and sovereignty, and so forth.

Yet couldn't we also say most people experience most legal materials as determinate most of the time? Experience their favorite theories and doctrinal solutions as brilliant antinomy resolvers? I want to locate this experience in the qualities or potentials of the materials, not only zooming in from ideology or whatever. Meanwhile, even potentially indeterminate materials take a lot of things off the table—they frame the situation as *this* or *that,* not as something else altogether. Isn't all this—"framing," if you like—part of what it means to show that law is power?

Martti: Absolutely. It is one thing to demonstrate law's formal or logical open-endedness as I did in *From Apology to Utopia* and another to show that, as a historical or sociological "thing" or a frame, law binds its practitioners or users to prefer certain types of practice or decision. I now think that what that book did was to show how relations of power were *translated* and *reproduced* in competent uses of legal language. It demonstrated the links that existed between certain philosophical vocabularies (I called them "liberalism") and technical formulations that were generally regarded as important parts of the professional vocabulary of international law. It explicated what could be called the conditions of validity of international legal speech. It then showed that with this toolbox anything could be argued. It did not, as it were, contain an inbuilt image of the good society.

Nevertheless, despite the indeterminacy of this—logical—type, the social and historical world of law communicated and consolidated among the general public the belief that the world was composed of firm meanings and solid identities—rules, principles, institutions and regimes, and that these were the instruments with which the crises of the world could be held under control. In this way it confirmed the status and position of its practitioners, the authority of the institutions where they worked, as well as a received conceptualization of the hierarchical relationship between the elements of the international world. A project that presented itself as progressive, even necessary, confirmed and reproduced over and over again an altogether familiar and unjust world.

But I was also keen to suggest that there was no reason to set international law aside. *From Apology to Utopia* presented the way power operated in or through the argumentative structures of the law; because those structures were indeterminate, there was no reason—no logical or intrinsic reason—why they could not be used to challenge any existing structural bias as well. Quite optimistically, I followed the early critics by presenting law's necessity as *false necessity,* allowing legal institutions to be turned into counterhegemonic projects as well. I used that type of analysis then in a number of essays on individual legal topics collected in *The Politics of International Law.*[9] All of that was very close to what your *International Legal Structures* did. I think I have since moved beyond those types of analyses. What would you say about yourself?

David: I'm not sure I moved away from structuralism. I would say I tried to broaden the canvas of things to which structuralist insights might be applied. Lévi-Strauss, after all, was not talking about texts but social relationships, interpreted and built around the transformation of recurring antinomies—the "raw" and the "cooked." You find this sort of thing all over the international legal world—public and private, the economic and political, the North and the South, the developed and the underdeveloped—as the central preoccupation of one field after another. I was struck—and perhaps we'll talk about this next time—by the strange way the intellectual history of the field, the movement among preoccupations and theoretical priorities, seemed structured in a way parallel to the doctrines and theories we have been discussing. And then the poststructuralist moment pushed me forward—the interesting binaries are *hierarchical* and *unstable* in particular ways. There was a lot still to figure out.

I'm still wondering about your statement that it "was power and not truth." Yes, if you mean the truth claims were constructed, not *really* true in some way—but isn't the assertion of truth a kind of power? International law folks are constantly asserting truths, both factual and normative, as authority. Effectively in many cases—and in any case their framing of the situation is somehow always already performative.

I'd also like to say more about "indeterminacy." But first, could you say a bit more about how hierarchies are *translated* and *reproduced* in legal language? Do you mean textually—they express the hierarchy—or do you have a sociological mechanism in mind through which these effects occur?

Martti: I have always found it hard—maybe harder than you—to separate between language and the world to which it is addressed. I think of "truth" as a propositional quality of language—that is to say, using a Kelsenian idiom, the "validity" of an utterance within a language and "power" as an aspect of its use in practice. When I say the law translates and reproduces human relationships of power, I say it *asserts* them authoritatively and then expects those addressed to yield to that assertion. Althusser would, I think, speak of "interpellation." The validity of two sets of power relations are declared: the right/duty relationship (or hierarchy) in the social world, and the law's (and lawyer's) authority to determine it.[10] The one who yields, thinks they yield to what is "true" about the law. But it is not "true" in the sense that its content could not be denied validly in that language.

David: I do like the formulation "it asserts authoritatively and expects those addressed to yield." A person does that in legal terms, but the statement, the assertion is also performative—it is the authority to which one yields, something like that.

Before we move on, though, what you said a moment ago made me wonder if we are thinking about indeterminacy and structural bias in the same way. It might be useful to pin down the differences. First, some common points. The legal materials are full of gaps, conflicts, and ambiguities opening opportunities for interpretation. If you think legal work is the logical unfolding of deduction, you have underestimated the gaps/ambiguities and overestimated the persuasiveness of deductive assertions that move a long way from a general proposition to a specific outcome.

Rather, the interpretive practices on display in international legal materials have a structure—grammar in your Chomskian sense, in which assertions are made, assertions of the type available in the legal vocabulary—to generate a feeling of closure in spite of the gaps and contradictions by rearranging the available terms in ways that transform, reverse, elide, or otherwise maneuver the contradictory alternatives in ways analogous to what Lévi-Strauss thought was going on when people used their cultural inheritance to talk about the world or Chomsky thought was characteristic of language itself.

Here we may part ways a bit. You are drawn to the idea that the materials as practiced by the interpreting professions are "indeterminate" in the sense that definitive legal conclusions are not *possible* under some theory of what it takes to be definitive and possible. Or that indeterminacy is an attribute of the materials, given their structure: there's always a contradictory alternative waiting to rear its head, making it possible for a determined legal worker to unravel an apparently satisfying resolution by pulling on the other thread. Or perhaps the materials/practice promise a resolution which their own terms prevent them from offering—that kind of a conundrum.

If the materials are indeterminate in this sense, it is hard to see how they could be constraining. And, therefore, also difficult to see how they could be malevolent. If there is a justice problem, it must come from somewhere else, which takes us out to context, placing any bias in the structure or the agents—which could include their "ideology." No question, one could imagine a squishy professional tool being used by evil agents in an unjust structure to reinforce their position, crush or exploit their enemies. But I do think this takes international law—the materials, the profession, the interpretive practice—off the hook. Which is not at all what you intend, I think.

Martti: No, not at all. I agree that professional people are constrained, just not by the linguistic or logical aspects of the law.

David: Like you, I've been struck by the ubiquity of contradictions and antinomies or irresolvable polarities in legal materials. The grammatical element, if I can call it that, which has seemed most significant to me I associate with Derrida and the word *deconstruction:* the repeated discovery that even the extreme ends of what seemed like polar opposites contain a shadow of one another, which is what opens the way to their reinterpretation. These reinterpretations—what you thought was sovereignty should really be understood as justice—are the grammatical operations that do, often, get people to yield, generate the experience of closure.

Now we both think this isn't the end of it. There's a linchpin of interpretive instability in the Derridean formulation: differences *between* recur as differences *within.* The listener might see that straight away and not experience closure. Or a determined legal worker might pull on that thread to reverse a seemingly settled interpretation. But often there is no determined legal worker and, as a practical matter, the interpretation does settle. I suppose you could call this *potential* interpretive instability "indeterminacy," but that is easily misconstrued to mean things always fall apart when in real life they rarely do—perhaps because of some outside power, but also just because no one thought of it, had the time or energy to pursue it. And that's why the *hierarchical* dimension of the polarity itself—public *over* private, private *over* public, sovereignty *over* community, and so on—is also crucial.

With that in mind, I've tried to restrict the term *indeterminacy* to connote an experience, a social/psychological event, rather than a textual attribute: the experience of an interpretation that seems settled unraveling—often in the face of determined legal work by somebody—which unsettles, even reverses, the experience of their relative hierarchy. All those attributes of the materials—conflicts, gaps, ambiguities, contradictions—may or may not make the experience of indeterminacy more common; a lot depends, for example, on how skeptically people approach them, how robust or adversarial the discussion is, and so forth.

If you think about it this way, the bias issue looks a bit different. This kind of contradictory vernacular may run on quite narrow and hierarchically organized tracks. Interpretive instability says nothing about *range* of possible interpretations or the experience of the relative position for the contradictory elements. Indeed, the obsession with a few recurrent contradictions suggests that people using these materials will have a hard time thinking about much else. Everything is either "raw" or "cooked"—it's not mineral or spirit or interplanetary or who knows what. And cooked sounds tastier—or not.

So, you could have bias in the "structure" *internal* to the legal materials which might otherwise be overlooked by too fast a turn to all those bad people in unjust structures. Although the materials are contradictory and unstable, there are some things that you don't see, there are propositions that are hard to bring into them. So, for example, "God gave me this" is not one of the things you can say in international legal materials no matter how you twist the contradictions around.

Martti: Not now.

David: Right, not now—nor can you say "I have a bigger nuclear weapon and so I'm going to take it." A nuclear weapon may be there, you might take it out and test it as a kind of assertion . . . but then you need a reason—"They're committing genocide, they violated our territory, our sovereignty, they're not really a country"—something. You might have to manufacture that reason on the ground—"false flag operation"—but you do that because you need a reason of a particular type.

The terrain of reasons can constrain even if the reasons come with counterreasons, are ambiguous, and so on. Where the imagination is constrained by an incessant focus on states and sovereignty, it's very difficult for nonstates to get a grip on international law despite all the modern efforts to disperse the locations of norm making, techniques of implementation or fora for dispute resolution. Or it is more difficult for the people on the periphery to express themselves in the vernacular of an alternative universality than for those at the center whose vernacular has become universal. That kind of thing.

The interpretive instability and internal contradictions of the materials may exacerbate these effects by raising the bar for sophisticated professional work, thereby distributing the capacity and opportunity for determined legal work in ways that advance some interests and stymie others. It is striking that sophisticated professionals both act as if the materials were determinant and understand that they're not—that is, that they need to be suspicious of one another's apparently compelling articulations. The result is a range of particular professional styles that require training; not everyone can play.

Skeptical antiformalism at the center, formalism at the periphery is a real thing in the world. Just whom that privileges in a given situation is hard to say, of course—but important to figure out. Does formal rule following favor the weak? Well, not if the strong made the rules. And not if the strong approach formal rules in a spirit of skeptical antiformalism—ready to devote energy to the transformation of their uncertainties—when the weak lack the skills and the energy to respond in kind.

Martti: So, there is, on the one hand, an openness and endless revisability that you would call grammatical and, on the other, a phenomenological experience of relative closure that is sociologically "real." I agree, and I think people come to that discrepancy differently prepared. There are those whom you call sophisticated professionals who are very aware of both worlds: even as they know that you can argue that Kosovo both is and is not a state, they also know that for some audiences the matter is simply one way or another. And they will formulate what they will say in accordance with that (sociological-psychological) understanding. And then there are those others who, for whatever reason, are committed to thinking that the truth speaks only with one voice—and I suppose most people most of the time think this in a way that counts for the stability of our institutions. Like a language, a hermeneutic of suspicion can be learned; you can learn it by legal training, but also through intuitively experiencing the world as unjust and its explanations of itself untrue or hypocritical. I like your distinction between actual and *potential* interpretative instability: even a hermeneutic of suspicion can exist only in a world of experiences, some of which are stable.

I agree that some legal meanings have a very powerful pull—that even as it may be technically, grammatically, quite *possible* to challenge them, as a sociological fact, everyone is constrained. In moving from *From Apology to Utopia* to *The Gentle Civilizer of Nations* I tried to shift the perspective accordingly, from linguistic to ideological structures embedded in and communicated by law as historical practice—what I there called a "sensibility." Even as you may plausibly disagree on whether Kosovo is a state, you cannot really, or meaningfully, challenge the fact that France is one and expect anyone to yield. Or claim that your right is based on your owning a nuclear weapon. The law as a historical social phenomenon compels seeing or believing some things and not other things. In that sense, not everything is "flippable."

David: Conceptually or practically? I can imagine arguments against French statehood—start with the German/Austria customs union case and apply Montevideo. We find France in the European Union—they call it a *union,* no less. With Schengen, a common commercial policy, territorial authority is muted; government is shared, the population can float around, capacity for foreign relations restricted . . . and so on. Couldn't we imagine a situation in which someone might make an argument like that—and even find some resonance? That France is not a state for some purposes? Think of Putin and the nonexistence of Ukraine.

Martti: I can imagine those arguments as well. Most international lawyers can. But I cannot imagine an institutional decision taken as authoritative based on the argument that France is not a state. Maybe we can think of something like the quantitative aspect of structural bias. I acknowledge the psychological aspect, the depth of "feelings" of closure and openness, of subjective possibility and impossibility. *The Gentle Civilizer of Nations* aimed precisely to sketch an ideological field where it had become possible to say certain types of things but not other types of things. The formation of a "professional ethos" in the 1870s limited the ability of those who shared it to think and say things that were nevertheless said by, for example, participants to the Second International in the 1880s.

But when I wrote *From Apology to Utopia* I was conducting an analysis of the features of language, though I can now understand that it was also an analysis of the features of the world. For some people, I suppose, the relationship between the two seems very fixed and deconstruction just meaningless wordplay. These may be legal or technical experts working in stable international institutions, people who feel in control of the way the world operates. But many others are puzzled and feel not at all in control of things; these people experience the discrepancy between language and the world very acutely; the justifications of the former group appear random, unjust and somehow ideological. I guess to the extent that we talk about the quantitative aspects of the structural bias, we must bear these kinds of distinction in mind. Here attention moves from open-endedness and obscurity of language to the constraining power of the world itself.

David: Let's turn to our intellectual history work. How do you see power in the story of your men of 1873?

Martti: These were elite Europeans with an agenda; some of them were members of government, parliamentarians, and so on. They had excellent international contacts. But the principal power in their story lay in the institutional and the framing effects of the international law they developed—especially during the interwar period, but also earlier. Diplomacy would be increasingly legalized—there would be multilateral treaty-making conferences with state representatives, suggesting a kind of international legislation. There would be courts and tribunals, international "unions," a framing tension between domestic and international jurisdiction. The frame was *good,* its value lying in the way it would oppose a narrow-minded nationalism, the politics of sovereignty, on the one hand, and an aggressive imperialism, on the other. The world was dangerously poised between extreme alternatives like that and it was the task of law's "civilizing process" to bring everyone to understand the wisdom of the modest middle.

At universities, "public international law" would be taught as a real "legal system" with its textbooks, case collections, and complex formalism; it was *law* and not some sort of peace activism or charity work. It represented professionalism, internationalism, and enlightenment; the more it intruded in political debates, the better for the world. The power of the law to which the men of 1873 gave professional form was the framing power of public law in putting together cosmopolitan progress (international institutions, free trade, and human rights) and liberal statehood (self-determination, development, and solidarity). It embodied the enchanting power of moderate liberalism, reason and authority enshrined in legal rules and the profession tasked to manage them.

David: I like "enchantment"—there can be something so charismatic about professional style.

Martti: In *From Apology to Utopia* I had sketched the grammar of that vocabulary. Like any structuralist work, it was quite static, describing possibilities and techniques. It had little to say about how that vocabulary had emerged and been employed. With *The Gentle Civilizer of Nations* I wanted to examine how the international law profession—my profession—had come use the vocabulary for the practical projects in which it was engaged through the interwar period and into the 1960s.

I felt that the profession had a very thin sense of itself as a moral and political *project* and I wanted to create an account of that project. Where had it come from? What things had it supported and what had it been against? How had it experienced its successes and failures along the way? Looking around, I could see enthusiasm about some efforts—distribution of proceeds from deep sea mining to the developing world, for example; UN peacekeeping; Protection of the ozone layer. But there was quite a bit of cynical consciousness, also, about anything of the sort. I wanted to understand international law by examining how lawyers in the past had related to its achievements and failures: How were we to think about the dialectic of idealism and cynicism?

David: Your guys were certainly pursuing projects *with* or *through* international law. I also liked the way you drew attention to the project *of* international law—more important for a lot of people than what can be done with it. And the way their sense of the world took shape in its terms. Their sensibility also comes, as you describe, with cynicism—or pragmatic savvy, to put it more affirmatively. There's an economy of cynicism within a profession that also has effects on the people and the world.

We've both experienced the gap between the way professionals talk about their work in official and unofficial settings—at lunch and in a meeting. To give an example, when I was at working at UNHCR it struck me that they managed their engagement and cynicism in part through a division of labor in the organization—pragmatism/plasticity in the field, sanctimoniousness/normative clarity in the headquarters.[11] People felt these were also roles required by the two situations. Although there remained an underlying *potential* for cynicism in both places, it was kept in check by this sense of institutional role requirements. In headquarters, people might say at a party that they worked in the "if you can't feed them, film them" department—but they also felt that making such films was necessary and ultimately, if obscurely, related to feeding them. And the films were the very opposite of cynical; cynicism was the domain of realism, public facing was all ethical. In the field, the front foot was pragmatic and politically savvy rather than sanctimonious, with a reverse lunchtime cynicism about ideals compromised.

We've talked about international law's oddly doubled self-image: the product of both a rough-and-tumble realist history and an ethical history of ideals slowly realized. It has always astonished me how easily international lawyers—and students—could believe both: a legal fabric wrought in sovereign accord expressing civilizational virtue.

Martti: We were both surrounded by this economy of moral virtue and professional savvy and interested in its institutional manifestations and role in reproducing the hierarchies of a profoundly unjust world.

I now think that the modest reasonableness of the "gentle civilizers," their careful embrace of contrasting alternatives such as cosmopolitanism and nationalism, was part of this economy, keeping the doors open to both moral virtue and solid realism. This was the ideological frame that was reflected in the perceived authoritativeness of an open-ended set of concepts and the institutional practices of the legal diplomacy as it arose within the League of Nations first and the UN thereafter. I wanted to make the point that, contrary to most historical accounts, this type of "sensibility" had emerged quite recently, in the context of late nineteenth-century debates about European political order and the progress of civilization. It expressed an aspect of the modernizing consciousness of European legal elites, the efforts to push forward liberal laws across European parliaments and civilize—but maintain—colonial rule. It would pass through a creative but traumatic period in the interwar. But as I had come to it in the 1970s, it had frozen into a rather stale set of formal doctrines and institutional practices. I was interested in recounting that narrative, a story of a profession in its prime—*rise and fall.* What had the men of the 1870s been looking for? How did they stabilize the tensions in their intellectual tools and professional activities?

David: You bring them alive in that way, in the more innocent spring of Victorian possibility. I tried something similar with *The Rights of Spring* for the early innocence of the human rights movement.[12]

Martti: These late nineteenth-century ("Victorian") legal professionals believed that legal modernity would bring about peace and order among European sovereigns. This would involve, among other things, what they sometimes called "a more elevated patriotism"—an enlightened consciousness that would assist state elites to cooperate with each other.[13] They understood and agonized over the Janus-faced character of statehood: on the one hand, a force for egoism and war, on the other, a platform for just rulership, development, and welfare. They believed that law would enable the benefits of statehood win over its dark sides, that law embodied a progressive spirit that would gradually overtake even reluctant or backward states; it would endorse their welfare-oriented cooperation and bring about an increasingly integrated world, Europe's idealized image of itself. They might be more or less "optimistic" or "pessimistic" in this respect, depending on how soon or with what likelihood the law would be able to carry out this task.

David: And the rest of the world?

Martti: They were "liberals" but also imperialists. They were conscious of the avarice and rapacity of Europeans in what they called the "Orient" and wanted to turn colonial policy into civilizing direction. But they turned a blind eye to the worst atrocities—King Leopold's Congo or the suppression of the Herero Revolt, for example. In due course, they would switch from a civilizing to a modernizing vocabulary and speak of development in the third world. Their very strong investment in public international nstitutions—the League and the UN—was accompanied by the domestic analogy. The international world would eventually have its legislators, its courts, its functional administrators, they believed—some more, others less firmly. The "sovereign equality" promised by the UN Charter and international law generally would eventually become a reality. Indeed, this might be helped by pretending—as the rites of multilateral diplomacy suggested—that it was so *already*. Whether as optimists or pessimists, none of them could really convince their opposite number of the reality of this perception, but each could leave the debate satisfied with having said what always needed to be said. Indeterminacy was handy to keep both groups in the same camp.

Here is how *The Gentle Civilizer of Nations* came to the theme of power. The book pointed to the paradoxical way in which a small group of modest professionals could consolidate a normative worldview, a small number of apparently "true" propositions about the international world, its present status and prospects of development. Because those propositions were formulated only loosely, and pointed in different directions, they enabled powerful institutions to use them quite freely, to liberate and to constrain as needed. On the one hand, there was sovereignty; on the other, there was solidarity. On the one hand, there was equality; on the other, a firmly trenched system of hierarchies. If this seemed confusing, a strong progressive undercurrent explained that things would eventually fall in place once the world found its way from separation to unity, fragmentation to system. The ironic title of *The Gentle Civilizer of Nations* suggested that if you believed in international law, then you were thinking in nineteenth-century terms, but also that perhaps that was right, that many of the world's important features still the carried a "Victorian" spirit. That would at least explain a lot.

David: I like that description of contradictory propositions enabling a practice loosely stabilized by an image of historical progress. So the *power* in the practice lay in their development of a picture of the world that became widely shared among the ruling elites, enabling and limiting their sense of what it was appropriate to do. After 1945, Kelsen imagined international law similarly—emerging as legal, as centralized, as history advanced—*if you saw it that way*. He was also proselytizing: After what we've just been through, are you with civilization or are you not? He wrote to bring into being what he described as the product of a progressive history.

You identify your "gentle civilizers"—what we might now call "influencers"—as people who were able to naturalize their vision of the world, a description of "how things are that implied a set of projects, authorities, limitations for elite action. They were, in this sense, sort of Gramscian intellectuals, expressing and forming the consciousness, the ideology, of at least some parts of a ruling elite.[14] I like the way you leave somewhat open whether they were the tail or the dog.

Martti: Right. But I think that "Gramscian" gives them too much credit as sophisticated strategists; they were professionals, not versed in positional calculation.

David: Well, as organic intellectuals of a class, you don't necessarily have to strategize; you articulate the vision of the class to and for itself. But you might *think* you're being terribly strategic. The late twentieth-century US tradition felt that way to me. I leaned toward treating the texts I studied as *evidence* of an elite sensibility, while you seemed to lean more toward your guys as the originating mandarins of a profession with projects in the world that made a difference—until they didn't.

So, for example, I looked at Hans Kelsen and John Jackson as exemplars of a postwar "international style."[15] They were big figures, certainly, influential in their way: Jackson really was the intellectual origin and acknowledged leader of a legal subdiscipline with serious institutional clout. But I read them to take the temperature of the American policy elite—its legal face—more broadly. These guys could illuminate how that broader elite imagined the world, the law, their role as well as their professional style in approaching the puzzles of global governance. There, also, I found conflicting propositions, vague generalizations, stabilized by a kind of mental geography and sense for the direction of history.

This all raises the question of the power of *style,* if we can call it that. I've used the term to embrace something broader than the "beliefs" of an elite which we can imagine steering "use" of their authority or power. That's a conventional way to think about ideology—people (usually other people) are in the grip of strange beliefs which explains why they do the things they do. I imagine *style* to include something like beliefs, but to be both less conscious and more embodied—like a language, perhaps, with its underlying grammar; a shared vernacular and modes of speech; a shared sense for what's possible, appropriate, out of bounds. But not just the grammar—also the content, the topics, the preoccupations. So "raw" and "cooked" plus "kinship" as the thing to be worked out. We could call it a professional "consciousness" and mode of practice, perhaps. As a mode of imagining and asserting, a style like that is performative and is also a mode of power. The kind of knowledge/power mash-up to which Foucault is always drawing our attention.

In *The Gentle Civilizer of Nations* I think you distinguish this kind of professional sensibility or worldview among your men of 1873 from what we might call their "ideology," which you identify as "liberalism" and describe as a set of shared cosmopolitan beliefs and projects. Their liberalism in this sense is a kind of parallel expertise, alongside their international law expertise. Some of what you trace—imagining and building the world on the domestic analogy, distinguishing public and private in particular ways, and so on—seemed deeper and more open-textured than what we usually imagine an *ideology* or *interest* to entail. So one could imagine ideological "conservatives" framing the world in the same way and having robust arguments with "liberals" about what to do in a world they *all* imagined as your guys came to imagine it.

When you say they were Victorian, I imagine a lot of their liberalism sinking beneath the waterline of conscious ideological commitment to become the sea in which everyone was swimming for most of a century. I think of their Victorian "sensibility" as an embodied style that would endure in a generation, despite all the shocks and setbacks these nineteenth-century people experienced in the twentieth—until they seemed to a new generation like everyone's grandfather. Nevertheless, a great deal of their vision endured, took new professional forms. A vision of liberal free trade and the legalization of interstate relations as a mode of universalizing the European imagination turns out to have some staying power—certainly way down beneath that waterline.

It is too soon in the history of the American century and its potential end to know how that turns out, but your disentanglement of the specific projects, the particular ideological tendencies, and these deeper world-making conceptions are incredibly useful as we try to figure that out.

Martti: It does sound right to me . . . style, sensibility, something that came naturally as part of a certain experience and education. Not the conscious adoption of an ideology or a set of theses but a predisposition that allowed patterns of decision to emerge even when working with an indeterminate vocabulary and a grammar. Just one little footnote that I would like to add. You suggest that I remained agnostic about the causal relations between the world and these men. Were they influential producers of this world or just illustrations of it? I am not sure that it would be useful to think in causal terms. People have very different assumptions about how ideologies (sensibilities, styles) operate. You don't want to commit to assuming trajectories of influence that are impossible to prove. What you want to do is to describe something that people intuitively recognize as true, or illuminating, even though they don't have a clear view of it, and even if that might stand in contrast to other things that they believe to be true or right.

David: I agree completely. In this kind of intellectual history project, the reader needs to experience the ideas, and your interpretation as significant. Here are some documents which express these ideas, some people who embodied them and that can help us understand their contours and limitations, what they enable and what they impede.

Martti: I'll just add here that although people have paid a lot of attention to the starting year of this narrative, 1873, they paid much less attention to the ending year, 1960. When I put that ending in the subtitle I thought Wow, well, this will arouse strong feelings. But it did not. That it does not seem scandalous to say that international law is dead as an intellectual discipline by 1960 shows that it not only is *not* an intellectual discipline but that it never was and that thinking about it in those terms—as a kind of series of derivations from a (liberal, cosmopolitan) philosophy—is utterly wrong, even though that is often how academic political scientists deal with it. I find those writings (in the "philosophy of international law" genre) usually without much interest.

A second point about that ending date is more practical: it gives expression to the sense that large chunks of international law seem somehow irrelevant, or anachronistic, today. In an earlier conversation, I asked whether there is any way a person's life might be influenced by anything that the International Law Commission does. I asked this question as a one-time member of this body, assigned to "codify and develop" international law within the UN. The body had all kinds of tasks in the early years of the UN that it accomplished reasonably well—the various Vienna Conventions, for example, giving professional form to customary ways of diplomacy. But since the 1960s, what? *The Gentle Civilizer of Nations* ends around that time because one idea of a universal public law had by then run its course. Of course, international lawyers still operate in New York or The Hague. But the law that mostly counts is dispersed all over; it comes in a myriad of projects and preferences—global, transnational, private international, and so on. While "law" is everywhere, the idea of a public-law-governed world isn't.

David: Being on different sides of the Atlantic makes a difference. When you say "international law died," you have in mind those 1873 guys and the profession that came in their wake. International law in "the American style," if that is even the right term, doesn't end in 1960 but was just getting going and continues to provide a robust legal and political imaginary for the management of global affairs. It has nothing to do with the International Law Commission and very little to do with what your Victorians imagined the doctrinal corpus of "international law" to be. Not to say they didn't inherit the basic framing images—a horizontal world of notionally equal states, law as their joint product and better nature, and so on.

From that starting point, however, UnitedStatesean legal elites were enormously innovative, again and again—often building on innovations that had their intellectual origin in Europe, if not in European international law. They were grabbing pragmatic ideas about law, ideas about the social function of law, about the complexity of the global policy process and the relationship between the legal and the political blended together with ideas about the ethical universality and progressive imperative/destiny of a global legality. The American ascendency came with a mode of law—of legal thought, practice, professional style. I say *came with* to leave room for the relative autonomy of law and for the circuit by which law also constituted the authorities whose tool and mode of expression it then became. Far from fading, this legality is everywhere as a mode of claims making, dispute resolution, institution building, and management and professional practice.

I understand the impulse to identify a mode of analysis, a professional project, a disciplinary style as over, out of fashion. I have claimed for some time that "human rights" is past its sell-by date, although people will doubtless continue arguing and getting jobs in its name for years to come. Alongside that lies the impulse to stress the continuities—"liberalism" not as the political convictions of one party of opinion in the late nineteenth century but as a deeper and more widespread framework of thought. From my perspective, there is both continuity and innovation in the move from your Victorians to the postwar American legal folk.

In that spirit, perhaps we could go back to your idea of *legal imagination* as it extended beyond the professional communities of international lawyers, certainly for the diverse professional communities you canvas in *To the Uttermost Parts of the Earth,* as well as for your men of 1873. In *To the Uttermost Parts of the Earth* you expand the aperture to trace a legal imagination embedded or reflected in theology, economics, politics and more. Not because these fields are normative in a narrow sense, although they often were, but because they shared in projects of imagining sovereignty and property at home and abroad. Can you say a bit more about the distinctiveness of legal imagination as a mode of power—here expressed or inhabited in quite different vocabularies? As we've talked about *To the Uttermost Parts of the Earth,* I've been struck by the parallels to my *World of Struggle* in the engagement with a wider range of adjacent vocabularies—expertise, if you will—in the legal imagination.

Martti: As you say, *To the Uttermost Parts of the Earth* was a study of the legal imagination as it is expressed itself in authoritative professional-technical vocabularies in Europe from the late Middle Ages and through the period commonly called the early modern era. I wanted to step backward to examine the very constitution, by the use of legal vocabularies, of a world from which the late nineteenth-century activist moment had arisen, and that still accounts for so much of present-day experience of the international world. From a kind of prehistory of "modern international law" it grew into a much wider analysis of the rise of the "modern world" as one framed by states and capital and by the many forms of imperial hegemony they support. *International law* or *law of nations, ius gentium,* were only parts of a much wider arsenal of legal words with which Europeans had become accustomed to justifying, consolidating, and occasionally critiquing relations of power and subordination.

Beginning from the late medieval period, when the first graduates emerged from the first law schools in northern Italy and France, there was a story to tell about how the idioms they had learned—especially the notion of *dominium*—would spread around Europe to help them imagine authority not only at home but everywhere. As the religious content of *dominium* gradually diminished (though never disappeared), its forms received increasingly technical articulations as "sovereignty" and "property."

David: Your recovery of that moment before the sovereignty/property distinction is incredibly useful—I'm sure we'll come back to it when we discuss law's relation to political economy.

Martti: You ask how *To the Uttermost Parts of the Earth* treated the distinctiveness of legal imagination as a "mode of power." First of all, the *legal imagination* gave people a legal interpretation of the hegemonic relations in which they lived. For example, "This demand is valid because it is issued by a lawful prince." This is an articulation of a world ruled by "sovereigns"—and there would be a whole litany of explanations of what sovereignty means, how it is possible to become a sovereign, what sovereigns may do, and where the limits of their sovereignty lie. Or "You are not entitled to use this piece of land because it had been enclosed as property for that landlord." Again, there would be a whole set of positions about common lands, enclosures, direct and indirect dominion, about specific and general use rights, and so on. But, by and large, with many local variations, the legal imagination created sophisticated notions of sovereignty and property with innumerable local variants that, as I like to put it, became the *yin and yang of European power.*

Secondly, I wanted to highlight the autonomy of the legal imagination from any specific intellectual construct or job description. It was available for everybody—theologians, political advisers, philosophers, diplomats, judges, academics, merchants, and so on. It gave all of them the ability to assert relations of superiority and subordination in an apparently authoritative way so as to seek to attain whatever they wanted to attain by it.

David: To interject—that's how I saw "expertise" in *World of Struggle:* modes of imagining and articulating power available to pretty much anyone in one or another vulgate—even, as I argued there, my grandmother (who was not legally trained) speaking in the vernacular of legal entitlements and limitations as she argued with a tourist merchant in some foreign location.

Martti: Did the king want to challenge the emperor? Well, sovereignty would be the way to do it. Do you want to have access to those resources? Well, then, imagine a contract, build a fence, or plant some grain, and it might be yours. None of this took away struggle, but law would provide its terms. Through the constant interaction of law speakers in royal chambers, courts and public institutions, universities and merchant houses, an increasingly complex legal language arose that included all kinds of idioms: public law of Europe, *ius gentium,* law of nations, merchant law, common law, custom, royal prerogative, and so on. These provided both an interpretation of the world and tools for people to push forward their projects: supporting somebody, criticizing somebody, staking a claim on something, and so on.

To the Uttermost Parts of the Earth was about how the legal imagination kept producing and reproducing powerful interpretations of the "international" world in the period of the half millennium preceding the gentle civilizers. It organized hierarchies and allocated authority. It decided questions of just distribution. There was some innovation as well—new idioms crystallizing as hierarchical structures while others lost their former self-evidence. When did interest cease to be usurious? Was noble status really incompatible with mercantile activity? May common lands or people of an alien race be owned as property? Did colonial companies have war-making powers?

Such items emerged both as specific interpretations of human relations and as platforms for struggle; people differed with respect to them. But they were relevant questions treated under complex languages of natural law, public law, private law, domestic law, and so on. That legal imagination often took quasi-philosophical modes of literary expression underlined its connection with elite formation. But elites have always struggled. I was interested to survey how legal authority migrated from one elite group to another, from theologians to political advisers, from advisers to philosophers, from philosophers to natural lawyers, and finally to political economists.

David: Recapturing those struggles is crucial; otherwise it can seem like legal authority just rolls along, expressing a—shifting—elite consensus.

Martti: In that sense, *To the Uttermost Parts of the Earth* resembled a little the work on fragmentation of international law I carried out in the International Law Commission in 2002–2006. That study, too, examined how forms of legal authority rise and fall in globalization: public law lost authority to human rights, human rights lost authority to security law, environmental law arose as a challenger to trade law, and so on.[16] But you have done much more work on this, examining in your *World of Struggle* in great detail the ways in which the languages of law and political economy today help us imagine a world of power and struggle. I found your use of the expression *articulative power* especially useful and attractive for my purposes. So, those ideas you presented in that book, are they different from what I've explained here?

David: No—that sounds like what I had in mind. People have projects, pursue them on a terrain shaped by the successful and unsuccessful projects pursued previously. They have little backpacks full of expectations, entitlements, arguments. If we could look inside their heads, we'd find a stack of unconscious or semiconscious stuff they take for granted—at least until it is contested—beneath factual material, large ideological or theoretical positions they realize are in contention with one another, and technical differences of degree which are often marked in legal terms. On that basis, they pursue their projects by articulation—not always, or even mostly, in language. More often, probably, by doing things; the obvious international law example is probably sailing your ship through a strait to *say* it is open seas and thereby keep it so.

This can all sound very horizontal and interactive: everyone can play, if with different things in their backpack. I think Foucault has often been misunderstood in this way; power is interactive, social, and one loses sight of hierarchy and domination. In *A World of Struggle* I tried to focus on the operation of a Foucauldian performative knowledge/power as domination—treating hierarchy and domination as effective assertions of authority, claims to which others yielded, made in the available expert vernaculars. So, "Off with his head" is not outside the legal field but an act of legal assertion which might or might not be effective. The guy with the axe is also asserting and performing—yes, to physically remove a head, but also to *say* "That guy over there is the one who can get this to happen." Similarly, "You are a colony" or "You are not, congratulations, but you owe us a lot of money."

Martti: Right. And it was the migration of those "effective assertions of authority" from one type of expert formation to another that I examined in *To the Uttermost Parts of the Earth.*

David*:* Absolutely. And the material in play these days is a kind of mishmash of expertise from various fields—law, certainly, but economic development expertise, war-making expertise, political and international relations expertise, ideas people attribute to the national sciences and lots more.

In *A World of Struggle* I focused on "knowledge work" or "articulation" or "the performance of power" for the same reasons you landed on "legal imagination." But tell me if I'm wrong there. I thought it would bracket the more common approach of first identifying the structures and the agents and then treating the impact of ideas in that frame: these agents exercise the authority their structure provides by using this language, or these ideas legitimate that structure and those agents. I wanted to focus attention on the *identification* of "structures" and "agents" as articulations, claims made for a purpose, just like "The world is flat" or "Off with his head" or "I'm the sovereign here" or "That's my property." People usually make assertions like that both to themselves and to others to get something to happen. In both cases, it sometimes works. When it does, power is verdictive, performed in the assertion. Although we can make predictions about when that will happen, one only knows ex post facto whether it did or not. So power is not something one "has" that can be used—you have it *as* it is successfully used.

All of this, which sounds jargony, is borrowing from the basic sociological turn in legal science: the norms are the propositions that turn out to be effective. So it is not "power" that operates in the world through norms, but people perform having power by making assertions—about facts or norms—to which people (including themselves) yield. That is what I take from the slogan "knowledge/power"—that power is effective knowledge. Of course, there is lots of social theory aimed at explaining the conditions of effective articulation: Weber, Nietzsche, Freud, Foucault. How the effect lands depends—maybe someone has a submissive character or slave morality, or finds the person charismatic, or accepts the bureaucratic form, or finds the other's authority already inscribed in their body and self.

What has struck me in our field is the overestimation of "persuasion" as an explanation and the underestimation of expert claims which are not made as arguments but as statements of common sense; or which need not be stated at all to be claimed; or are made with coercion, implied or actual, historic or threatened—for all of which "persuasion" is an odd way to think about what's going on. Your *legal imagination* seems to focus on the foundational ways we divide the world up into public and private, and what's a state, and so on and so forth, that we don't interpret as norms but *as facts of the situation,* the meaning of history. If you need to argue about these things or persuade someone, the game is half lost.

Martti: I sometimes wonder if anyone is ever "persuaded." We assent all the time, and give up. We yield to articulations that we think are authoritative or because we fail to see the point in resisting. Or then, perhaps, just don't even think about it. As you say, classics of social thought have had much to say about how or why such relationships emerge or break down. Ideology is important, of course—Althusser's interpellation. Normative assertions have long played a diminishing role vis-à-vis factoid ones: economy is not morality—only facts and mathematical inferences.

David: Absolutely.

Martti: But more than justifying or critiquing the mechanism of authoritative articulation and submissive yielding, I have been interested in just describing it. Sometimes the process is quite explicit and unproblematic; more often, things happen with scarcely anyone noticing. For critical analysis, describing those situations often may well be enough—trying to figure out complex ideological causalities may in fact be quite hopeless. I often think of Anne Orford's work on the critical power of description; to alert one's audience to the injustice of something it is often best just to describe a relationship and refrain from the morass of normative language.[17] If you do not get it when it is shown to you, then there is often no point in pushing forward. I suppose this is a feature of the weakness of "persuasion" in matters where we feel, and maybe should feel, strongly.

David: Although now you are also preferring the power of factual over normative assertions.

Martti: Factual, yes, but in a narrative mode, as a kind of hypothesis to see if the reader can fit it in their experience. That is why *To the Uttermost Parts of the Earth* has little language that seeks the reader's assent in celebrating or condemning anything. The brief descriptions of the *encomienda* system or the theory of natural stages of development address structural relations of power that most people would find problematic already as they are described—though perhaps not necessarily. One does not address rational persuaders but the experiences and background ideas people have about the world. Assent may often, perhaps usually, depend on the *how* that description fits them. No need emerges to supplement the description with normative language. The best case, as I said earlier, is when the reader finds a description that articulates something they "knew" already but did not have the words to express.

Then there is another thing. Say you describe the contents of the Carolina slave law or the Trade-Related Aspects of Intellectual Property Rights (TRIPS) system with regard to COVID-19 medication. What happens to that description if you, as author, add "And it was/is all terribly wrong"? Not only nothing of importance, but foregrounding of the authorial opinion will diminish the power of the fact description. You invite your audience to a *moral* debate that is likely to bring no enlightenment to anyone.

David: That seems a condition of the current elite situation—like no longer being able to speak theologically with much hope of effect. One denounces with "facts" instead. I remember my mother: "See what you've done!" She didn't need to denounce it. Still, quite parental.

Martti: Hmm. Would asking you to sit down and discuss have made any difference? In the bit on the sixteenth-century Spanish scholastics in *To the Uttermost Parts of the Earth* I situated an important moment in the history of legal imagination in the confessional relationship as developed within the Catholic Church in its struggle against the Reformation. Here was a formalized system of authoritative assertion and yielding, controlled by an ideological vocabulary mastered by a powerful global institution. The requirement that Christians should confess their sins at regular intervals created an intense relationship in the exercise and articulation of power—perhaps paradigmatic for the understanding of counseling generally, the relationship between an expert and a layperson, perhaps a decision-maker, elsewhere and in later periods.

The fact that the frame was theology did not make it essentially different from situations where that frame is law or economics, say. The point was to make visible that relations of power are articulated, over and over again, in systemic contexts even when they take place in bilateral exchanges. They are not about moral persuasion or rational proof but factual assertion of some state of affairs (this act was a "sin" or a "violation of a right") by a source already experienced as authoritative. But the system is far less a well-articulated ideology than a mishmash of factual and normative assumptions that nevertheless converge in some specific type of authority. And then they are often articulated as law. I'm not really interested in *why* confession or expertise works or *why* people yield to assertions of authority—a psychosocial question. It is much more interesting—and also more powerful, I believe—just to describe the way assertions of authority are made and complied with.

Mind you—and I think you agree—that power happens is no tragedy. Mothers serve a purpose. The point of the analysis is not to get *rid* of authority but to make it visible so as to understand and operate with it—and sometimes to learn to oppose it. Anyway, I'm much more interested as a writer in describing those situations than trying to use them as mere evidence for the truth of some normative claims I would follow up on later.

David: Indeed, *power* is no scandal; *domination* and *poverty* and *injustice* are scandals. One thought: it's not obvious whether saying "Jesus says, 'Do this'" is a fact or a norm. Aren't norms always invoked as facts, and facts relevant because they indicate a normative direction?

I wanted to raise a quick question about the word *legitimacy*, often used as an umbrella framework for understanding the social function of international law. I think this is part of where the overestimation of "persuasion" gets going. Draping what you're doing in legal norms is said to *legitimate* both you and what you are doing. The power of the norms—or their "normativity"—resides in their ability to stimulate a complex *legitimation* reaction in an audience which changes the power of the asserter and the assertion. No doubt things do sometimes work like this. I remember voters in the streets with signs claiming the Second Iraq War was "illegal." It seemed not only unusual but somewhat perverse: The reason to march against the war was a complex interpretation of the UN Charter's procedural requirements? But it may have influenced someone in the war machine—hard to know. May have made them more determined to proceed, as well, I suppose.

But the sociological mechanism for legitimation is pretty complicated. It is not that the addressee yields to the truth/authority/good sense of the assertion. You need a person exercising authority and an audience whose reactions—their views, their actions, or both—are valued by the actor either as to this action or more generally. And that audience needs to have an evaluative posture toward the action or actor and see legal norms as relevant evaluative criteria. That is, they need to *have a view,* a legally informed view, about the appropriateness of the action. And then they need to be understood by the actor to be willing—likely—to act on that view in ways relevant to the actor. So they won't vote for him next time if they are not *persuaded* by his assertion that the action is legal. Or won't allow use of their airfield. Or whatever. So you are not persuading the person you want to do something; you are persuading a relevant audience that is important, relevant, and somehow highly attuned to being persuaded normatively.

As I said, I'm sure this does happen, and statesmen and government employees and military commanders and soldiers and activists all might be adjusting their actions in light of an image they have about the legal evaluative conclusions of a relevant audience. But that seems a very narrow way to imagine the power of *legal imagination,* as you call it. And I wonder if the imagined audience isn't really a kind of dim and distant mirror which has folks glancing over their shoulder at . . . themselves. Talking about *legitimation* is a way of interpreting law's power—your professional power—as socially mandated or ratified.

In historical work, you find the word *legitimation* used in a more general way: international law *legitimated* colonialism or war or slavery. The mechanism by which that occurred is usually unspecified. It has to be right that some—many—people who were in an evaluative posture toward slavery or colonialism felt the legal arguments in favor—or against—persuaded them to pursue it or not oppose it. But again, the world-making impact of legal knowledge about sovereignty and property on slavery or colonialism seems underestimated in this framework, which places power with the colonizer or enslaver, with law only getting into it only to confirm or solidify those authorities rather than being constitutive of slavery or sovereignty or colonial authority in the first place.

Martti: *Legitimacy* does tend to suppose a series of encounters between agents or between an agent and an audience where power is "used" in the way you critiqued earlier, as something outside the discourse that then gets *legitimated* by recourse to that discourse. As you say, it fails to account for the law's framing power that extends also to the supposed legitimizer. The vocabulary of legitimacy often appears as part of empirically oriented political science that needs a kind of phlogiston to explain the work of power in a social relationship in order to avoid alternative vocabularies such as those of moral rightness, juridical lawfulness, or economic effect. I read it as a move in a struggle for disciplinary jurisdiction: "This is not for moral theorists or jurists to argue—it is a matter of political science," where it can be measured through studies of inputs and outputs and the debate can end in a proposal for liberal procedural reform. I much prefer the less technical language of ideology that points to a more complex reality and does not carry those kinds of disciplinary consequences. I try to use it without the apparent implication of speaking truth to ideology, however, so as not to claim that my own beliefs are excused from a hermeneutic of suspicion.

David: As we've discussed, I do worry about the word *ideology* for its association with something like self-conscious *belief* in a space of contending beliefs. So liberal and conservative, socialist and market, Left and Right. My worry has its origins, I suspect, in my experience of religious identity and consciousness in the Protestant world I grew up in. On the one hand, lots of strongly felt differences, but they did not seem to be experienced internally as *beliefs* or the adoption of a kind of platform. They were matters of identity, style and good ordering, shared understandings of what "religion" was and how it ought to be practiced. These background matters were powerful and easy to arrange in a structure of social differentiation—how close or far from the poles of agnosticism and Catholicism, how "high" or "low" church in practice, where on the spectrum of reason and mysticism, dogmatism and relativism. If you went to a morning service, the congregation would recite a creed of belief, perhaps subtly different from the church down the street, but this was pure ceremony; the differences were forged in these other ways. And, of course, by race and class, and so on.

Translated to the world of politics, "liberalism" did not seem to function the way people described "ideology" in just the same way. Its world-making powers seemed to transcend Left and Right, operating at a more organic or commonsense level. The "liberalism" critiqued by the critical legal studies people in those years—and by Roberto Unger in *Knowledge and Politics*[18]—was a whole world of thought and action. That's why I prefer your term *legal imaginary* to *ideology.*

We have been talking in different ways about the *immanence* of power: power immanent in the legal materials / profession / practice / social situation. But let's go back to the more conventional image of law as useful to a power outside it—to statesmen and war criminals and environmental despoilers and human rights activists, and so on. Perhaps we could distinguish law's framing and constitutive relevance from its usefulness in this sense. For example, international legal ideas and arrangements—territorial sovereignty, property rights that roam the world—are "constitutive" in the sense that they set the background conditions for lots of things, from commerce and war to the distribution of activities and risk in global value chains. Within that frame, a hodgepodge of diverse bits and pieces from all sorts of legal regimes are picked up by actors with particular axes to grind.

Mapping the law that both constitutes the terrain, the actors, the interests, and that is then useful to those pursuing malevolent projects, has always struck me as a terribly important terrain for inquiry—particularly in the international field, where the focus has so often been on law as a balm for the weak and limit on the powerful. It is not an inquiry I have pursued, but there is a burgeoning literature tracing law's impact on the allocation of powers, wealth, status among groups contributing to the reproduction of inequality and racial hierarchy.

What do you think? Was (international) law *useful* to the Spanish in their colonial engagement with the Indigenous people of the Americas? Or to the crusaders or slave traders or capitalists or kings and queens of the worlds you examined in *To the Uttermost Parts of the Earth*? How do you think about that?

Martti: I like your example of religion. Most of law's power, too, relies less on conscious beliefs than on truths, rituals, literatures, stories that the professional vocabulary conveys. Suddenly it becomes natural to think of some killing as "armed conflict" and derive things from it. Or that people are "citizens" or "refugees" or "Indigenous," with much about their lives then beginning to depend on that description. In the interwar era, philosophically oriented lawyers sometimes did focus on law's world-constituting elements—statehood and the role of individuals, for example, or "responsibility." A neo-Kantian lawyer like Kelsen had no difficulty to think of law as an interpretative scheme that people imposed on the world and his student Verdross even wrote about the "unity of the legal world-image."[19] We may now look upon those texts—there were others—as idealistic or unprofessional. Wrongly. There was some hermeneutic there, maybe as a result of the Great War, and of the intellectual situation—Viennese high culture—that oriented those people quite fruitfully to thinking about law's background assumptions that vanished as lawyers turned to more pragmatic institution-building tasks.

Of course, world-creating terms, such as *sovereignty* and *property, armed conflict* and *jurisdiction,* have not disappeared—even as analysis of them is often flattened within something like a new historicism: "Can sovereignty survive in the conditions of globalization?" But they do operate in more straightforward instrumental talk, too, as fighting words and assertions of authority. The kings and merchants and intellectuals that I study in *To the Uttermost Parts of the Earth* certainly *used* legal words to assert claims or yield to them. There were many reasons for the Castilian crown to think law useful as a vocabulary to defend and organize its actions in the Indies. It satisfied the theological requirements, it communicated those claims in shared language to other Europeans, and it opened an institutional door for further action. But law is a complex instrument. It also tied the hands of the crown somewhat, reconfirmed the authority of Dominican theologians often critical of official action, and offered channels of bureaucratic decision-making not always under the crown's control. I make these points to highlight the limits of a simple instrumentalism: law's power is fickle, the legal vocabularies as free-standing imperatives (as the Scandinavian realists once called them), available for a variety of uses in the hands of imaginative claimants.

David: Take the civilian/combatant distinction—certainly *useful* to privilege combatants to kill and civilians to be spared. You can imagine warriors and peaceniks finding uses for such a distinction. But the effects seem so much broader—on how we think of women, for example, or of war itself.

Martti: I do think law can be *useful* for both benevolent and malevolent projects, as you suggest, though rarely in any straightforward manner. Rights may benefit people you would like to benefit—but as you have pointed out, they also have "dark sides" that may come to haunt those very same people. When firmly embedded in institutional hierarchies, law can certainly support the projects pursued by those institutions, though again it may also be used to oppose them. But you asked specifically about the usefulness of international law. I suppose one answer emerges from the very proliferation of alternative idioms (transnational law, trade law, human rights law, environmental law). It does not provide much support to anything, really, in the instrumental fashion, outside the old structure of diplomatic interactions. Its power remains above all of the framing variety.

David: That sounds right—and why we've been focusing more on framing.

Martti: What makes instrumentalism disappointing is that it often comes in rather simplistic *problem-solving* terms, with the assumption that law is there to solve problems that have been already given by the world somehow. True, lawyers are also problem solvers. How to access that resource, for example? Well, make a legal claim over it! How to prevent those people from benefiting from this technology? Well, stake a claim of intellectual property rights! But I worry when legal scholarship goes this way. This both ignores the indeterminacy problem—that as long as a problem is described abstractly, many alternative rules or policies apply. And it subordinates intellectual work to some supposedly authoritative determination of what in the world are its *real* problems.

Of course, practicing lawyers manage problems all the time; this makes sense in the institutional world, where they assert and yield to claims. But as scholarship it is intellectually unsatisfying and politically objectionable. It upholds a managerialist mindset. I mean an overall sense—very common among elite educational institutions—that things are more or less under control, that modest reforms are always available to correct problems that appear. But for many people, the world is not like that. It seems chaotic, unjust, and out of control.

Managerialism tends to ignore the way most problems are experienced differently by different groups, and no problem falls from the sky; they are actually expressions of hierarchical relationships. This is the way of *plus ça change* . . . small reforms offering more of the same. Despite your doubts, I still think the word *ideology* does some useful work to describe the world of managerialism that, among other effects, makes us assent to international law's hollow promise.

David: That routinization of reform as a reinforcement of elite privilege and the status quo is certainly familiar.

Martti: We have both spent much of our careers among students and colleagues anxiously trying to figure out whether international law can be used to challenge that privilege and the status quo by recourse to legal concepts such as self-determination, the New International Economic Order, racial justice, gender identity, and so on. However, your text "The International Human Rights Movement: Part of the Problem?" demonstrated the many ways it deradicalized transformative agendas.[20] The entry of a first generation of third world lawyers in multilateral diplomacy in the 1960s failed to bring about the kind of substantive change some expected. The call today to "decolonize" the legal curriculum is an expression of that frustration.

On the other hand, people like Antony Anghie, and others, insist law's performative power is open to heterodox maneuvers.[21] Learning to speak international law is insufficient. But its open-endedness may sometimes be used to address unjust distribution, or to destabilize the structural bias. It's not easy, and requires complex strategic thinking. Which legal institution should I choose to be active in? How to articulate my claim so as to maximize chances of success? And what might "success" mean? What costs are involved by accepting it as the legitimate forum for my claim? If I make a legal claim *here*, does it constrain me *there*? There's need to open up the legal imagination for such critical thinking, plus doing it in such a way that one understands that it is ideological work, and not speaking truth to power—that at issue are *choices* on both sides.

David: Enabling heterodox strategies, certainly. Although I've always been suspicious of moving too quickly to embrace the idea—or fantasy?—of such heterodox uses. If for no other reason than that the continuity of things—unjust things—can be blamed on critical voices not being clever or persistent or savvy enough to play for change. And anyway, for all its openness, the prevailing vocabulary is certainly less useful for revision of what we've called "foundational" questions—maybe at some cost to that.

Martti: Activists sometimes think they represent the *real* law, the law understood in a just way—while it is the adversary who is ideological. This is wrong, but often hard to accept. Nevertheless, realizing that these struggles have not been *already* resolved by law is, I think, necessary for developing the kind of strategic thinking that pragmatism calls for. You have often stressed the need to think clearly about the consequences of one's legal maneuvers on the ground. A paragraph in a resolution is not the same as money for a project. I think pragmatic legal work accepts the reality of choice and the need to measure the target as close to the ground as one can get. The difficulty, a real difficulty, is that in international law we do not often get very close to the "ground."

David: Fleshing out Tony's suggestion, Arnulf Becker Lorca has a piece detailing the ways semiperipheral nations have used international law rules and entitlements over the last century.[22] It is difficult to bring that kind of (relatively everyday) problem-solving practicality together with a sense that one is making choices—political choices. That you are acting, not channeling the law as actor. *Pragmatism* is a strange word—like *problem solving*. Who could object to that? People talk about pragmatism in the sense of being savvy or realistic in bringing law to bear, as if it were waiting out there to be used. There might be some delicate matters of interpretation, but pragmatism figures law as kind of cold thing, outside the ethical—like a shovel or an algorithm. And you are its servant or mouthpiece. But shovels and algorithms have political and ethical backstories. Law has that and is also open to political or ethical alternatives. In this kind of pragmatism, the ethical gets lost, just as the pragmatic can be lost when law is seen as a kind of ethical theology.

Pragmatism encourages a focus on the middle—doable—way, law as instrument for progressive and evolutionary social development. In American legal thought, anyway, the call for pragmatism encourages the association of law with the positive action of public authorities acting in the public interest. A lovely image, if one that obscures law's significance as a problem creator and sustainer. That image also serves as a kind of fable, short-circuiting critical inquiry. Even a problem solver ought to want to know how the problem gets going, but somehow the urge to action, to the *solving* part of problem solving, gets in the way of deeper inquiry into law's role in the problem itself.

There are some positive elements—a focus on what law *does* can help disrupt the image of international affairs, diplomatically and commercially—unfolding on a transactional terrain of notional equals. What people are *doing* with law is distributing resources, authority, and status and exercising authority over one another. Following that thread, you see a world of hierarchy and domination. It is not surprising that a hegemonic authority would devise, promote, and enforce legal arrangements favorable to it, nor that it would promote these as universal values, reflecting equality and justice for all. But one must get below the promotion to see the motion. That is where a—let's call it *pragmatic*—what-does-law-do stance can spur inquiry into inequality, colonialism, racism, wars, slavery, and environmental damage both as *legal institutions* and as *people doing things with law.*

A final idea I associate with the American tradition of philosophical pragmatism would take us back to the "action under conditions of indeterminacy" discussion we had earlier, echoing the decisionism of people like Kierkegaard or Weber or the European existentialists. Given what Weber calls the "irrationality" of the world, the ubiquity of unintended consequences and uncertainty, acting demands a kind of *responsibility.*[23] That sense of being responsible *when one cannot know* is precisely what I think today's legal/technocratic experts and rulers are in flight from. It was not their decision; it was the rules or the situation or the facts or the science or something else which they were merely channeling. Where a strand of pragmatism can also serve as an antidote to this escape into expertise, so widespread in contemporary technocratic rulership, it seems just what we need.

Martti: Right. Contingency, choice, responsibility. One does come back all the time to those problematic themes, Weber and the existentialists. A foothold might be found also from earlier religious traditions, discourses of virtue and confession. But I don't think either one of us feels comfortable with those. Hence, their invocation comes often as a gesture at the end of some analysis or other, as if from that point technical debate ought to give way to some other language appropriate for the inner world (of faith?).

But might it not be possible to work a little more on the notion of expertise—I mean, to reconceive expertise as a realm of precisely, contingency, choice, and responsibility instead of something firmly nonideological and technocratic? I think one thing we have learned from interdisciplinarity has been that no expertise is a coherent black box but that, just like law, it tends to be divided into orthodoxies and heterodoxies; even when best practices are settled, there are disputes over principles. There are also fields of indeterminacy and choice. This takes us back to where this conversation started, the power/knowledge nexus, the way any expert knowledge involves claims about authority and the invitation for others to yield. The challenge would then not be to step, as it were, outside the vocabulary of expertise, into virtue or "politics," say, to challenge the assertion (although that remains an alternative), but to conceive expertise itself in a more open-ended way, an aspect of rulership and subject to the kinds of debates and controls we feel ruling ought to be subjected to.

David: Absolutely. That's a great description of what I was trying to do in *A World of Struggle*—in the way what one was trying to do always appears more clearly in retrospect!

Notes

1. Kennedy, *A World of Struggle;* Koskenniemi, *To The Uttermost Parts of the Earth.*
2. Koskenniemi, *The Gentle Civilizer of Nations.*
3. Hans Kelsen, *Law and Peace in International Relations: The Oliver Wendell Holmes Lectures, 1940–41* (Cambridge, MA: Harvard University Press, 1942).
4. Hans Kelsen, *Der soziologische und der juristische Staatsbegriff,* 2nd ed. (Tübingen, Germany: Mohr, 1927).
5. Kennedy, *International Legal Structures.*
6. Kennedy, *The Dark Sides of Virtue.*
7. Koskenniemi, *From Apology to Utopia.*
8. Noam Chomsky, *Language and Mind* (Cambridge: Cambridge University Press, [1968] 2006); Noam Chomsky, *Reflections on Language* (New York: Pantheon Books, 1975).
9. Koskenniemi, *The Politics of International Law.*

10. Louis Althusser, "Ideology and Ideological State Apparatuses," in *Essays on Ideology. Ideology and Ideological State Apparatuses. Reply to John Lewis, Freud and Lacan. A Letter on Art,* no translator given (London: Verso, 1976), 44–51.

11. Kennedy, "International Refugee Protection."

12. Kennedy, *The Rights of Spring.*

13. Koskenniemi and Kari, "A More Elevated Patriotism."

14. Antonio Gramsci, *Selections from Prison Notebooks,* eds. and trans. Geoffrey Nowell-Smith and Quintin Hoare (London: Lawrence and Wishart, [1971] 2005).

15. Kennedy, "The International Style."

16. Study Group of the International Law Commission, *Fragmentation of International Law: Difficulties Arising from the Diversification and Expansion of International Law: Report of the Study Group of the International Law Commission,* finalized by Martti Koskenniemi (Helsinki: Erik Castrén Institute of International Law, 2007).

17. Anne Orford, "In Praise of Description," 25 *Leiden Journal of International Law* 609 (2012).

18. Roberto Mangabeira Unger, *Knowledge and Politics* (New York: Free Press, 1975).

19. See Hans Kelsen, *Introduction to Problems of Legal Theory,* translated by Bonnie Litschewski Paulson and Stanley L. Paulson (Oxford, Clarendon Press, 1992), 10–14; and Alfred Verdross, *Die Einheit des rechtlichen Weltbildes. Auf Grundlage der Völkerrechtsverfassung* (Tübingen, Germany: Mohr, 1923).

20. Kennedy, "The International Human Rights Movement."

21. Antony Anghie, "The Evolution of International Law: Colonial and Postcolonial Realities," in *International Law and the Third World: Reshaping Justice* (Richard Falk, Balakrishnan Rajagopal, and Jacqueline Stevens eds., Abingdon, UK: Routledge-Cavendish, 2008); Antony Anghie, "International Law in a Time of Change: Should International Law Lead or Follow?," 26 *American University International Law Review* 1315 (2011).

22. Arnulf Becker Lorca, "Bargaining with Sovereignty, Fighting Global Inequality" (unpublished manuscript, 2022, draft on file with the authors).

23. Max Weber, "Politics as a Vocation" (1918), in *From Max Weber: Essays in Sociology,* ed. and trans. H. H. Gerth and C. Wright Mills, 77 (Abingdon, UK: Routledge, 2009).

CONVERSATION FOUR

Many International Legalities: Hegemony and Differentiation

David: We've both studied aspirationally universal projects undertaken by legal intellectuals in the North Atlantic. Despite—or perhaps precisely to sustain—their pretensions to universality, these traditions have been preoccupied with diversity: managing it, denying it, overcoming it. Of course, when international lawyers speak as the voice of the universal, they obscure the specificity of their tradition and any differences within or beyond it. But think of how they remember what they call the Westphalian system: religious diversity accommodated by lifting the international legal and diplomatic order above the water line of sovereignty—the management of difference is at the core of it. Perhaps we can focus our conversation today on diversity or difference *within* this international legal imagination.

Martti: I suppose the very suggestion that there should be "law" is premised on the perception of the irreducible diversity and dangerousness of the prelegal situation. This may be a specifically Christian narrative; I mean one where the cardinal sin had been committed. At least thinkers from St. Augustine to Hobbes were clear that difference was real and had to be tamed by public enforcement of rules. Liberal universalism may not share their realist attitudes, but as a "universalism" it is nonetheless about managing difference—hegemony, in other words. Let me just say at the outset that I am frustrated by the old debates that juxtapose "genuine" with "false" universalism and treats difference as a problem of moral philosophy instead of history and social practice.

David: Me too. So let's focus there, on difference as a history of social practice, but also as an intellectual (and sometimes political or ethical) preoccupation of the professional. One starting point might be the way differences in international law are expressed as national traditions or schools of thought. Of course, it's a different job to be an international lawyer in Helsinki or Paris than in Washington, DC—in a way, international law *is* a game of the middle powers. And it feels different at the center and periphery of things: in London or Brussels and in Portugal or Slovenia, in the United States and in Canada or Australia. These differences are accompanied by divergent professional sensibilities, preoccupations. Perhaps we could say more about the national legal cultures, professional projects, political and ideological priorities of international lawyers within which these vocabularies were developed.

I'd also like us to talk a bit about the *hegemony*, for lack of a better word, of the North Atlantic legal imagination. Neither of us has focused on the normative authority or impact of our traditions elsewhere; how a North Atlantic legal idiom—its rules, institutions and modes of thought—fell upon the rest of the world, the legal worlds upon which it fell, and the strategies of engagement or resistance that emerged elsewhere. I've bumped into these issues in thinking about development and European law: what happens as the European Union (EU) forces acceptance of the entire *acquis communitaire* by candidate nations in its periphery, when Latin American lawyers bring British or American commercial models and legal forms into their domestic practice, or when legal conditionality exports administrative forms to the sites of investment or foreign aid.

Martti: Or when European historical experience is translated into the "rule of law" or "constitutionalism" that is then expected to operate as a universal benchmark.

David: Exactly. Britain as the mother of parliaments, Europe as the apogee of human rights—such strange ways to summarize British and European history in the world. We've spent more time on strategies for conjuring universality *within* the North Atlantic legal imagination: how our guys have imagined other countries, projects and legal traditions, and the intellectual frameworks they use to manage the differences they perceive.

One way to define intellectual hegemony would be as the ability to define who is in, who is out and the conditions of assimilation—the vocabulary within which projects must be articulated to be heard. In international legal terms, normatively to be the benchmark of civilization, professionally to set the standards of competence. What roles does that leave outsiders and how have our traditions handled challenges to their uniformity and universality?

As the traditions we've studied have become influential and widespread, what globalized was less a uniform set of rules or institutions than a mode of work and professional vocabulary preoccupied with conceptualizing and managing difference—more, even, than with establishing a "system" or "order." Indeed, we might say the ideology of contemporary hegemony *is* "difference" or "diversity," understood and managed in a variety of ways.

Can we generalize about the directions that preoccupation has taken? So, for example, less codification or harmonization than techniques for accommodating doctrinal difference. Or less universal principles than celebration of pluralism in a framework of procedures, institutions, and normative arrangements to interface between them. I'm thinking of your International Law Commission (ILC) study, offering professional practice as the antidote to fragmentation, or of recent enthusiasm for "comparative international law." Or the celebration of functional specialization, multiple systems redescribed as constitutional orders in a pluriverse of technical expertise.

Let's start with our home traditions—their specificity and the diversity within them. I'm thinking about *From Apology to Utopia*[1] because the geographic and temporal specificity of your analysis there is *least* on the surface. The book reads as the identification of a philosophical and practical conundrum; one just can't not keep oscillating between apology and utopia in something like a magnetic field. Does this have a time and place or is it a *universal* human dilemma that international legal projects are bound to encounter?

Martti: The target of *From Apology to Utopia* was an utterly European philosophical account of the law of nations, in the form it had passed from late nineteenth-century Victorian lawyers to the present. That account believed itself to be universal because, after all, Europe, in its own philosophical view of itself, represents the universal. That view also led generations of European lawyers to think of what they were doing as a kind of philosophy, or at least a pragmatic transformation of a philosophy. This is also why the problem of difference, of fitting diversity within a single normative mode, was always treated in such abstract fashion. It was believed to form a philosophical conundrum above all.

Nobody suggested that this way to treat the field either dealt with the *wrong* problems or that the philosophical issues had actually been already resolved somewhere. The point was, of course, to show that the conundrums to which the legal vocabulary pointed—how to subordinate many sovereigns to an international order, problems of consent, of deriving uniform norms from heterogeneous practices—were raised within a specific political philosophy that had not only never resolved those problems successfully but which were not at all for philosophy to resolve.

In *From Apology to Utopia* I tried to show that European law bought its apparent universality by its substantive emptiness. In the end, anything could be justified by it—which is to say that nothing really could. This was an immanent critique of the European universalization project in its legal-philosophical format. But as you say, the "North Atlantic tradition" itself is not that homogeneous. Not only was international law as we encountered it in the 1980s a European one, but I also came to realize that it arose from a specific German story that can be traced back to the way lawyers in the Holy Roman Empire struggled to fit the *Landeshoheit* of territorial princes with the supremacy of imperial law. The "order among states" problem had already been articulated in a really complex political history and academic discourse.[2]

David: So, if I understood you, the apology/utopia conundrum arises from quite particular—German—ideas of what philosophy is and how international law should relate to it. The critical bite is less this origin than the legacy. The critical finding is the grip of that contradictory and inconclusive inheritance on the world's legal imagination. Plus, that conceptual practice arose to address a set of practical set of questions—*Landeshoheit*/empire relations—which became something of a model for practical questions in our day but are a poor fit for the range of issues that now draw professional and political attention.

When I wrote *International Legal Structures* and "Primitive Legal Scholarship," I hadn't thought it through this clearly.[3] I wasn't thinking of the field's specificity. I was accepting—even promoting—the significance of the texts I was analyzing to establish a baseline for criticism: treating the multivolume *Classics of International Law,* reprinted early in the last century, as if they were what they purported to be rather than the idiosyncratic project of James Brown Scott and the Carnegie Foundation.

When I picked up those volumes sixty years after their publication, they already seemed musty and forgotten.[4] Their vision had become a footnote here and there in a rapidly developing and internally diverse postwar practice which had a *Landeshoheit*/empire project of its own—fitting a newly dominant America into a global order: for some, training an American elite to mobilize law toward the global public order they preferred; for others, encouraging American engagement with the United Nations (UN) system and adherence to what they saw as a virtuous international normative framework. The provincial nature of their projects came home to me when I attended the 1984 oral hearings at the Hague in the Nicaragua case: it was an intramural legal debate between Yale and Harvard and a foreign policy struggle between Republicans and Democrats.[5]

I told the story of postwar UnitedStatesean international law as a "tradition" held together by a grammar of contradictory alternatives and a professional style rather than as a set of "American" doctrinal or theoretical positions. I suggested that the authority and influence of the style might rest in part on its flexibility or compatibility with diverse legal particulars.

There are conditions of plausibility and effectiveness in putting such a story together. Do the participants recognize themselves? Does assembling things this way seem like a telling critique to others who come to the field with a skeptical eye? Does the whole thing meet the routine canons of academic legal history or legal sociology? You don't have to hit all these notes, but they provide some goalposts. I wonder if this is how you understand your historical work—as inventing, as much as unearthing, a tradition while focusing on these underlying "grammatical" patterns.

Martti: Inventing, or discovering?—I think that performance is the key. Although you and I have talked a lot about it, up to now I have been very sparse in producing any account of "my method." This is because I have never really followed any clearly definable style of writing beyond aiming to sound true to my targeted audience—academic and professional colleagues. When I said that *From Apology to Utopia* examined a tradition that thought of itself as philosophy, I was not engaged in philosophy myself but in a rhetorical analysis of the technical and stylistic tropes—the grammar—that made the participants think of what they were doing as a kind of philosophy.

David: I think you tell the story quite differently in *From Apology to Utopia*, in *The Gentle Civilizer of Nations*, and in *To the Uttermost Parts of the Earth*.[6]

In *The Gentle Civilizer of Nations* you identify a very specific political and intellectual project pursued by a small group of Europeans *as international law* starting in the late nineteenth century and petering out sometime in the second half of the twentieth. The whole book is a radical narrowing of the aperture: this international law was just these guys and these ideas in this time. If I read it right, the dominant note is unity—shared ideology, method, language, style.

To the Uttermost Parts of the Earth takes a more expansive tack over several centuries: there are identifiable legal people in France, England, Germany and Spain. There is an identifiable legal vocabulary—words like *jus gentium*. And there are repeated themes you're interested in—sovereignty/property or *imperium/dominium*—invoked and invented by people with all kinds of political and ideological projects. In this story, the domain of international legal imagination ranges far beyond what we—or your Victorian gentle civilizers—would see as international law, including topics that have been lopped off as private or domestic or commercial or religious/ethical. This is a kind of one, two, three, many *Landeshoheit*/empire problems.

Placing these three stories alongside one another—international law as a German public law philosophy, as the project of Victorian cosmopolitan liberals, as a five-hundred-year tradition of legal imagination among European notables concerned with property and sovereignty—illustrates how much "the European international law tradition" is open for invention and reinterpretation. An effect, at least in part, of historical work, including your own.

Martti: There is certainly a sense in which *From Apology to Utopia, The Gentle Civilizer of Nations,* and *To the Uttermost Parts of the Earth* illuminate different aspects of the "European tradition." One focuses on a discourse that imagines itself as philosophical, another describes its object in historical-sociological terms, while the third examines the relations between a heterogeneous set of legal vocabularies and the professional and intellectual practices that mutually construct each other over a lengthy period of time. They are also about provincialization, although that attempt was conscious only in *The Gentle Civilizer of Nations.*

As you say, what that book aimed at was to further specify the "European tradition" in its different variants: there were the French and the German and the British, as well as the UnitedStatesian, approaches that together suggested that to speak of "Europe" or "the North Atlantic" was still too general. This was a realm of plurality, not of homogeneity.

Later I found out that this was what legal historians had always thought; they had always been fascinated by the way European law was differently articulated in the different domestic legal cultures. Most critical were lawyers from the United States, not because I had proposed to "end" international law in the United States but because I had not quite comprehended the relations between the various legal and political realisms there. But I'll let you say more about international law in the United States.

David: Right, over here they didn't think it ended; they thought they had a new and improved version.

Martti: *To the Uttermost Parts of the Earth* shares the view that "Europe" is too grand and that there are various legal idioms in Europe that each have their specific way to present and seek to deal with the problem of diversity. I wanted to break the "law of nations" (*ius gentium; droit public de l'Europe; Völkerrecht,* or "international law") down into local and technical vocabularies that competed with and eventually penetrated one another, determining the frame within which legal imagination would have to work when it directed itself to the international world.

But I also wanted to make the point that this was not just a matter of variants in a *legal* tradition but that "law," so called, also interacted with and sometimes incorporated or was incorporated by idioms that presented themselves as *theological, philosophical, political,* or *economic.* This was not "legal pluralism" but something larger having to do with the formation and re-formation of intellectual and ideological constellations in Europe during a half millennium. It had to do with the struggle for intellectual hegemony in the form of the "conflict of the faculties." So far, surprisingly few readers have noticed that the book is also a narrative of the rise of "economics" as a master language of government today that is full of assumptions about international lawfulness.

David: Let's turn to the relationship of these traditions with everybody else. How has international law in Europe or the United States imagined everybody else? As "states" that are "just like us"? As divided by a boundary of civilized/uncivilized, Christian/infidel, developed/underdeveloped, democratic/authoritarian? How should we think about—and evaluate—the authority or impact of legal vocabularies and professional styles we have associated with our own national traditions in the larger world? Could we call them "hegemonic" in some sense?

Martti: Agreed. But let's remember that most of the time that imagining did not take place as "international law" but as "natural law" and, moreover, a natural law of divine inspiration. If that was how one saw the law, then it became natural to think of it as applicable everywhere, its rules binding over everyone. Hegemony, yes, but experienced as a gift to humankind.

David: In that sense, they both knew they had something specific—and knew it was and ought to be embraced as universal. We might start by revisiting authors like Tony Anghie or Arnulf Becker Lorca who have focused on the ways this international law tradition engaged with people in the world beyond the North Atlantic.[7] In Tony's case, engaged to dominate; in Arnulf's case, engaged by assimilation, opening a field of tactics for players on the periphery.

Attention to those who were left out all together is a different inquiry—the absence of women, of subaltern voices, social movements. Their absence has also shaped the field and the field has arranged things to ensure their absence. I'm thinking of Balakrishnan Rajagopal's *International Law from Below,* for example. [8] Or the way the alignment of public and private with international and national has reinforced the absence of women's voices and concerns in the field. In my "Spring Break" rumination on representing male and female prisoners of conscience as a human rights advocate, I aimed to engage this question.[9] But let's leave that aside for the moment to think about those outside the North Atlantic world whom the field has engaged—or at least imagined.

In *Imperialism, Sovereignty and the Making of International Law* Tony was looking at the same texts you and I were reading and saw something different: a European tradition "forged in the colonial encounter" as his work is often read to mean. I mentioned this before: he interpreted the classic texts to find an alternative continuity. I had taken the field's self-defined central issue—relations among sovereigns—as a focal point, noting that it brought faraway peoples into its universal frame in ways that turned ruthless wars of conquest into doctrinally comprehensible entitlements. Tony says, in effect, "Well, yes, but this relation with faraway peoples was at the center of their project, not an incidental site of its application."

In Tony's reconstruction, international law has been preoccupied less with European sovereign authority and the relations among putatively equal (European) sovereigns than with the relations Europeans had with those who were culturally different and for whom sovereignty was a lack or a goal or an ongoing problem. In relations with the culturally different, with the not or not yet sovereign, structuring inequality and domination edges out the management of intersovereign equality as the field's focal point, giving projects of universalization a very different feel. Although the philosophical frame may have its origins in German public law, its international extension was a matter of cultural differentiation and colonial hierarchy.

Martti: This was a fundamental critical insight; it certainly revolutionized the way we now think of sovereignty's historical significance.

David: Tony then follows this preoccupation from Spanish colonial wars through the nineteenth-century colonial mapping of Africa to the League of Nations' mandate system, postwar economic development and beyond—a *longue durée* consistency to replace "managing relations among sovereigns" as the field's central project. In each period he identifies a *hierarchy* established as the culturally distant are brought within a framework claiming to be universal.

The field, in short, is about hierarchy rather than order among equals—or about an order of domination among unequals. In an early work, legal anthropologist Annelise Riles expanded Tony's argument, identifying two aspirations in nineteenth-century international law writing when confronted with difference. Within Europe, she argued, the aspiration was communication and community; in the colonial world, it was control—two dimensions of a single sensibility treating culture as essential.[10]

It's worth noting that Anghie and Riles were not asking what actually happened in the colonial encounter or how significant international law was to the colonial project. This was not "colonialism as a legal institution." The focus was leading international law thinkers, what they thought, and how they thought about it. Tony does suggest the result was legitimation or facilitation of colonial conquest, but he leaves the sociology of that effect pretty unspecified. The authors they analyzed imagined themselves both atop a hierarchy and as arbiters of placement within in it: violation of norms as they interpreted them or departures from standards they exemplified defined the lower rungs and measured progress upward. If we think of hegemony as the ability to set the terms, they were imagining themselves as hegemonic.

Riles's later anthropological work has followed the complexity of reception for international legal forms and professional styles, from Fijian women's movements to Japanese financial markets. Others have worked to reconstruct the legal architecture of colonialism to see how international law played a role. It turns out that international law did express some baseline assumptions shared by colonial officers who often used international legal arguments within the colonial administration, with other colonial powers, and with subject populations. But the legal foundations of colonialism were a complex mélange of local and national, official and informal law reflecting the diverse institutional arrangements for colonial conquest and administration in different settings or characteristic of different colonial powers at different historical moments.

What about your story of the men of 1873—European liberals uniting the European civilization—or the legal professionals of *To the Uttermost Parts of the Earth*, picking up legal ideas to sort out the authority of the king, relations with the pope, commercial rules of the road, and the priority of property? Was all this also "forged in the colonial encounter?"

Martti: Well, I think Tony was right in that much of international law as we received it is such as it is owing to the Spanish conquest and the elaboration of its principles, first by Spanish theologians, then by Grotius, then by people like John Locke, Adam Smith, and so on. I think he is right, especially with regard to the emergence of a binary world of sovereignty and nonsovereignty and the continued significance of the distinguishing criteria—I mean Christianity, civilization, development, modernity, criteria for distinguishing two types of community, and two types of law to deal with intercommunity relations. I have no problem with that, although, as you say, that was not the critical project I think we were engaged in. But does it mean that if there had been no colonial encounter, there would have been no sovereignty as we know it?

David: That phrase—"forged in the colonial encounter"—can certainly suggest not only a tainted origin but colonialism as *the* origin.

Martti: Right—and I don't think so. Social struggles within what historians now are a little wary of calling "feudalism" brought the idea of the prince's sovereignty to the fore—the position of kingship as something higher than a mark of a powerful member of the nobility. But the way the word *sovereign* moved from being an epithet of a person to that of a community, and eventually of a "state," was clearly connected to colonization. The idea of "criteria of statehood," for example, is a fully colonialist concoction that emerged in legal writings toward the end of the nineteenth century. Historians of political thought, especially of the Cambridge school, have done a lot of work to uncover the genealogy of statehood and of sovereignty; so far they have not paid sufficient attention to the effects of colonial expansion on that notion but have, until very recently, been satisfied with describing intra-European developments.

As for property, it is true that the justification of land ownership, especially in the Anglo-American settler context, was powerfully influenced by the colonial encounter, though it also played on the old English theme of improvement. Your right to the land depends on your commitment to improve it, and improvement would mean the specific European way of land use. On the other hand, however, it would be strange to suggest—and I do not think this is anything that Tony was suggesting—that the concept of property, even property over land, would have been *created* in the colonial context. The Roman law notion of *dominium* has a long history, and even as colonization belongs to that history, it still just one part of it.

So, yes, the colonial encounter is an important context, but nevertheless it's just one context where law of nations arose. In *To the Uttermost Parts of the Earth* I have tried to show how sovereignty and property were employed also with respect to struggles inside Europe, within territorial communities and between European powers, indeed quite crucial in constructing what "Europe" would mean. Roman law notions of *dominium* and *imperium* were extremely important in crafting an image of European kingship. And the eventual formation of consensus on what "property" might mean and where its limits might lie have been powerfully indebted to debates inside the church about the morality of wealth and interest taking.

The question of debt, both public and private, has been an unappreciated aspect of the formation of social relations in Europe. People forget, for example, that for Grotius its recovery was one of the official justifications for just war. To reduce all of that into the colonial encounter does not seem to me very credible—as I said, I do not think Tony meant to go that far, either.

David: That's helpful—nor, as you say, does Tony take it that far. He shows that the colonial encounter was important for international law and—less definitively, I think—that international law was important for colonialism. How this channel of reciprocal influence compared to other factors and forces, how the colonial encounter should be weighed with other encounters, he leaves aside. Nor does he focus on the ways international law was harnessed in resistance to colonial hierarchies. I think part of the force of his argument comes simply from the recurrence of this universalize-to-dominate pattern, from conquistador wars to contemporary arbitration, bilateral investment treaties or the World Trade Organization.

Martti: It first arose in Christian-universalist terms, then became scientific-naturalist, cultural-developmental, and eventually humanitarian-economic.

David: I know Tony has sometimes been read to have identified a *logic* of domination rather than a series of projects for which people found bits of international law useful—often in similar ways. But if there were a logic, it's unclear whether it resides in the colonial project or the international legal imagination. That pattern of embrace-to-dominate is a joint project of soldiers and lawyers, traders, and government officials. We might think of the international legal vocabulary as carrying the pattern around, available for rediscovery as people imagine and pursue various projects.

To the Uttermost Parts of the Earth tells it this way. There are legal advisers, they have some intellectual and textual resources, something of a shared, if loose, lexicon. They have various power projects that they pursue with assertion and argument, drawing attention to facts and norms somewhat interchangeably. Perhaps they're trying to get someone to accept or reject papal authority over this or that.

Or there's Vitoria, trying to figure out how to guide the confessional practices of Spanish clerics with believers who had done something regrettable overseas. He draws on his lexicon and offers a way to understand what (he imagines) to be going on there and to give it normative shape. He refers to the facts on the ground as part of his argument—invoking the context is one of his tools. Military pastors in Iraq talked that way when counseling American servicemen: the context of battle, the "rules of engagement," and so on.

One advantage of your story in *To the Uttermost Parts of the Earth* is to multiply the "contexts" or "projects" in which people exercise their *legal imagination,* tweaking and reinventing the vocabulary as they go along. An idea that worked with the pope might not with someone else, and you have to come up with something else. So there are all kinds of origin situations, with lots of accidents and confusions and innovative suggestions along the way. Although the continuities you identify—legal advisers, shared vocabulary (*jus gentium,* etc.), preoccupations with sovereign authority and property—might lead someone to think there is an unfolding logic, I'm sure that's not how you see it.

Martti: No, no logic—apart from the logic of rivalry, struggle, and ambition. I suppose the most important thing lost along the way is the understanding of *dominium*—the sense, palpable still among the theologians in the sixteenth century (and maybe with Kant)—as justified power that in its character as sovereignty and property (that is, today, *dominium iurisdictionis* and *dominium proprietatis*) is identical: there is no essential difference between the ruler and the owner or public and private power.

So I would say it is amazing how so much seems to depend today on that quite convoluted and accidental distinction in a history that has been teleologically understood as "state building." Many alternative forms of institution we lost on the way: the city, the province, the land, the university, the guild, the commercial company. Each used to have its hierarchies and claim the allegiance of its members. Each provided, if I can use the word—a different *context* for human interaction.

At the time of the American Revolution, influential thinkers were already speculating about a commercial order that could be formalized against the order of states; there were even formal proposals for Europe's rulers to get together to turn their commercial outposts into a formalized network to administer this global order. In the epilogue of *To the Uttermost Parts of the Earth* I reference the striking effort by some of the lawyers who took part in the revolutions of 1848 to imagine an "international society" as a legal realm of solidarity, separate from states and governed by the kind of laws that became the social laws of the industrial state in the late nineteenth century. These are just some examples—but they point to ways of thinking through law that might have framed the "international" world differently from how it then came to be.

David: Recalling the lost forms really opens space, denaturalizing the "state" that has become so mandatory, if also shot through with more complex and uncertain legal possibilities. But let me turn to a different "rest of world" inquiry illustrated by Arnulf Becker Lorca's book *Mestizo International Law.* Arnulf expands the people who count as creators to include legal intellectuals of the "semiperiphery" active alongside the canonical European voices, at least since the late nineteenth century. He argues that their innovations within international law were shaped by their projects *outside* the North Atlantic, on their home turf, as much as by their participation in a shared cosmopolitan world.

He also stresses the relatively marginal position of international law mavens within Europe—so, the Belgians in *The Gentle Civilizer of Nations,* but also the Russians and Finns, alongside the Latin Americans and Asians he identifies. To be a legal cosmopolitan at the center may have been more marginal than being an internationalist on the semiperiphery—often men from the most elite circles. In Arnulf's telling, international law is less built at the center for reception on the periphery than in the borderlands of the European experience.

In the UnitedStatesean tradition, the leading international lawyers were always a bit outside state power, if often leading figures in the commercial bar or the professoriate. Particularly in the postwar decades, the leading international law figures were also often immigrants. You've concentrated on German, French, and British innovators—can you place them in this picture? Were they also marginal in some sense or in a collaborative, if unstated, dialogue with Arnulf's semiperipheral "outsiders?"

Martti: I was delighted that Arnulf resuscitated the role of non-European or non-US lawyers, in the late nineteenth and early twentieth centuries, as many of them began to get admitted to international law tables. But it seems to me that the condition for their accession was that they behave like the Europeans, something that was not hard for them, as they had received their legal education either in the United States or in Europe anyway. They became influential in Europe because they shared the idea of legal competence of those around them.

This did not prevent them from being innovators, but the scope of their innovation was limited by, on the one hand, their interest in supporting some supposedly local variation—such as "Latin American international law," for example—and otherwise their broad agreement with their North Atlantic colleagues of what international law was about. But what they could—and did—do was to use the law to support the elites in their own countries (to which they mostly belonged) against European influences, as well as sometimes to subordinate the Indigenous populations in their own countries.

This difficulty was also visible with the first generation of postcolonial intellectuals with a powerful presence in the field in the 1960s—men like T. O. Elias from Nigeria or P. S. Anand from India. They were admitted because they did not challenge the gentle civilizing spirit. In their historical writings, for example, they made over and again the argument that African and Indian traditions were just like the European traditions—they, too, had a just war theory, diplomatic immunity, sovereignty, and a widespread practice of treaty making.

It is completely understandable that these men, despite the obvious difference of their backgrounds from those of the North Atlantic elites they intended to join, would refrain from putting to question the basic forms of international law. This did not prevent them from being reformers; that is what they became. But their reformism was strictly confined to proposals that did not put to question the basic frame of the law. The only clear exception that I can think of was the Algerian, Bedjaoui, of whom Umut Özsu has written interestingly.[11]

David: I wonder about Bedjaoui—in 1979, I picked up his *Towards a New International Economic Order* at the UN bookshop in Geneva with enthusiasm—but I didn't find much beyond the well-trodden paths of (French) sociological realism long since mainstreamed in American legal thought. But back to their situation . . .

Martti: The only alternative would have been just to stay out, and begin throwing bricks into the windows of the Palais des Nations in Geneva or the UN. This may also be a way to power. But it, too, involves risks. If the people I mentioned earlier faced the risk of assimilation, the brick throwers risked remaining eternal outsiders. You may be able to protect your principles, but only at the cost of not really knowing what happens inside and how to influence that happening. This is the paradox that both being included and staying outside may, at different moments, be either an act of political wisdom or political stupidity.

I often feel dubious about the call to "include" the "other." One of Tony's merits was to show that such inclusion may actually lead to binding and disciplining that other—with the powerful example of the Spanish Dominicans of the sixteenth century. Refraining from inclusion may, by contrast, be an act of respect—though, of course, it may equally well arise from discrimination, refusal to grant benefits to those not part of the in-group. It's a hard choice.

For third world legal intellectuals in the first, second, and third postcolonial generations, the matter presented itself differently—the third world approaches to international law (TWAIL) people continue to debate this with some urgency. If neither difference nor integration is valuable in itself, then the issue breaks down into strategic choices—but addressing the world strategically has its own problems, and so you seem to turn around in circles.

David: It is true that a postcolonial couldn't get in the door without accepting the constellation of institutional and doctrinal arrangements that attended decolonization: succession to sovereign debts and colonial boundaries, and so on. Nevertheless, I read Arnulf to be challenging the frame of castrated insider or brick-throwing outsider. He opens the book with an evocation of people like Alvarez, men of letters arriving in Europe. Their situation is more elusive. It's not clear that but for their Europeanization they would have pursued more radical political projects. Often their project was precisely to belong, to insist their nation belonged.

Your image of brick throwing captures something of the hegemony of the situation: the vocabulary of engagement is ours; join or you cannot be heard. You picture the brick thrower aiming at the legal order, consigned to modes of engagement that insiders understand as outsider challenges. But insiders also throw bricks around—enforce their prerogatives, make legal war. And throwing a brick—like invoking the brick throwers back home—is also an articulative strategy.

I remember a meeting at the UN at which the secretariat was being urged to focus diplomatic energy away from the Middle East, where prospects for a breakthrough were dim. International lawyers from both Israel and the Arab world immediately invoked the brick throwers back home—"Stay focused on us, else our terrorists get the upper hand." It was Cavafy who reminded us that the barbarians "were a kind of solution."

I see that "situation in the borderland" as one indicium of an intellectual hegemony in the sense of an authority to manage the line between inside and out. Your Belgians were making up the European tradition that confronted Arnulf's semiperipherals with that choice: participate or be an outsider. There was room for a range of strategies, but the further you get from Belgium, the more difficult it is to establish an *alternative universal* with the potential to become hegemonic in this way.

I can imagine it feels this way in Beijing or Russia—or Bangladesh—today: the West and North offer lots of strategies of engagement but there is no visible path to establishing our own universal vocabulary, reflecting our national legal traditions and political projects. This kind of intellectual hegemony has effects, but they are hard to pin down—even if we intuit they somehow reinforce and are reinforced by (unequal) patterns of trade or political influence, modes of finance, and so on.

Martti: I think most people would today feel that the choice between following the Lenins or the Bernsteins of this world is too starkly posed and the demand for alternative universals may only lead to disappointment and cynicism. It did not take long for the hugely ambitious Brazil, Russia, India, China, and South Africa (BRICS) project, just a few years ago, to dissolve into limited financial and development initiatives among the larger non-European countries, each wary of the others' hegemonic ambition. In the late nineteenth century, hegemony may have seemed fixed, at least if you looked at it from the center; things have become way more fluid since.

David: There's more to be said about projects to break the frame, to establish an alternative universal and about their destiny. I'm thinking of the Soviet project; the Nazi project; at various moments, decolonization projects; perhaps the third world/Bandung/New International Economic Order projects. It is easy to reinterpret them retrospectively as having used—or abused—international law for diabolical purposes before falling in line or being defeated. But that tangle of inside and outside, of legal assertion as brick throwing against the order—or brick throwing as legal assertion against the challengers—is unlikely to be best understood exclusively from the perspective of the universal that survived.

But let's turn to the other side of Arnulf's story: the marginality of the international legal imagination in the center. It is tempting to picture international lawyers in the control rooms of European (or American) power as they colonized the world. Your men of 1873 were a bourgeois elite, but I wonder if their cosmopolitan intellectual/political project also reflected some estrangement from national power. In the formation of the American imperial mind in the 1950s and 1960s, public international lawyers were quite marginal.

I'm sure we'll come back to this when we focus directly on the history of international law. But in the United States, political scientists, sociologists, and economists were more important than legal intellectuals—the prestige of the social sciences and the centrality of the "study" in policy was on the rise. These were the people who thought about nuclear power, nuclear weapons, and national security and who reframed the West as the "free world" in a new global struggle.

The lawyers who were in the control room of American war making, colony making, and trade making were elite American corporate lawyers and American constitutional and administrative experts with international interests, experiences, clients. When the American president decides he needs a lawyer to go run the colony in the Philippines, he picks a commercial New York lawyer rather than someone from the world of diplomacy and public law. After 1945, American public international lawyers were a discredited Republican bunch in a Rooseveltian world, remembered for their piety about neutrality and isolation from European conflicts.

The legal architects of American power borrowed bits and pieces from commercial law, private law, banking law, and the American regulatory practice to build the scaffolding for an expanding national market, outbound investment, the stabilization of international finance. They were rooted in the history of American legal thought and largely ignorant of the "international legal tradition" of the Carnegie projects, let alone their European predecessors.

Martti: It is, of course, true that the outsiders who became respected international lawyers were not usually of the revolutionary variety; they may not only have shared the preferences and conceptual frames of the North

Atlantic mainstream but may, as Liliana Obregón has shown, actually have used them to forge a domestic distinction between the "civilized" elites (usually with European background) and the Indigenous inhabitants.[12]

You are right that the "borderland" is more elusive; there is space between castration and brick throwing. In my own experience, there have been many international lawyers from the Global South who have been very conscious of that predicament and have straddled between the extremes. Again, however, to understand that middle space it is necessary to see clearly the opposite poles.

And I wonder if the gentle civilizers of the late nineteenth century were that marginal at the time. All were politically active. Many were members of government; Mancini was foreign minister, and his "principle of nationalities" resounded across Europe; Bourgeois was both foreign minister and prime minister and chaired the first sessions of the League Council. One of my predecessors in the Helsinki chair, Rafael Erich, once served as prime minister, as well, in the 1920s. Twiss and Arndt convinced the US Congress to recognize the flag of King Leopold's Congo Free State. They were influential members of the delegations of their countries at various late nineteenth-century treaty-making congresses. They came from the post-1848 liberal ascendancy across Europe but, as you say, were now challenged by a more powerful type of nationalism, socialism, xenophobia, and disappointment with liberal rule. They did represent a mindset that was influential—perhaps even "hegemonic"—until the Great War and the early years of the League of Nations but were gradually sidelined even in their own countries. They were clearly that group with which it would be easiest for outside lawyers to contact for the purposes of influence.[13]

Can I then just ask you something that has been puzzling me in your American story? The Europeans, the gentle civilizers, were very focused on certain types of institutions and institution building—the "unions" of the late nineteenth century, the League, and the Permanent Court of International Justice; you have described it in your article on the "move to institutions." After the Second World War they shifted their commitment to the UN and regional institution building in Europe. Their universalization urge had a very clear institutional emphasis.

But I don't see anything of the kind in the United States. The field there is so much more fragmented, with these commercial lawyers and security lawyers and civil rights lawyers, and so on operating mostly in institutions situated in the United States and have none of the Europeans' interest in the League or the UN. Their language is often so . . . parochial. And yet I believe they also share a universal ambition; it's just that it is so different from the language, and the mindset, among the Europeans. How would you characterize the legal "exceptionalism" of the international style of which you spoke?

David: It *is* strange—both parochial and ubiquitous in the legal affairs of the world. I don't think the lawyers think their style is exceptional in the sense of being particularly "American"; they think it is good lawyering, just rare to encounter in people not trained in the United States. But I don't want to get too focused on "national traditions." In all the cases we are talking about, the vocabularies and professional practices are hybrid—that's one benefit of Arnulf's insistence on the presence of semiperipherals in production process.

People geolocate intellectual traditions for a reason. You root international law in the European experience to "provincialize" Europe in an international law discipline that understands itself to be global. A hundred years ago, Alvarez invoked an "American" legal tradition he imagined as a fortuitous blend of civil and common law practices in order to introduce the social-interdependence-oriented perspective he had actually studied in France to the international law of the day.[14] I've heard you say your men of 1873 seemed to delight in transforming one another's idiosyncrasies into "national traditions" as evidence of their cosmopolitan bona fides. Or take the "regional custom" idea, promoted to solidify a couple of Latin American doctrinal peculiarities around asylum and foreign investment.

I claimed there was a "UnitedStatesean" professional style to focus attention on a grammar of professional practice that has its roots in American legal thought. I hesitated because naming it this way also suggests that it expresses the interests or enhances the power of "the United States," a different kind of argument. The ubiquity of this UnitedStatesean style means it has been used to further interests in lots of directions; we might better return to the phrase "law in global affairs" to identify the object of study.

Martti: I agree, "style" is better than "tradition." It also relativizes the drama of "outside" versus "inside" and focuses attention on the elements of professional competence, what it is to learn such competence and how it can be used to support varied purposes.

David: At the same time, international lawyers do bring national political projects, historical sensibilities, and shared professional experiences to their work. For a century or more, American lawyers with an international orientation have experienced the traditions of "public international law" as artificial, ill suited for global problem solving. That experience has roots in their professional work, more often commercial than diplomatic. It also has roots in American legal thought, which has long tried to shed nineteenth-century doctrinal specializations like "public international law" in the name of a more pragmatic and functional style, able to cross conceptual boundaries in the search for practical solutions. Philip Jessup's 1928 manifesto, promoting the functionalist and realist perspectives familiar in American private commercial law and corporate practice, captures the sensibility.[15]

Two quick examples. I mentioned Abe Chayes before; in his US Senate confirmation hearings to serve as legal adviser in Kennedy's State Department he was asked how many judges were on the International Court of Justice (ICJ) and he was amused to admit he had *no idea*. The senator was reassured. It was a matter of pride that he had never taken a public international law course and saw himself as an American constitutional lawyer, interested in the limitations of federal power. He then becomes the guy who develops the legal arrangements for the quarantine of Cuba in the Cuban missile crisis.

Or later, Harold Koh, a dean of the Yale Law School who has repeatedly played an important role in the State Department, cites the American proceduralists of the 1950s and 1960s as his most important intellectual influences, inspiring his vision of a transnational legal process.[16] For both of them, American legal thought was the keystone. And I think we could say much the same for the many human rights and environmental law activists who flooded the global stage after 1989.

Martti: But problem solving and functionalism are also important elements in the bureaucratic ethos of international institutions as they arose during the interwar era.[17] Still, I do not see US lawyers having played a big role in them.

David: Right, you had asked about international institutions. They're certainly less the focal point for internationally oriented American lawyers than for those you found in your diplomatic practice. I do wonder if that's both Finland and the way the public international law experts have been channeled in European ministries, think tanks, and universities. In the US government there are lots of lawyers focused on various international institutions. Still, I think you are right that the UN system is more central in the international legal imagination elsewhere—in middle powers, certainly in major donor and recipient nations. Looking back, the spurt of interest in intergovernmental institutions after World War II in the United States was unusual.

Although the League was an important project for a subset of the American elite—and for numerous social movements—the globally oriented legal community was less enthusiastic. Elihu Root, founder of the American Society of International Law and a well-known opponent of American membership in the League is more representative. After the Second World War, public law specialists with experience in wartime and New Deal government were "present at the creation," in Dean Acheson's famous phrase. As the UN system dwindled to a third-tier instrument of American power, legal attention moved elsewhere, despite the repeated assertion that the institutions of the postwar settlement were "American made, funded, and hosted."

For some international lawyers, the UN did remain the touchstone, but it was a focus that shrank their influence as the Cold War stymied the UN as a great power project, as decolonization pluralized it to irrelevance other than as a public diplomacy platform, and as its functional regulatory and humanitarian arms became routine. The foreign policy action was in the operations of the American government, American industry, American military expansion, American cultural production, development policy, and the activism of what came to be called civil society.

There is always this strange moment when students come to talk about pursuing an "international law career" and you have to explain that they will more likely find engaging work with the US Treasury than with the State Department, in state or city governments rather than the UN, in corporate legal offices or nongovernmental advocacy projects rather than the ICJ, with Boeing or Chevron—or Greenpeace. After all, the most significant "international institutions" today may be global supply chains, elaborate and complex legal edifices constructed across innumerable local and national jurisdictions. The most significant international norms are regulations promulgated in Brussels or London or Washington—or invented by private actors and only occasionally visible in places like Basel.

Nevertheless, global value chains, payment systems, military supply lines are legal constructions forged in the American style. That is what led me to think about the influence—hegemony, perhaps—of the American "international style," or, in your terms, the grammar of the American legal imagination. The EU is an obvious example. Its legal culture has been so influenced by American legal thought, for all its doctrinal and institutional distinctiveness.

This American style also draws a line between inside and out, often in quite prosaic ways: getting your client access to global capital markets means practicing law in the New York/London manner. Beyond that, a world of economic life cut off from the global economy, with an enormously porous borderland between.

Arnulf's outsiders could pinpoint the boundary and identify the password to come in: our country is civilized, we don't crucify prisoners of war. They could strategize about overthrowing the distinction between civilized and noncivilized, a victory won in the Montevideo Convention. Decolonization meant crossing a sharp line to statehood and sovereignty. The hegemony of American legal thought has a bit of that—the terrorist, the Islamic fundamentalism joins the pirate and international criminal beyond the line.

But a boundary etched in *legal thought* is much harder to pin down. The borderlands of today's legal hegemony are marked in modes of law firm practice, in comfort with antiformalism, with legal pluralism, and with the policy and normative self-confidence that characterize American legal professionalism. You can feel the outside air when professional styles or modes of argument sound outdated, traditional; Americans long disparaged European international lawyers in these terms as less sophisticated, not "up to the standard our clients expect," and so forth.

But let me stress that whether the globalization of American legal thought benefits "America" is a different question. American lawyers, at least in the leading firms, certainly benefit, along with American law schools. We'd need a clearer sense of "what America wants," to coin a phrase. And whether this legal imperium advances the cause.

Martti: Such a different world, the United States. It reminds me a little of the position of Britain and British lawyers in the nineteenth century—I discuss this in *To the Uttermost Parts of the Earth*—whose universalism was rarely, almost never, channeled through a "law of nations" of the continental type. They operated internationally through domestic principles of prerogative law, colonial law, and the common and commercial law regulating British companies and travelers abroad. The legal essence of British empire was to think about the world through types of British law—that's the parallel with the United States.

But it never became a more widely used idiom. By contrast, something like UnitedStatesean legal thought—or style—has indeed been globalized in the more recent decades. In law firms around the world, US practices today form the professional standard. The cultural figure of the "gentleman lawyer" seems hopelessly old-fashioned. But I think the conflict with European law remains quite open in public and criminal law. Meeting lawyers from the US State Department at the UN, I remember that not only their background but their style, their conception of what it was to be lawyer in a multilateral context, was very different from what I had learned. The anxiety with which US negotiators—I am thinking of the law of the sea, and of international criminal law—were looking over their shoulder to what members of the Senate might be thinking. And what was the "foreign relations law" to which they kept referring, anyway?

I ended *The Gentle Civilizer of Nations* in the 1960s, a moment when the style and sensibility of the generation of the 1870s would no longer represent changing legal culture or provide access to positions in government; it had now become something between a minor technical aspect of public diplomacy and utopian speculation about peace and humanitarian rulership. The type of cosmopolitanism that had been inherited from the League period had come to be seen old-fashioned, unable to meet the challenges of decolonization and the growth of US power, as well as the increasing technicity of the law itself. New specialist fields were developing their own, often conflicting, types of internationalism that sought distance from old ways of international law—human rights and environmental law from the 1970s onward. And ambitious jurists in Europe would now invite the EU to flex its muscles; public international lawyers could only dream of "direct effect" and "supremacy."

Where do young European lawyers go today? No longer to international law. Instead they choose EU law, investment law, environmental law, human rights law. They become experts in transnational corporation law, migration law. As Erasmus students much of their attention as potential future wielders of hegemony is directed to the EU, not the UN. As activists in human rights or experts in transnational finance their perception is not organized by public international law but by the techniques of specialist institutions, with their specific practices and ideals.

It was no accident that the new generation of European lawyers learned first of all to stress the distance of what they were doing from international law and diplomacy; they were consciously building something new as an amalgam of, as you said, US legal styles, as well as distinct and easily detectable influences from French and German administrative, financial, and constitutional law—not forgetting novel theories of bureaucratic governance.

David: Absolutely. That phrase *sui generis* was so important to everyone in the European law world: "What we're doing is *sui generis*!" American law firms were quickly able to dominate practice in Brussels—and did so for years—in part because they were familiar with that kind of amalgam of ad hoc, pragmatic constructions from the multi-jurisdictional American commercial world. Part of this American rulership style is also the blurring of boundaries between "legal" and other expertise, the rise of a management and problem-solving sensibility. In *A World of Struggle,* I painted a more general picture of "expertise" in contemporary transnational governance, a sophisticated technocratic sensibility shared among human rights people, military people, development people, UN people, and so forth.

Martti: The genealogy you developed in *A World of Struggle* certainly made me ask whether what you were proposing was a new type of universality. The aperture was so wide that everything that we call "global" or address in terms of "governance" is covered in the technocratic practices and the mindset that you label *expertise.* Although it may have had its specific starting points in local practices, to what extent has it now become the successor discipline or mindset for everything else? I have sketched a trajectory from Christianity to civilization to science, development and globalization. Will the next thing now be *expertise*?

David: I put that forward as a hypothesis with examples from sites I had had the opportunity to observe. If technocracy and expert rule is our fate, perhaps this is how it works. You said earlier that the apology-to-utopia grammar of international law was rooted in an identifiable philosophical and practical situation. In *A World of Struggle* I argued that transnational expertise also expresses a historically and geographically specific situation:

a late twentieth- and early twenty-first-century mode of thinking influenced in its expressions and phenomenology by American legal thought.

Martti: One question that emerges from reading *A World of Struggle* has to do with the role—if any—of that older universalizing governance-related idea of the "state." What has happened or is happening to it?

David: A big question!

Martti: I have always found myself—maybe weirdly—as a defender of the state; not any particular state, of course, and even less any nationalism connected with them, but statehood as a specific form of human togetherness. In an early text, which I titled "The Wonderful Artificiality of States,"[18] I made the point that we always need institutions to live together, and the fact that statehood—or the language of statehood—pretends to be or has the push to be *substantively empty* provides a way of figuring out the ways in which one lives together in a really open-ended fashion. I mean, the idea that you do not need an identity fixation to become a citizen. Of course, both Europeans and Americans have often grasped at fantasies about substantive nationhood, civilizing role, or manifest destiny. But even though the state has sometimes been captured by such ideas, it has also had some historical resistance to them; it often seems to me that it is hardly more than a systematic effort to resist such reduction. And I think that's a really good contribution. I wonder how you see the role of state in US history, or the history of US universal imagining.

David: Before I get to "the state" in particular, let me just say that I do think professional style often trumps institutional form. I'm thinking of all those students oriented to problem solving rather than to the UN or the EU or any other institutional arrangement. They're off for the summer to solve the water crisis in this or that spot—if they need an institution, they'll invent one, crowdfund it, harness whatever other institutions they find to their project as it evolves.

Martti: But then there's property rights, another figment of a universalizing imagination, terribly complicated, and I wonder about its role, too, in your *World of Struggle*. That work is not, it seems to me, a world of struggle over property—or is it? In case it is, then the role of the lawyers would seem to become accentuated among the experts to talk about its history, its limits, and the way it is distributed.

David: If I understand that right, lawyers certainly seem to feel they "own" disputation about "property." But I can imagine many others dabbling in just that—back to my grandmother on holiday, arguing with a hotelier. The way you put property back in the story alongside sovereignty is great, raising questions about how the great distinctions we live among arose and were consolidated.

Part of modern expertise, I think, is the skill of making and unmaking those distinctions. The public/private distinction—like that between national and international—has priority, is easy to treat naturally, but the work of expertise is managing the links, turning the one into the other, tricks like that. I wanted to focus on those practices of intellectually managing, deploying, modifying—formalizing and relativizing—the big classics: property/sovereignty; international/national, but also things like "development" or "progress."

Martti: Which then leads me to think about the way grand terms such as *Christianity, imperialism, colonialism, capitalism, socialism,* or *neoliberalism* have proposed general views on sovereignty *and* property—and on their relationships. But they are often, in fact, unhelpful for analyzing situations. What does *communism* mean in China, for example, or how does *neoliberalism* capture the reality of Finland and the United States? These words point to more or less vague ideas and historical analogies; they may act as names for political tendencies. But as analytical instruments to think about the constellations of statehood and property rights they really do not go far.

I think we've had this conversation before. As nominalists we both feel that critical analysis should break through such large notions and refuse to think of them as good or bad in a universal way or in themselves. This does not mean one should never, in political engagement, invoke them as "fighting words." They may be associated with solidarity, peace, human rights, justice. They are part of good brick-throwing politics.

But so often they are simply obstacles for thinking clearly. Much of your critique of human rights, say, has been about the enchanting nature of such words. So, how to draw a line between when to use them—and when to critique those who do so? Can one say that being a political activist and an engaged, critical intellectual, sensitive to the complexities of political language, are two different things? I mean different in the sense that you have to choose, you cannot be both at the same time. I often think so.

David: People *do* do both, all the time. Perhaps it is too easy to say one can't escape approaching that strategically—if also fallibly. We are back, in a way, to law's constitutive/background import and its usefulness. You invoke property and the rest of the human rights and justice vernacular as "fighting words," grounds for resistance to the power of another. Absolutely. Like all legal entitlements, sovereignty and property are about both the resistance *and the assertion* of power. Just as they are available both to be insisted upon and to be relativized, broken apart, reallocated. Nor is there a sharp line between asserting and resisting; they travel together, a kind of joint boundary work for the practices of power as their relative ambits are repeatedly contested and adjusted. It's not surprising to find both—the "grammar" of legal practice, if we are calling it that, is in the rhetorical, procedural, and institutional forms of their interaction.

Martti: But what about the problem of the state—the specter that always haunted international lawyers? The gentle civilizing generation had a really ambivalent attitude toward it. On the one hand, the state was the great obstacle to their cosmopolitan objectives; much of the law they created was about limiting and taming it. On the other hand, they were also keen to defend ideas about self-determination, and nonintervention, and certainly believed that their own states were worthy of practical and principled defense. As I said, I have found one aspect of statehood—its bureaucratic formalism—as a useful structure for thinking about politics, democracy above all. But you don't see it like that?

David: No question, "the state" has always been right there, a preoccupying possibility to be invoked, defended, maligned, transcended, overcome. If I understand you correctly, I've never seen the analytic/political potential you identify—the state as a promise, something to hold on to, rather than a central conceit to be interpreted, deployed, resisted, promoted. Descriptively, it could be that technocratic/expert rulership is what "the state" has become. But once one empties the state of the many associations it has acquired it is a rather empty vessel—the idea of "institutions we need to live together." So many of the institutions we routinely rely upon are not the state and have been set up in opposition to the state, that the state, "emptied of substance," seems an odd way to embrace them. I'm not sure *expertise* is much better—I was sorry I'd chosen that word even before I sent the manuscript off.

People often contrast American and European society by saying we treat the state more as an artificial legal construction than an organic reality. There's something to that. Lawyers here have been trained to dissolve both property and sovereignty into their component legal relations: in Hohfeldian terms, they are both just "bundles" of rights, duties, and so forth. We claim that makes it easier to imagine them taking other forms, transnational forms, private forms. And it foregrounds relations of relative power: for every right, someone else has a duty. At the same time, the institutions of national government often seem the *only* common reference point for national unity: the cargo cult of the US Constitution, the procession of presidents, and so on. However powerful and ubiquitous in American society, as a dominant reference point, the state occludes the knowledge and power deployed everywhere else.

That's also true of international law. The image of a central government ruling a territory and population in the general interest barely characterizes modern European nations and is an utter fantasy most everywhere else. As a model for global governance, it could hardly be more misleading. Think of the utterly fantastic notion that international law is *like* national law . . . except horizontal, enforced by auto-interpretation rather than higher authority. Or that global "governance" is *like* state government . . . except distributed. Or that international courts—or criminal law—are *like* national courts . . . except primitive, neonatal. What massive misreadings of legal power in the world! Or think about what is missed: Dan Danielsen aimed to upend the state-equals-public-power association by refiguring corporations not as "influential" but as *governing*, exercising what we should—or certainly could—reframe as public power.[19] The Institute for Global Law and Policy hosted a research project that aimed to reimagine global value chains as transnational "governing" institutions along parallel lines.[20]

As a utopian vision of government—one territory, one people—the state is *also* difficult to assess positively. What violence has been undertaken in its name! What other solidarities crushed. It was a catastrophe for the colonial world to discover that the only way to be postcolonial is to be a state—with the colonial administrative boundaries, no less! Nevertheless, people remain attached to this strange fantasy—and international law eggs them on. I suspect people hang onto an international law among "sovereigns" as they do precisely because they also know most so-called states are Potemkin overlays on deeply divided, unequal, and artificially cobbled together societies. Invoking the state enables rule by some combination of leading families, kleptocrats, oligarchs, foreign investors, gangs, or military elites. It enables private actors to offload responsibility for the harm they cause.

So I guess I'm pretty down on the state as a model or focal point in our fields.

Martti: Well, of course, there's all that. But, historically, states also arose against centuries of violence by empires from above and feudal lordships from below.

David: In Europe, anyway—or quite differently in the European heartland and elsewhere: settler colonialist societies, postcolonial societies, and so forth.

Martti: Struggling for statehood has given meaning to the pursuit of emancipation and peace across the world. As an "empty vessel" it has provided a vocabulary that has been and continues to be used to separate legitimate government from mob rule. Is it possible to live without thinking in terms of some such distinction, never mind that we may have seen it collapse in practice many times? Or let me put it this way: with the history of forms of rule that we have had in Europe, one of the avoidable directions seems to be one where government is understood as a means to enforce an identity formation or the image of a supposedly natural type of government over a people.

The hegemonic group sees itself having the task to impose an identity or purpose on the rest. Surely that result would be likelier in an imaginary nonstate situation than in one where the structures of statehood and citizenship are available. I suppose this is a variant of the point about a culture of formalism that I made at the end of *The Gentle Civilizer of Nations* or, perhaps, takes up the distinction that some have made between a civil association and a teleological project. The point would be to base the association on something—rules, institutions—that have been agreed on, instead of some external purpose imposed on everyone, with all the caveats about hegemony that may attach to manufacturing that agreement. Still, I do not see why that would invalidate that standard.

David: What would it have meant for the world had the US Civil War turned out differently—a North America of multiple units with different destinies? I've often thought the attachment to "one" United States a political and cultural mistake. Or, on the other side, what if Africa had come to the postcolonial world whole? Without statehood, a different destiny for South Asia? How long should we expect the states strung between the Balkans and Burma to survive in their current forms? Surely we ought not be carrying a brief for the "statehood form" against whatever distributions, hierarchies, or violent clashes accompany their challenge and defense? We're now engaged in an ethnonationalist statehood conflict in Europe. How many should die for that cause?

But maybe you are imagining "the state" as a kind of ready-made theory of justice—a placeholder for something like "power on behalf of everyone." I know there are lots of theories of justice that try to put legs on "the good of all" or "the public interest." When they get applied, it turns out they enable some and not others—others who are unlikely, unless you're really lucky, to find the "theory of justice" persuasive. Here, also, the state seems an odd choice. I'd sooner go for "what reasonable people would design behind a veil of ignorance," or whatever that Rawlsian formulation was.

In so many places, the state *is* mob rule—or so malevolent that one might want to take a chance on mob rule. I know that's not what you mean, and for lots of purposes, the Finnish state could be a standard of criticism—I often invoke it to criticize American carceral practices. But the Chinese or Russian or Hungarian states could also be standards of criticism, as well as the global practices of Microsoft or the Vatican or Hollywood.

As I've said before, I think there's a better way; rather than working against a loose historical standard or comparing to a fictional form, we might evaluate hegemony or rulership by asking what it distributes and among whom. When international law enables a professional elite to imagine and manage the line between an inside and outside, the normal and the deviant, the center, the periphery and the beyond-the-periphery, it distributes capabilities and roles. One could examine who is in and who is out and make a judgment, make a political or ethical judgment from a standpoint. I have a hard time imagining assessing "good power" other than from a point of view—that's what got me off the "theory of justice" project. I think you need to "carry a brief" for some group and figure out how they fare.

Martti: Well, I do not buy into those theories of "justice"—in fact, I do not think much about moral rationalism or abstract debates on governance architecture—and I agree that the good can most of the time only be assessed from a standpoint. That's precisely why I think valuable the idea of an "empty vessel," perhaps in the mode of a regulative idea, a rule of thumb, or even more prosaically as a fallback for people (such as myself) who feel very clearly the limits of what they know, including what they know about the "good."

David: Like you, I wouldn't stigmatize hegemony—the question is who benefits, not whether the hegemony is "like a state." After all, James Scott gave his *Seeing Like a State* the subtitle *How Certain Schemes to Improve the Human Condition Have Failed.*[21] In the hegemonic eye, some problems are easy to see, some arguments easy to make, some authorities obviously significant. Perhaps it is easy to think about exchange and hard to think about domination; or easy to think about equality but hard to think about structural inequality. To figure out whether "that's a good thing or a bad thing"—back to my grandmother's question—you'd have figure out who those assumptions empower or disempower and make a judgement.

This would not be an easy inquiry. When we say the contemporary international legal framework is both hegemonic and somehow American, we would need a whole picture of what America *is*—itself quite complex an interpretive task—to see how the hegemonic frame distributed in its favor. Very unlikely to be easily done. As an American legal scholar with an elite training, I've personally benefited from the intellectual hegemony of American legal thought on the world stage. But lots of American citizens and institutions have also been dragged into military quagmires, deindustrialization, and cultural marginality in its terms.

Martti: You and I have both tried to resist the temptation to figure out those ideal distributive forms in the abstract as an academic exercise. We have had difficulty with the kinds of writing that seek to come up with ideal forms of government or just ways to distribute powers and vulnerabilities across groups of contestants—in abstraction from being oneself, actually a contestant in a situation. Political moot panels? But I wonder how far that sort of perspectivism can go. It is really important to realize that for every utopia, there is an apology lurking around the corner. But surely that does not mean one cannot have utopias?

David: Well, I've always kind of liked that image of a public policy jury in the clean room; you want to start a war, so you assemble a jury and let the experts try to talk them into and out of it. Anyway, as a thought experiment.

Martti: I mean, we began these debates by pointing to an impulse or a posture of critique we shared. This may be hard to define, but if I try, I find distinctions such as legitimate government/mob rule helpful for explaining to myself why I have those feelings.

When one breaks down distinctions the way you do, by pointing to hegemony as the power of distributing positions—of power and vulnerability, say—that is very useful analytically. But it immediately raises the question of the engaged voice. There's a big difference between brick throwing—actually struggling to attain or attack hegemony in the name of something—and sitting down with friends to analyze hegemony. You have often been critical of the human rights people for being wary of thinking of themselves as men and women of power—distributive power, I suppose. Now, imagine they have sat down and agreed that that's what they are—from that point onward they must carry large words such as *justice* and *state* and *property* as part of the arsenal of ruling, of distributing.

This takes nothing away from a more structural idea—such as was put forward in 2000 by Hardt and Negri, say, who talked about empire without supposing that the empire serves some specifically identifiable interest, that it was concocted by some plan, you know, in the attic by some guys.[22] I am completely sympathetic to that view of hegemony as an impersonal thing. These languages and idioms of which I have written operate a little bit in that way—platforms over which people struggle, but that also control access to and terms of the struggle—until they collapse, of course. But I wonder whether that *empire* or *the state* is really more than a redescription of what it is for there to be a hegemony.

David: I thought Hardt and Negri were on to something in their very disembodied image of empire, and we've both said the ubiquity of the international legal idiom is connected to its plasticity and dispersion. That doesn't mean it is neutral; the trick is figuring out how so open-ended a vernacular can also subordinate, keep some players or projects or problems off the table. As I remember the book, Hardt and Negri were vague about that—more stigmatizing everything they tarred with the word *empire*. But what was bad about it? In *A World of Struggle* I proposed some analytic steps to identify some people with projects, inhabiting an expertise—its institutions, its language, its cultural, political, and commercial significance—and evaluate the distributive effects of their performative authority. What was their standpoint for assessment? Some people clearly benefited, others didn't; perhaps Hardt and Negri had a view about that, but I don't recall it.

Still, you're right. As soon as you start to rule—to carry that brief—you're both positioned and in the soup of reasons, standards, forms, and technical expertise. You start figuring out what's in the interests of "landlocked states" and you're in the domain of expert assessment and argument. There are interests you can see and say and imagine—and ones you cannot. As you go along, the interests also take the shape of their expression, and vice versa. So there's no stepping "outside" into a free space of knowledge and assessment. In a hegemonic situation, being outside is also a position, the way barbarism is a back-formation of civilization. Like brick throwing, it seems to be speaking a different language all together. In *A World of Struggle* I tried to map these insider/outsider relations and vocabularies as expertise.

A classic European example: discussions a century and more ago between *civilization* and *Kultur*. In the middle of the First World War, Thomas Mann filled a volume on German opposition to the entire world of civilization, democracy, political rationality, and so on, situating the German people as the historic protesters against imperial and Catholic Rome and the Triple Entente as carriers of everything that *Kultur* was not—he wrote, and soldiers marched to resist hegemony.[23] In retrospect, everything he said seems *inside* a shared European heritage, an opposition that continues in a thousand forms. Not at all how he experienced it then. Or how at least some folks in Russia seem to be experiencing it now.

Martti: I suppose we move here between hegemony as an abstract description of a relationship and a concrete situation of domination. In *To the Uttermost Parts of the Earth* I tried to capture both in the historical description of succession, in Europe, of hegemonic languages, together with the forms of expertise gaining control over them. I imagined them somewhat like how other people—classical analysts of hegemony—have treated the succession of more tangible empires—Spanish, Dutch, British, American—each both dominant and split against itself by leading and opposing actors.

When religion was hegemonic, it could set the conditions for some leading group of theologians to draw their distinctions by using the conceptual dichotomy of faithful/sinful. This was overtaken by a scientific critique and the accompanying distinction used by dominant scientists between fact/illusion, followed by politics (right/wrong), philosophy (true/false), law (lawful/illegal) and economics (profit/loss), each basic distinction allowing both internal struggle over its mastery and the consequent use of the basic distinction for boundary work.

For five hundred years such vocabularies have followed each other, framing with authority how human relationships were to be conceived and offering places of intellectual and political dominance to groups successful in their employment of these vocabularies against rivals. A combination of persuasion and coercion. I was interested to see at what point law came in, and at what point it went out, and what subsidiary role it played within other vocabularies. The struggles between law, on the one hand and, say, science, theology, politics, and economics, on the other, have displayed many of the strategic conundrums we have addressed—integration and "othering" are ubiquitous. For example, to make a last footnote on this, I've found very interesting the move by lawyers, to often redefine law as science, even as a metascience that would then adjudicate disputes between other sciences, but also moments when that idea has come to seem utterly ridiculous.

David: Yes, what is "science" and what is not, and what prestige and what limitations does that bring along? The same for "technology" or "ethics." A recent example of this parade of disciplinary claims would be the rise and fall of economics and law as master templates for analyzing and pursuing "development," itself the hegemonic topos for thinking about political strategy across the developing noncommunist world since the 1950s. The terms of the discussion were set by economists in waves of self-confidence punctuated by bursts of uncertainty during which policy discussions turned to law and institutions as the royal road to development.

And all along you find sociologists and historians and political scientists tossing this or that finding into economic or legal/institutional discussions. At least some of what we might remember as the rise and fall of neoliberal ideology was this rhythm of alternating disciplinary hegemony.

But let's turn to the question of what happens to difference in a hegemonic situation. If norms are generated by everything from treaties to parliaments to rock star norm entrepreneurs, you'll get a lot of diverse norms, administered and adjudicated in diverse institutional settings. How do the traditions we've looked at imagine handling all this diversity? I suggested that the global legal imagination is far more preoccupied with managing and celebrating difference than with unification. Not managing and celebrating *within* a hegemonic frame, but management and celebration in some way *as* the frame or, in Star Wars terms, the "prime directive."

The idea that "global governance" could be strengthened by ever more plural modes of norm generation, administration or implementation, and dispute settlement, certainly suggests a healthy appetite for pluralism and a confidence in the ability to say what *doesn't* count as a contribution. The ILC's fragmentation report has such confidence in the hegemony of a *practice* and the skill—or vision—of the practitioners.[24] You talked about that: they *will* want to hold it together and *will* have the tools and skill to do so. There's a parallel in the many global institutional techniques for seeking consensus after hearing all the voices, consulting all stakeholders. The institution and its cadres will know when to turn from appreciating difference to a unifying action.

I often feel there's a nascent goal of unification in this embrace of difference. I found something similar in comparative law: a typology of "national traditions" or "cultures" at various technocratic "stages of development" facing universal "functional problems" from which one could generate a range of stories about how differences masked similarities.[25] Same culture/different functions or different culture/same functions, that kind of thing.

These projects all have a hegemonic dimension; they situate the international or comparative lawyer as the arbiter, establishing the differences which can and cannot be accommodated. There's a studious inattention to questions of relative power and distribution, as if recognizing and including differences somehow levels the field between them. Or picturing them in a hierarchy would distort the comparative endeavor—they're not independent variables, something like that.

I recall Drahos and Braithwaite's comprehensive sociological study of the global regulatory structure that showed how many of the laws on the books in Australia had been written in administrative agencies and law firm conference rooms in either Brussels or Washington.[26] If we focused on these questions of relative power and distributional effect, normative diversity would have a different feel. Less pluralism than hierarchy, center/periphery, dependence—something like that.

Martti: Sure, the globalist legal sensibility is not about *ignoring* difference but embracing and, as you put it, managing and celebrating it. In the international legal world this often takes place by lawyers having chosen a social sciences vocabulary—anthropology or systems theory, for instance—as a kind of novel naturalism that is purified of political or strategic considerations. Plurality managed by science. I see this also as the preferred technique by international institutions as they approach diversity within a historicist theory of modernity or "modernization"; all this difference is framed as part of a natural "social process" responding to a description of the present as one of increasing complexity. And complexity is understood as both natural and good. "Let all flowers bloom! Let's all be legal pluralists!"

But I worry over the often uncritical attitude involved, an almost programmatic tendency to avoid judgment. As you say, merely stating *difference* is often insufficient; surely most of the interest is in relationships—subordination and hegemony, for example; patterns of distribution. But the thrust of the "global" is often elsewhere—namely, in describing and ordering, that is to say managing, but in an ostensibly neutral, unpolitical way.

I was very interested some years ago to survey the simultaneous celebration and anxiety over *pluralism* in the systems of international governance. When I was member of the ILC in 2002–2006, the anxiety appeared under the general rubric of *fragmentation* to which you referred a moment ago. At a certain moment around 2000, lawyers from the public international law center—the UN and the ICJ—began to express their anxiety over the proliferation of new courts and tribunals, new treaties and new secretariats, new conglomerates of states' parties, each regime apparently following its own rules under its specific ethos. These bodies and these regimes were constantly extending their jurisdiction to wider areas and subjects, something the lawyers in the center felt encroached on their powers and on the received hierarchies. *Is the center collapsing? Is no one in control?*

David: One could feel that anxiety in the profession at the time. I think the Ford Foundation funded a project on the "proliferation" of international courts and tribunals—a very dubious development.

Martti: But it did not take long—some five years or so—for the lawyers and other technical experts to conclude, "Well, actually, there is no chaos but just differentiation and plurality; so why not celebrate the richness of the system, its ability to 'respond' to the complexity of its tasks." I was struck at how ready everyone was now to use social scientific idioms to reassure each other that there was no reason to worry. The center responded by offering techniques to deal with the resulting boundary conflicts.

As you know, I was assigned by the ILC to head the composition of a 250-page study on how to manage plurality, on how to think about the relations between the World Trade Organization and environmental treaties or deal with the conflicts over the jurisdiction of human rights bodies vis-à-vis other international organs. In the end, what initially appeared not only as an issue of diversity but as a frontal challenge to the old hierarchies was managed by referring it to further debates among the concerned legal experts, to be resolved in an ad hoc manner by bureaucratic adjustments and interpretative techniques. As a result, plurality would be both celebrated and managed by what would be called "systemic integration" that, I suppose, sounded pleasingly technical. All flowers would bloom, while everything would continue more or less as it always had.[27] As you say, from that insider perspective, confidence in the skill of legal practitioners was unlimited—no reason to assume that the same would be true with outsiders as well.

In the end, I began to think that *difference and similarity are in the eye of the beholder* and that once you are able to produce a persuasive narrative about relationships—it may be historical, sociological, or framed in terms of identity—then the sense of friction and loss of control diminishes. Difference is managed, or even celebrated, as plurality, and things can go on as usual.

I now think of this as an example of the way pluralism glosses over the struggles—struggles for jurisdictional power, assertive power, waged both aggressively and defensively between global institutions and expert vocabularies, their conflicting scales of value and crisscrossing distributive projects. Was something a human rights matter or a security matter? A trade or a development matter? Once one knew which institution would deal with a matter, one would know how it would be decided.

David: The American postwar "legal process" people—so influential for Harold Koh—focused similarly on institutional competence rather than substantive outcomes. So long as one could figure out who should settle disputes, pluralism was almost—or even especially—a virtue.

Martti: If *pluralism* is a big word in comparative constitutional law and international law today, this is because it embodies a particular type of liberal toleration that is notable for its absence of critical power. In recent debates on international legal history, for instance, pluralism tends to become an endless process of describing exotic difference. Pluralism is like a plane flying over earth and showing that "Well, there's a lake, and here's a mountain; look at those houses and that field," and so on, and because the world is round such flying over can continue endlessly. It tends to exoticize its objects in an often uncritical and self-satisfied fashion.

David: I really like that plane-flying-over image. In public international law, cases often turn on whether something is "on the international plane"—cases like *Nottebohm* or *Barcelona Traction*—establishing jurisdictional rules for "claims on the international plane" to square the circle of contending sovereigns.[28] There's a parallel fantasy—up there, passionate sovereign differences fade because we can handle them procedurally. This embrace of pluralism is certainly an elite practice and sensibility—you have to imagine yourself up there.

Martti: My own sense is that *pluralism* is best seen as a name given by someone thinking of themselves as an outside observer to a situation that from the inside appears as a struggle between competing identities and projects. I suppose this is what you are also saying about the internationalism that both celebrates and seeks to manage difference. From the inside, people struggle for new rules, institutions, or resources; the perspective is that of simultaneous solipsism and imperialism. Each competing identity in the international world of governance—trade, say, or human rights, environment, or security—interprets the world by reference to its own priorities and seeks to make its own project and perspective also the *universal project and the universal perspective.* Pluralism intervenes in this process as an outsider that explains that it seeks nothing else than to describe and compare.

But in seeking that descriptive authority it also strives for control in a way that is often hidden by the social scientific or historical language in which it operates. It becomes an insider. This seemed obvious in respect to the treatment of the theme of "fragmentation" by the ILC: the concern was both to describe and control a situation in which the authority of old law had become challenged by the formation of new specialist types of law. For the ILC to take upon itself to describe that process was to seek to gain control over it and restate the authority of the older law—or at least its representative institutions.

I often think of the pluralism of global governance as an updated form of the old *Landeshoheit* / empire or sovereignty / international order problem. New regimes of knowledge and authority are first established to challenge vertically the priorities and institutions of the old law and to struggle for jurisdiction in a horizontal way against countervailing priorities and knowledges. The established institutions may then try to assimilate the challengers ("There is no such thing as environmental law, only international law applying to the environment") or at least limit their jurisdiction and claiming higher status to themselves (which is what the ILC report on "fragmentation" tried to achieve).

This is the "world of struggle" you have described. There is no space for neutral description in this process. Instead, every suggested description is an interested intervention, an effort to arrange normative and institutional hierarchies in some way suggested to become authoritative. Although I have used plural "legal regimes" as an example of the theme of managing and celebrating diversity, I think it can equally well be extended to the managing and celebrating of the ubiquitous claims for recognition and respect of distinct identities, their autonomy and ordering in a world of plural choices. My worry is that all of this struggle, vertical and horizontal, tends to take place in an apolitical fashion, between legal and technical experts in the world of regime conflicts and between nonnegotiable claims to authenticity in identity conflicts.

David: The pluralist imagination certainly has those limitations and dark sides. And that depoliticization does seem to go with management by expertise. On the other hand, I've also experimented with framing pluralism as an *experience:* things don't add up, coherence fails, some kind of incommensurability or difference must be acknowledged. So, pluralism as that first moment you describe, when it all seemed chaotic, before your plane has enabled you to arrange it all neatly in commensurate categories. Somehow in such an encounter—with the other, with contradiction, with multiplicity—one experiences a loss of confidence. One is defeased of professional knowledge or certainty. And then you have to figure out how to be in that experience—or how to manage it until it fades. Only then does pluralism become a system of accommodation that calms the experience. But you don't have to go there; you could use that moment of experience to innovate, stretch the boundaries, glimpse the foundations and determine to adjust them. My own utopian wish, perhaps.

There's no getting around the international legal wish to comprehend it all in the same framework. You'd think systems theory would offer a counterpoint: dispersion and differentiation is foundational and cannot be overcome. As it comes into our field, it tends to get put together as an alternative comprehensive story. There's functional differentiation gone wild in the world—all those divergent domains and no central coordinating committee. But each is governed by the logic of its functional competence, which is then institutionalized and professionalized as a kind of constitutionalism—or flywheel—behind its assertions of authority. No global order, but the interaction of a thousand constitutions.[29] It is hard to imagine the terrain on which that occurs without a background expectation of balance or equilibrium; functional differentiation would be over if one of them triumphed. At a minimum, there is an aspiration for cognitive control in this interpretation of modern legality. One can get to power and domination within and between functions, or to the world outside these functional operations, but these remain second-order inquiries, submerged beneath the narrative pleasure of identifying history's functional destiny.

I prefer your formulation: similarities and differences *in the eyes of the beholder.* It puts the emphasis on the intellectual and political work of asserting difference and similarity. Your metaphor of a pluralist plane flying around comes with the fantasy that one is up there in the plane assessing differences made down below. Up there, clarity about the priority of functional differentiation or cosmopolitan tolerance, down on the ground, functional—national and religious—difference. To get up there, you have to put your religion, your patriotism, your specific expertise in a little box.

The *in the eyes of the beholder* metaphor brings everyone down to the same level, contesting how to behold.

When you get up in the plane, you don't actually leave all that behind. The global administrative law project, certainly in its initial phase, is a good example.[30] The breakthrough idea was the identification of a universal function—internationally significant "administration"—which, like legislation or dispute settlement, was being done all over the place by all kinds of institutions. The insight launched a project: once identified, "international administration" could be improved, rendered accountable, and so on.

In national legal orders, one does that by linking administration to political control policed by judicial oversight. But in the globally dispersed space, the administrative function floats free; there is no political spot you could link it do. If you've brought along that idea of what "good administration" is, you end up with familiar accountability remedies floating free of a context where they might have made sense. As I recall, the original manifesto for global administrative law sidled up to these issues but couldn't quite engage them, acknowledging that stronger administration might end up strengthening an unjust order.

Martti: I like the way you point to the distance of the pilot from what's being described from the plane. Can I just say one word in defense of systems theory? When theorists such as Niklas Luhmann or Gunther Teubner think about a perspective from which functional differentiation operates, they are very aware that their standpoint is also functionally differentiated, so it's not a lonely plane up there in the sky. I've always admired the irony with which especially Luhmann addresses his own standpoint and tries to elaborate on what the function is that is operating within him when he perceives the operation of other things, that sort of self-reflection.

David: I agree. But that irony and self-positioning *within* the system world being narrated is tough to sustain when functional systems analytics gets going as a framework for mapping the world of global legality or when the word *constitution* drifts from a theoretical property of imagined systems to something recognizable from its more routine use in public law narratives.

Martti: What you say about global administrative law—it is true that it's a very specific notion of administration that is being generalized in that project, and that the conditions of its acceptability or operation in the original situation from which that "model" was taken are not present in the global situation because there's no political community. Which means that it, too, is a hegemonic project, though I wonder whether that's such an important critique of it—or a critique at all.

Is it not more significant to seek to assess a project such as global administrative law or global constitutionalism by reference to what they might achieve in the world in case they succeed in becoming new types of legal Esperanto? I mean the case where more and more people would address the world through an administrative idiom. This would gradually bring into existence a community to be administered together with the need for more "administrators" with authority over that community—perhaps like the call for "constitutionalism" has expanded the numbers and power of constitutional experts and the massive transfer decision-making power from the political realm to supreme and constitutional courts.

These are examples of the performative aspect of those languages—the way they condense a world of plural standpoints so as to distribute authority and resources. Coming back to the fragmentation theme, you could see that there were two stories to tell. One was the narrative of diversification, a story of positive progress and identity; another was that of disorder and chaos. Neither has, of course, any intrinsic priority; they are both perceptions but they involve different values and do different things. Going by one or the other is a manner of actually *creating the reality it purports to describe* and *supporting those forces and identities that are dominant in that description*. The question seems to come down not to what is the "correct description" of the situation but what is the description that supports the forces you favor.

David: Absolutely, on both counts. First, that hegemony can best be evaluated for its effects, in the "who benefits" sense, the distributional impact. And second, that those effects may include community—or autonomy/alienation—production. This performative dimension is critical to understanding what's going on. People narrate difference in these ways to create an effect—and they do. I think that's how we get to the issue of hegemony's impact: what worlds they are creating, who is visible and invisible. I see the observation that global administrative law brings along assumptions from its home terrain as analogous to your claim about *Landeshoheit*/empire relations. It doesn't prove it's a bad thing, but it opens an inquiry: how did the mentality of that setting shape—or limit—the way people comprehend things now? Perhaps in useful ways, perhaps not.

Before COVID-19, I was in China and there are plenty of extremely sophisticated people in the Chinese intellectual, academic, legal, and foreign relations worlds who understand and manipulate all the norms and rules and institutions we've been talking about. They are participating across the whole structure of articulative power in that way, often extremely effectively. If they were ever Arnulf's semiperipherals, you wouldn't know it now—they've crossed over and are, in this sense, inside. For these people, "Chinese international law" is not a thing—other than a description of Chinese government practice and positions. Comparison would pass them by.

But Chinese international law professors are often preoccupied by "China and international law" questions. And they inhabit a completely recognizable professional world differently from you or I in ways it is difficult, certainly from the outside, to pin down. What is the role of an international legal intellectual in China—what is that job, compared to a Finnish ex-diplomat law professor? They are living a different historical situation, a different past and present. In the Atlantic world, if you think about the history of international law, for example, slavery is a big deal, as obvious a part of the shared legacy as the two world wars or the Holocaust or the Reformation or . . . the list goes on.

It's just different in the Pacific world: different colonial relations and unequal treaties and experiences of humiliation are among the historical punctuation marks. And in the personal trajectories of these professionals there are all kinds of important turning points—for some I met, Tiananmen Square remained a positive touchstone; the "rule of law" resonated with what did not happen. For others that was all a long time ago, the trajectory of Chinese economic growth alongside internal disruption and inequality, the dilemmas of a newly robust global role, disenchantment with a hobbled West were the touchstones.

Rather than approach global legal affairs as a problem of "diversity in universality" I'd propose that what needs explaining—and what is being managed—is hierarchy, relations of (unequal) power with distributional effects. We might start with obvious hierarchical relationships—secular over religious, white supremacy, capital over labor, center over periphery—and try to figure out how legal projects to establish a "global market" or manage relations among "equal territorial sovereigns" affected, supported, or undermined them. This is familiar outside the international law world—Wallerstein's world systems project, much of the "history of capitalism" literature, the dependency analytic in development economics.

Martti: I agree that hegemonic relations are thrust aside in reigning legal discourse; its tendency is to assimilate difference by using generic criteria that set different identities alongside each other in the manner of the flags on UN flagpoles. All international lawyers know Vattel's dictum: "A dwarf is as much a man as a giant; a small republic is no less a sovereign state than the most powerful kingdom."[31] But it is cited usually in an ironic mode, covertly addressing what it hides rather than what it reveals, a little like that other cliché about "all boats" rising on a free market. And yet the irony produces no energy for change, perhaps perversely obstructs it.

Our analyses would indeed be much improved were "relations of power" and "structural effects" more prominent, no doubt. But that is a really hard objective to attain in a legal world that looks toward practice, the competent resolution of technical problems within the law as they emerge. Very little space is left for reflecting on larger questions. It may even seem that doing one's job properly necessitates setting that type of reflection on the side or taking an ironic attitude. Most practitioners do readily agree that the ideals of neutrality and impartiality that underlie official rhetoric are not fully realized but still form the professional ethos. This manifests the kind of "commitment" to the law itself that both of us have critiqued, being enchanted by law's promise rather than facing its reality. Or bad faith, simply. There have been sociological and historical narratives to contest these expectations, and to situate the lawyers in an already existing system of hierarchies and possibilities. But these have a hard time integrating in the world of legal practice. Legal sociology, ideas about "reflexive law," as well as "law and economics," "law and development," and many other "law and . . ." movements have in the past years tried to combine the two perspectives. With varying success.

Think again of the fragmentation issue, for example. Each expert regime has its formal rules whose mastery makes it possible to separate experts from laypersons and link functional objectives with technical practices. In operating within the regime, one has to keep one's eyes on those technical rules in a way that calls for at least momentarily bracketing the view to power and structural effects—while on the outside it is possible to produce all kinds of descriptive and critical accounts that have to struggle to penetrate the institutional practices. I suppose most legal experts imagine working in a center they perceive between the inside and outside; the result may often be limited to an ad hoc compromise in the name of "realism."

David: Experts do seem to work between the "trade or diplomacy among equals" conventions of their expertise and an awareness of their unreality. They know they need to frame distributive projects in the language of equality, although that ethos of working in an order oriented to equality colors everything.

We've been talking about the hegemony of the dominant discourse as it celebrates and manages the diversity it encounters—or recognizes. Before we stop, perhaps a word about all those others out there? The voices unheard, the people left out—we set this aside at the start of our conversation as neither of us have focused our research there. Can we say something, though, perhaps about Arnulf's semiperipherals who are *also* outside and often do get left out? He has been researching the Inca, their understanding and engagement with Spanish authority, for example. Or Balakrishnan Rajagopal's international law "from below" that focuses on social movements operating in a kind of parallel universe which he argues can be counterhegemonic even without that being their prime objective.[32]

Or what about women and feminist voices, queer voices? I know I've learned a lot about the structure and limitations of the legal world from those who have come at it from those angles; what's missing says a lot about what's there. Of course, that's a different question than whether you and I should focus there. What to say to those who argue we've left them all out of account? There could be both a project of recovery—they were always there, but not heard, forgotten, dismissed—and an account of absences; exclusions and silences were no accident but manufactured and reproduced with consequences both inside and out. Feminist work has certainly pursued both avenues very productively.

Martti: One early criticism of *To the Uttermost Parts of the Earth* was about its Eurocentrism; another was about the absence of women in its narrative. I have tried to think about that. But what would have been the alternative? I might have attempted to imagine the voice of that sixteenth-century Indigenous person whose life was ruined by the Conquista. Or I could have tried to do research on the lives of female slaves in Saint-Domingue. There are a thousand other things I could have done. But if I wrote this book, it is because it dealt with something I knew about—legal imagining. Did those other people engage in such? Perhaps, but there is little or no trace available about that. I remain puzzled about how to give "voice" to those other people; would not even trying something like that be an indefensible, even ridiculous, attempt at appropriation, bound to remain pathetic and wrong?

Arnulf and Rajagopal describe the actions and writings of activists—lawyers and nonlawyers—from the periphery in the nineteenth and twentieth centuries; people from outside the hegemonic center who have struggled over mastery of the languages of law and politics. The archive contains things they have said and done; their legal imagining in the late nineteenth century and through the twentieth has left a trace. Not so with my period from 1300 onward—at least not often. Lyotard once pointed out the problem of giving "voice" to those killed in the Holocaust: you cannot do that because the event is defined by the very erasure of those voices. If you claim you hear it, then there cannot have been any Holocaust.[33] Something similar can be said about the laws of the "colonial encounter." How could a European historian claim to produce the voice of those whose archives were annihilated? I know people have tried ways of writing that signal out the emptiness of the space that's left, that invites the reader to imagine that vacuum—how it was created and what was lost, and to feel sympathy, even rage. This has nothing to do with authentic representation of the "other" beyond tapping on narrative forms that evoke those responses in one's readership.

Then there is the question of violence. In *To the Uttermost Parts of the Earth* I argued that although British imperialists were occasionally quite violent, metropolitan actors were actually often averse to violence; they were capitalists and felt, rightly, that it was a costly detraction from the main business of profit production. I wanted to convey the sense that the specific evil of British imperial expansion in the nineteenth century was to force people to consent to the rules—the "rule of law"—that it imposed on the world it governed. You do not need violence if you can just make other people consent, right? I wanted to show that in that process law, legalism, and the rule of law are often deeply implicated and that in such situations calling for more law is not a liberating or critical thing to do. In demonstrating what could be called law's silent violence, something of the concern, I hope of those who wish to hear the voices of "others," is met and a critical pathway for historical legal studies is opened.

David: That puzzle, the relative costs of being inside, of relying on the state or the law, against those of remaining without has certainly been at the heart of postcolonial and feminist literatures. Misrecognizing law's violence and power's passivity makes it so much harder to assess. The absence of violence is as striking as its constant (background) presence in projects of domination.

Your focus on the legal invention of an empire of commerce and property, if I can call it that, is really helpful. Of course, I can understand why Sven Beckert wanted to place war at the center of slave capitalism, but that does take the focus off all the professional, institutional, and intellectual work that accompanied that violence.[34] In college during the Vietnam War, when dramatic, kinetic violence was front and center, I encountered Johan Galtung's phrase "structural violence."[35] It has stuck with me. My intuition then was that a half century of "economic development" had been more thoroughly and deeply violent than the vicious peripheral and postcolonial wars of the postwar decades.

I certainly agree that one has to work with who one is and what one knows in this business. Yet if we can imagine our way into the heads of people in sixteenth-century Salamanca or into the head of a nineteenth-century colonial legal officer, I'm not sure other cultural realities need to remain completely remote. I think we can get better at understanding the ways the discourses we are in are shaped by and shape their exclusions. Nevertheless, the critical approaches we've been talking about do require that one be close to the object of criticism, at least in one's imagination, reading a text and asking sympathetically what a person must have been thinking to write this in this way.

We're reaching the end of this conversation, and I want to emphasize how primitive our thinking is on these points. I think we are just scratching the surface on these issues of universalization, dispersion, hegemony, and difference or diversity in the international law world.

Notes

1. Koskenniemi, *From Apology to Utopia.*

2. Koskenniemi, "Between Coordination and Constitution."

3. Kennedy, *International Legal Structures;* Kennedy, "Primitive Legal Scholarship."

4. Arthur Nussbaum was about the only American international law historian who explicitly followed the "classic" Scott/Carnegie picture after 1945. See Arthur Nussbaum, *A Concise History of the Law of Nations* (New York: Macmillan, [1947] 1962).

5. Military and Paramilitary Activities in and against Nicaragua (Nicaragua v. United States of America), Jurisdiction and Admissibility, Judgment, ICJ Reports 1984, p. 392.

6. Koskenniemi, *The Gentle Civilizer of Nations;* Koskenniemi, *To the Uttermost Parts of the Earth.*

7. Antony Anghie, *Imperialism, Sovereignty and the Making of International Law* (Cambridge: Cambridge University Press, 2005); Arnulf Becker Lorca, *Mestizo International Law: A Global Intellectual History 1842–1933* (Cambridge: Cambridge University Press, 2015).

8. Balakrishnan Rajagopal, *International Law from Below: Development, Social Movements and Third World Resistance* (Cambridge: Cambridge University Press, 2009).

9. Kennedy, "Spring Break."

10. Annelise Riles, "Aspiration and Control: International Legal Rhetoric and the Essentialization of Culture," 106 *Harvard Law Review* 723 (1993).

11. Umut Özsu, "'In the Interests of Mankind as a Whole': Mohammed Bedjaoui's New International Economic Order," 6 *Humanity: An International Journal of Human Rights, Humanitarianism, and Development* 129 (2015).

12. Liliana Obregón, "Completing Civilization: Creole Consciousness and International Law in Nineteenth-Century Latin America," in *International Law and Its Others* 247 (Anne Orford, ed., Cambridge: Cambridge University Press, 2006).

13. For a recent sociology of the group of lawyers behind the Institut de Droit International in 1873, see Dzovinar Kévonian, *La danse du pendule: Les juristes et l'internationalisation des droits de l'homme, 1920–1939* (Paris: Éditions de la Sorbonne, 2021).

14. Alejandro Alvarez, "The New International Law," 15 *Grotius Society Transactions* 35 (1930).

15. Philip Jessup, "The Functional Approach as Applied to International Law," in *Proceedings of the Third Conference of Teachers of International Law* 1 (Washington, DC: Carnegie Endowment for International Law, 1928).

16. Harold Hongju Koh, "The 1994 Roscoe Pound Lecture: Transnational Legal Process," 75 *Nebraska Law Review* 181 (1996).

17. Jan Klabbers, "The Emergence of Functionalism in International Institutional Law: Colonial Inspirations," 25 *European Journal of International Law* 645 (2014).

18. Koskenniemi, "The Wonderful Artificiality of States"; Koskenniemi, "What Use for Sovereignty Today?"

19. Dan Danielsen, "How Corporations Govern: Taking Corporate Power Seriously in Transnational Regulation and Governance," 46 *Harvard International Law Journal* 441 (2005).

20. IGLP Law and Global Production Working Group, "The Role of Law in Global Value Chains: A Research Manifesto," 4 *London Review of International Law* 57 (2016).

21. James C. Scott, *Seeing Like a State: How Certain Schemes to Improve the Human Condition Have Failed* (New Haven, CT: Yale University Press, 2020).

22. Michael Hardt and Antonio Negri, *Empire* (Cambridge, MA: Harvard University Press, 2000).

23. Thomas Mann, *Reflections of a Nonpolitical Man,* trans. Walter D. Morris et al. (New York: New York Review of Books, [1983] 2021).

24. Study Group of the International Law Commission, *Fragmentation of International Law: Difficulties Arising from the Diversification and Expansion of International Law: Report of the Study Group of the International Law Commission,* finalized by Martti Koskenniemi (Helsinki: Erik Castrén Institute of International Law, 2007).

25. See Kennedy, "One, Two, Three, Many Legal Orders"; Kennedy, "The Methods and Politics of Comparative Law"; and Kennedy, "New Approaches to Comparative Law."

26. John Braithwaite and Peter Drahos, *Global Business Regulation* (Cambridge: Cambridge University Press, [2000] 2001).

27. Study Group of the International Law Commission, *Fragmentation of International Law.*

28. Nottebohm Case, Judgment of April 6th, 1955, ICJ Reports 1955, p. 4.; Barcelona Traction, Light and Power Company, Limited, Judgment, ICJ Reports 1970, p. 3.

29. Gunther Teubner, *Critical Theory and Legal Autopoiesis: The Case for Societal Constitutionalism,* ed. Diana Goebel (Manchester, UK: Manchester University Press, 2019). See also Andreas Fischer-Lescano and Gunter Teubner, "Regime-Collision: The Vain Search for Legal Unity in the Fragmentation of Global Law," 25 *Michigan Journal of International Law* 999 (2004).

30. Benedict Kingsbury, Nico Krisch, and Richard B. Stewart, "The Emergence of Global Administrative Law," 68 *Law and Contemporary Problems* 15 (2005).

31. Emer de Vattel, *The Law of Nations,* ed. Béla Kapossy and Richard Whitmore (Indianapolis: Liberty Fund [1797] 2008).

32. Balakrishnan Rajagopal, *International Law from Below: Development, Social Movements, and Third World Resistance* (Cambridge: Cambridge University Press, 2003).

33. Jean-François Lyotard, *The Differend: Phrases in Dispute,* trans. Georges Van Den Abbeele (Minneapolis: University of Minnesota Press, [1988] 2002).

34. Sven Beckert, *Empire of Cotton: A Global History* (New York: Vintage, 2015).

35. Johan Galtung, "Violence, Peace, and Peace Research," 6 *Journal of Peace Research* 167 (1969).

CONVERSATION FIVE

International Legal History as Critique

David: We've both written about international legal history, although you are far more the historian than I. As intellectual historians, we've focused on contesting the *history in international law*—the field's history of itself and its own history of the world—more than on international law's role *in history,* so we should probably begin there.

As I experienced it, international law, if we can personify it, had strong ideas about its place in history: that it civilizes history, that it holds high an aspirational candle of justice and peace in history. And at the same time, that it arises out of the rough and tumble of intersovereign competition and is a hard-wrought accomplishment that yields a hard-boiled perspective on what's possible and what's real. The relationship between those two quite different historical self-images animates the field. Is it real, is it ideal, can it be either, is it both, when which, and so on.

Together these historical stories—wildly inaccurate, partial, even a bit crazy—seem more about defending the field, grounding its normative claims, or lionizing its ethical vision than accounting for international law's actual role in history. Just for starters, so much was left out—colonialism, slavery, all but a couple of wars, pretty much everything outside the North Atlantic. We knew about 1648, but what was happening in India or China or Africa or Latin America in 1648?

When you think about it, international legal materials and the professional sensibility of international lawyers are redolent with dubious historical narratives. Where international law presents its history as a universal world story, we both stressed the particular cultures or places of its development. Where conventional histories stressed continuity, we pointed to ruptures and changes in the tradition. We have both criticized the common idea that international law's history has a teleology—the progressive unfolding of an idea or the working out of the unchanging dilemmas of statecraft—rather than expressing particular struggles here and there, or accidents of intellectual and historical influence. We tried to focus attention on the *work* that needed to be done to arrange a past of struggles and ad hoc inventions into so smooth a disciplinary narrative.

One objective, particularly in tracing the dance of real and ideal historical self-images, was to demonstrate how preoccupied the field was with *itself*—its very philosophical and practical possibility. Historical narration seemed animated by a worry about international law's possibility and virtue. The realist story answered the old Austinian chestnut: Can you have law "properly so called" among sovereigns? The ideal story supported the claim that a law so rooted in political practice could be other than politics redux. Together they were part of the field's ongoing rumination about itself, which served as a mode of engaging the world—as if reasoning about itself *were* reasoning about the world.

Anyway, that is what I was writing against; perhaps you were as well. My interest in disrupting the field's historical narratives has been a somewhat different project from "contextualizing" international law, placing it in the history of economic, political, and cultural life to assess how it was significant, who did what with it, what projects were supported or undermined, and so on. There is an overlap, of course: dipping into what "really happened" often does challenge the discipline's own narratives, although it may not take too much historical study to do that, as they are often quite fanciful. This difference of emphasis is what I have in mind by stressing my—and as I read it, your—preoccupation with *history in international law* rather than *international law in history*.

That's a quick introduction to some themes we might explore this morning. How would you summarize what you've tried to do in your historical work?

Martti: Well, I, too, have been interested in the tellings that international law has given of its past, and of situating—contextualizing—international law in history. Before saying something about those two modes, it might be useful to note the huge surge of interest among international lawyers in both, perhaps surprisingly also among historians of political thought and those doing global history. Interpreting the past through the lenses of international law has become more popular than ever before, and the new debates are often waged with great passion in the registers of the politics and method of writing history.

The reasons are probably not hard to find. Among international lawyers, I think there is a disorientation, loss of confidence—the end of the liberal hubris of the 1990s, difficulties in regulatory regimes such as the World Trade Organization (WTO) and the International Criminal Court, the stasis of multilateralism, the rise of geopolitics. Might looking to the past consolidate the field around inherited truths? And for "real historians," might integrating law in their analyses help in lifting their gaze beyond the purely national? Critics, too, have become historical; new postcolonial writing has focused on international law and empire, indicting the field's Eurocentrism and its complicity with the "civilizing mission." No doubt this both follows academic fashion and grasps at a problem specific to international law. It's hard to maintain progress narratives in a time of persisting global inequality, health crisis, looming climate disaster.

But I agree that we were dubious about the field's inherited histories already earlier and maybe indeed have had some effect in producing this "turn." For myself, venturing into history was a way to try to understand how these doctrines and institutions—at the same time pervasive and intellectually dubious—had once come about. What narratives gave them coherence or made them seem persuasive? The histories we met in textbooks and the few specialized works seemed vulnerable to many kinds of objections that were quite current in critical historiography.[1] As you said, we found ourselves producing at least three types of alternative stories.

First, instead of a single continuous and universal narrative, we saw all kinds of ideas and projects clashing against each other; there was no easily identifiable "tradition" out there but a very heterogeneous set of pursuits to which scarcely more was common than that they were expressed in a legal vocabulary. Second, and paradoxically, the historical narrative often consisted of a continuum of facts and names without much attention to the *frame* in which they appeared, maybe beyond oscillation between the abstract alternatives of "natural law" and "positivism," as if it were all about philosophical conversation. It seemed important to situate the events and names as meaningful aspects of wider historical struggles.

Finally, we both wanted to write against the idea of an international law as a universal "thing" that moves in some dialectical relationship with history. Instead we wanted to bring it down to earth, as the work of people with projects—professional, political, ideological—that resonated with the professional styles and expectations of the broader elites of which they were a part.

Maybe we could use those early critical ideas to discuss this history. What do you say?

David: That sounds good. So, identifying disruptions to contest the discipline's narratives of continuity; broadening the aperture to situate the tradition as an object for criticism, particularly where the field presented itself as somehow "out of time" or just a bundle of cases and ideas; and—probably the most interesting part—bringing the field "down to earth," as you called it, as the work of an identifiable elite.

Why don't you start, then—against the universal, how?

Martti: When I began work for *The Gentle Civilizer of Nations,* I bumped into eighteen volumes by the mid-nineteenth-century Belgian professor François Laurent, with the title *Histoire Du Droit Des Gens,* history of the law of nations. [2] *Eighteen volumes!* I almost stopped right there and then. This was somebody writing at the outset of the professional moment, imagining an international law that would begin with Assyrians and Babylonians, producing a full course of something akin to what we learned at school as European history. I then found out that he eventually gave the book two titles: *History of Humanity* and *History of the Law of Nations.* Here all past was "history of international law," structured within precisely those elements you laid out as basic for the traditional view—continuity toward the universal, a teleology of progressive statecraft. Large principles becoming mature as they move through the stages of the past to the present.

That was really old-fashioned work, of course. But it was understandable as an effort to ground an emerging profession. The nineteenth century praised historical self-awareness.

David: If one can call it that—sounds more like self-mythologizing into history.

Martti: A new generation of lawyers needed some such narrative or mythology. Others would provide it with more detail, adding breaks to mark its progression—1648, 1815, 1918, 1945, dates that outline what we think of as "the state system" read in world-historical terms.

Later works did not quite live up to this type of idealism. But they did tend to narrate the field in terms of a continuous story—mostly as progress, though not always. I am also thinking of Carl Schmitt's and Wilhelm Grewe's "realist" histories of international law as an instrument of imperial power, the succession of monolithic "epochs" within which hegemonic powers impose their preferences on others.[3] Postcolonial histories read like that, too, though in a different normative register. But everybody wrote about a state system—its rise and development, the way it was theorized, its expansion and the eventual realization of its universal promise. Many things were left invisible in that—essentially European—story.

David: With hindsight, that *state* focus is so much a symptom of the nineteenth-century European discovery of itself as "states"—"nation states," no less. Not peoples or empires or economies, or diverse authorities with diverse entitlements, but *states*.

Martti: By the time my "gentle civilizers" stepped in at the end of the nineteenth century, this story had become associated with the secularization and rationalization processes that were understood as the meaning of European history and incorporated in "modern" statehood. Here German historicism and public law took the lead.[4] They gave modern international law its founding problem: how to create order among sovereign states. My men of 1873 worried about this. Of course, international law was to stand for statehood; but, equally clearly, this would have to be an "enlightened" statehood compatible with the internationalization of things and a law to bind them in peaceful interaction. To explain how this would take place they chose the vocabulary of "civilization"—a cultural choice that projected European liberal and professional elites as the avant-garde of history.

Producing a narrative for the field in this way was rarely done in any detail; Wheaton's 1836 history was an exception, along with the works by Ernest Nys in the last years of the century.[5] Mostly it was evoked in brief sections at the outset of textbooks or as background materials to doctrines about state sovereignty and sources. Alternative frames available in the nineteenth century—international "society," for example, and solidarity instead of civilization—were thrust aside.[6] As we discussed earlier, this narration was split against itself. There was a *moral* story of high aspirations turning into law that would temper and eventually help to overcome the contradictions of the state system. And there was a *realist* story that would imagine precisely those contradictions as the heart of the interminable cycle of conflict and cooperation among power-hungry state structures.

These were "utopia" and "apology," rephrased in a historical idiom. Both could defend themselves by pointing to something in the past, but needed to leave other things unsaid. Both claimed universal validity, but also had plausible critiques of each other.

You could adopt either one as a matter of faith—but whichever you chose would have little consequence for how you'd go about your doctrinal or practical work. They gave a certain sensibility to practitioners—some were known as more "idealistic" than others. But nothing really important depended on them. They created some space for legal disagreement, providing themes for doctrinal debate, but were unhelpful as sources of historical insight. It was easy in the 1980s, even with standard legal theory, to put both to question as accurate or even interesting *as histories*. But structuralism did suggest that their point was not so much to tell a true history as to serve together as an intellectual frame for the legal project.

The two stories do constantly reemerge and, with them, the nineteenth-century German problem—associated with Austin in the Anglosphere—of order among sovereigns. We no longer reference "civilization" as the balancing vocabulary and instead prefer to speak of "development" and its derivatives.

David: Together the moral story and the realistic story preoccupy, or fully occupy, the field of historical analysis. If international law is both the carrier of the ethical and the carrier of the real, what else is there for it to be doing? It covers everything. Yet international law's *ethical* and its *real* are very specific to the particular world they imagine, the state system, which seems to be "the world" in part because the discipline figures everything else as its (unfortunate) precursors. Before 1648—or 1945 or whenever—you had anarchy or religious strife or empire or world war. That's what the state system replaced; who could want to go back?

Equally, international law's ethical and real are specific to what they imagine *law* to be. After the late nineteenth century, when these historical stories became the set pieces for the field, *law* among states meant *norms*—"valid" norms vouched for by juristic analysis—established by states to govern states in a kind of conjuring act that turned politics into law without a political enforcer. Such a trick could work if international law carried both universal virtue and political reality across the historical terrain. The jurist then had alternative resources which could be woven together into plausible arguments for normative validity.

Taken together, these historical stories give you the sense that this is the only possible—and quite a good—international law, suited to the world as we receive it from history. That seemed the takeaway from the history of international law as I was taught it: a continuous project to advance the ethical and the realistic in a world of states that started in 1648 and had kept going straight through to the present.

Martti: Both specificities displaying European experience; nothing else mattered.

David: Just as you describe, "history" lived mostly in introductory paragraphs or chapters, prefatory material for the real work of doctrinal elaboration. In American presentations of the story, no matter when it starts—1648, 1918, 1945—international legal history begins with a European trauma and its resolution in the European state system. Before 1648, whatever was going on with the Assyrians and the Egyptians and the Romans was not "international law"—can I say "properly so called?" Instead you had the domestic law of empires (Rome), religious authorities, various universal imperialist projects—and war, thirty years of it.

European intellectuals then spent several hundred years figuring out (secular) international law's place in their state system. For example, the "classics of international law" series put together by James Brown Scott and taken over by the Carnegie Foundation in the 1920s had put sixteenth-century Spanish clergy, seventeenth-century northern European Protestant lawyers, and nineteenth-century European liberals into a single evolving conversation toward what by 1980 had been defined as a traditional synthesis in the field.

You could study international legal history and learn nothing about European statecraft between Westphalia and the League of Nations. Instead, for that period, you had all the guys—Vitoria through Grotius and Pufendorf and Gentili and Vattel, and so on, naturalism giving way to positivism—you know the story. The list of big names could be arranged on a spectrum, whatever their own preoccupations and contexts, from more preoccupied with state practice to more concerned about justice. And somehow, back at the start, Grotius turns out to be the man of the middle way—as we now all should have become. An elegant story, that's for sure.

All that European cogitation reached an apogee in the late nineteenth century, perhaps culminating in the Hague Conferences—a European law gone global. But then Europe fell apart. When the rest of the world picked up the pieces after the First World War, after the Second, after decolonization, a "modern" international law with a more pragmatic/functionalist mode of reasoning and a focus on institutions and procedures rather than normative validity and adjudication took the field.

So, born in Westphalia, raised in Europe by great thinkers, and coming to flourish as a modern institutional problem-solving and dispute-settling resource once the United States got in the game. The twentieth century brought institutions and a dramatic expansion in the subject matter—and subjects—of international law. Along with a functional and pragmatic updating of the traditional synthesis. Wolfgang Friedmann embodied the shift to a new synthesis.[7] Of course, there remain old-fashioned European trained or influenced "positivists" and "formalists" and other traditional types, but the voice of American pragmatism remains the voice of the future, particularly so long as it has that traditional voice as its steady bad guy. So that's how I learned it.

Martti: I recognize that story so well, with all its nuances and shifts—sometimes it's power, sometimes philosophy; a moment when ships sailed on the high seas and another when professors composed large treatises. Both could be used to support the nineteenth-century project of addressing the possibility of order among sovereigns. In *From Apology to Utopia* I examined the rhetorical principles that helped make the story credible by condensing a heterogeneous history into two modes: an "ascending" one—up from sovereign autonomy—and a "descending" one—down from normative authority.[8] The past would manifest a movement between these two modes; it would be for late nineteenth-century lawyers to conjure up a legal idiom, derived from moral and philosophical verities, that would help controlling that movement through stable, "enlightened" state authority.

You did something similar when you contrasted modern modes of law against what you called "primitive scholarship." Can you say something about what you wanted to do with that text?

David: The article you mention, "Primitive Legal Scholarship,"[9] was part of an effort to break that sense of historical continuity and progressive development. Ever more and more refined doctrines; ever better accounts of their normative power as naturalism gave way to positivism; thence to functionalism, pragmatism, policy science, and so on; institutions proliferating through functional specialization. It took a lot of imagination to assemble the diverse and chaotic materials generated by legal actors over five centuries into these narratives, and lots needed to be left aside. Against this background, heightening the awareness of rupture in the foundational professional worldview seemed a possible way to resist the "there is no alternative" posture of the contemporary legal world.

What ruptured exactly? One could renarrate those doctrinal, theoretical, or institutional developments to highlight changes, accidents, confusions, and paths not taken: what Foucault taught us to call "genealogy" rather than a search for historical origins.[10] I was more focused on the underlying framework of thought and professional practice which made *these* doctrines, *these* theories, *these* debates constitute the field. I might have called it, influenced by Thomas Kuhn, their "paradigm."[11] I was equally thinking of Foucault's own work on the history of sexuality and punishment and my colleague Duncan Kennedy's work on what he called "legal consciousness" in American legal history.[12]

Anyway, the idea was that the early "classical" writers thought about things so differently that even doctrines and arguments with the same Latin phrases meant something different. The *rupture* I was most focused on was the twentieth-century break from—and continuity with—that nineteenth-century traditional synthesis we've been discussing. To get at that, I identified an early and more profound rupture between the sixteenth- and seventeenth-century Catholic and Protestant legal minds, recalled as "founders" of discipline (whom I somewhat ironically termed "primitive"), and all that came after. The world my "primitives" took for granted and what they imagined "law" was like were so different that I proposed we read them more as useful contrast than origin.

Martti: So it's a little like *From Apology to Utopia,* which I imagined as a description of an "order of discourse" with elements forced into a structure or constellation in contrast to whatever existed earlier on. The break that I sketched in *The Gentle Civilizer of Nations* did not rely on that kind of logical discourse analysis—though, of course, it presumed its correctness.

I was keen to show that what happened in 1870s Europe was not at all an outgrowth of a tradition going back a long time to Grotius, Gentili, or even further to the Spanish scholastics. The point was to make visible the Victorian consciousness of those new men and to argue that if you wanted to understand twentieth-century international law, at least up to the 1960s, then you needed to be clear about how late nineteenth-century European lawyers—in fact, European elites generally—situated themselves historically and how the legal vocabulary they developed was intended to respond to the lessons they drew from the way they narrated the past. It was that world—and neither that of the religious wars, of the sixteenth and seventeenth centuries, nor of the imperial wars of the eighteenth—that framed "modern" international law.

David: Absolutely. We were both focused on the specificity of the nineteenth-century tradition by contrast to what came before and after. Strangely, the distinctiveness of the primitive mode of thought was particularly useful for highlighting the difference between modern international law and the "traditional" synthesis associated with the late nineteenth century. Traditional preoccupations—with the validity of norms, the distinctiveness of public and private or of international and national—were all missing in the primitive texts. The late nineteenth century you describe—of German scientific rigor and Victorian sentiment—established distinctions unknown to the primitives, or even to Vattel, so important in the early American international law story.[13]

In his texts—or in early US cases touching on international law—you find a jumble of what we would call policy advice for diplomats, descriptions of diplomatic practice, principles drawn from here and there—all of which resembles contemporary legal reasoning in its rather unsystematic and blurred distinctions. The break into modernism was marked by the conscious unraveling of nineteenth-century preoccupations. As a distant mirror, the primitives raised a question about the modern situation: Did the unraveling of distinctions leave us where we would have been had they not arisen, or was our fallen modern world altered by the ongoing shadow of the cleft between traditional and modern?

Martti: You referred to a "traditional synthesis" of the late nineteenth century, but I think it is important to see its novelty. Unlike your "primitives," the "gentle civilizers" saw the future as open for innovation and had inherited a philosophical perspective that instructed them to expect universal "progress" from the scientific and technological innovations they were witnessing and that they hoped would also carry their legal ideas forward. But I agree with your temporal distinctions, of course.

David: Absolutely—I should put "traditional" in scare quotes. I had been taught that the twentieth century "modernized" a tradition otherwise unbroken from 1648, first, if splutteringly, in the League and then, post-1945, in the United Nations (UN) and the changes Friedmann listed: more topics, more institutions, more states, and so forth. There was an understated geography here as well—Europe stuck in tradition, America the place of modernization. All of which erased the distinctive and innovative nature of that Victorian moment—and its brevity. Duncan Kennedy had focused on the distinctive complexity of "classical legal thought" in the US tradition precisely in the late nineteenth century—I came to international law prepared to find something similar, and there it was.

I like the way you've recovered *innovation* from "tradition"—and identified the guys who innovated. For students today who want to change things—want to innovate—it is terrifically useful to illustrate how that's been done before. It's not an unbroken tradition they'd be the first to disrupt: it's a pattern of repeated disruptive innovations. I've long taught Nathaniel Berman's early insistence on the cultural modernity of the interwar guys to make this point.[14]

My objective was to set up a story of the twentieth-century discipline and professional practice as a repeated *interaction* between a traditional and a modern sensibility. Neither pole seemed fully plausible to contemporary professionals. Neither could they be easily combined. But they defined the range and occupied the field of professional methods or styles of engagement. Either norms needed to be validated to be norms, for example, or they could only be thought valid when they had been enforced or found persuasive. All one could do is try to square this circle in endless discussions of the normativity of international law, the best way to understand the relationship of international law to politics, and so forth. As a result, the modern discipline spoke with two voices, neither of them persuasive, relaying explanations between themselves in constant rotation.

This gave me a starting point for exploring other characteristic double narratives in the discipline, like "carrier of the ethical" and "carrier of the real" which we spoke about. The relationship among historical narratives was, in this way, parallel to the relationships between apology and utopia, or between sovereign autonomy and international community, which we were discovering in the corpus of modern international legal doctrine and theory. So it was structuralism all the way down—or back and forth in history.

Martti: And not just doctrine and history—also the ways of political energy and reform: strengthened autonomy for those deprived of it, binding everyone simultaneously to transnational systems of governance as we discussed, a kind of magic.

David: All this raised the question, What happens when a field becomes *aware* of (irresolvable) differences within itself? Perhaps they can be managed by an ever more sophisticated bit of doctrinal, theoretical, or historical analysis—but perhaps they can't, and then what? Again the primitive moment was suggestive.

The primitive field was also split—between Protestant and Catholic modes of reasoning. Neither was uniform—I included two quite different Catholics and two quite different Protestants—but everyone was increasingly aware of divergent doctrinal positions. So, for example, it was clear to everyone that in a holistic world only one side of any conflict could be *just*. But what if both princes understood their war as just? This seemed possible, even likely, but the intellectual techniques for managing the problem were weak. Things like, "Be particularly careful to consult your legal adviser before setting forth."

My hypothesis was that this awareness of irresolvable difference within the primitive vernacular contributed to its erosion, turning international law from religious analytics toward a meditation on "reason" which might be universal. And so began the slow working out of the traditional synthesis. All that seemed suggestive for the situation in 1980: increasing awareness of contradiction might open the way for innovation and foundational rethinking. A hopeful story.

Just to note, this is precisely the opposite story from my *International Legal Structures*, published roughly the same year.[15] Examining the modern mode of international law reasoning, I identified the interminability of a contradictory and open-ended discourse as how it kept going rather than how it might fall apart. The whole field was a sophisticated management technique of elision and deferral and repetition. So I was ambivalent about the then contemporary field: Was it fragile, able to be shattered by critique, or impervious, having long since internalized the practice of managing contradiction as its modus vivendi?

Martti: What you're saying is that a discourse or a professional field can be held together both by the way it offers closure to its fundamental dilemmas and the way it refrains from doing just that. That does relate to the way my *To the Uttermost Parts of the Earth* can be read as an account of a series of intellectual vocabularies emerging, becoming authoritative, and then withering away. What I thought I was seeing in the demise of religious modes of argument and those that followed—science, politics, natural law, economics—was often their excessive engagement in *casuistry,* read both as sophistication and open-endedness.

At some point, however, grappling with what you called the "irresolvable difference" within a discourse becomes so complicated, the rules so saturated by exceptions and ad hoc adjustments, that it begins to seem overly contrived and collapses under its own weight. I guess I was after a kind of Kuhnian view on how legal modes of speech, vocabularies, and types of competence rise, become authoritative, and then dissipate as the solutions they give to the questions they have taught people to ask no longer appear persuasive.

David: Kuhn was so hopeful—practices fall apart, become less persuasive. Perhaps uncertainty and contradiction could liberate us as well! Ah, if only . . .

Martti: If law's power is the power to produce convincing articulations of human relationships, then I suppose if people begin to feel that those articulations are no longer of this world, unhelpful or contrived, something will happen. Maybe the way down is casuistry—but I suppose it may also be toward increasing abstraction and rigidity; here, too, religion provides examples. In both cases, some contestant will arrive, a rival vocabulary to intrude in the space of the old system. We see it today in the way new vocabularies of the "transnational" or the "global" claim to speak with greater sophistication and authority on items previously allocated to international law.

David: They come not to kill but to honor—and reinforce—the field.

Martti: And then there is the whole fragmentation phenomenon. It has been interesting to witness new legal vocabularies mushrooming all over the field of the "international"—some powerful, others weak. But even a single vocabulary may appear both persuasive and unpersuasive, its practitioners living a kind of double consciousness, remembering and re-creating the bygone periods of self-assurance as against the complex internal knowledge that things are actually more complicated than originally thought.

David: Precisely—that doubled sensibility is crucial. It doesn't have to add up; you just need to keep the ethical over here, the real over there. In your head.

This kind of thing recurs in many of the professional disciplines I've had any access to, cycles of self-confidence displaced by chastened moments of self-doubt. As one might expect, in those moments some people double down, some try to innovate, while people in adjacent fields or heterodoxies within the field try to seize the wheel. So, I'm not sure casuistry is the mark of a field about to implode; in those I've encountered it is more hubris that precedes a fall: wild and ever more general propositions, broad rules of thumb, often contradictory but firm policy advice in the face of contradictory experience, incredible ethical self-confidence. Think about development economics, for example, in the late 1960s and again in the early 1990s.[16] Although I do think the *perception* that international law had become casuistic is part of what fueled the shift from nineteenth-century traditional to twentieth-century modern international law.

One odd aspect of our current situation is that the legalization of everything globally has accompanied the fragmentation and dissolution of the decisiveness of the vocabulary. The incredible spread of legal institutions, vocabularies, professional ways of thinking about things—among politicians, citizen advocates, corporate public relations folks, and lawyers—may have been fueled by the perception that the law is both malleable and decisive, or at least might be. Perhaps we should call this a new casuistry: the making of definitive sounding claims in a vocabulary understood to be plastic. But it seems to go with the expansion, not the collapse, of law's ubiquity.

Martti: That's a hugely suggestive point that touches upon the phenomenology of modern legal expertise. Simultaneous self-assurance and self-doubt. I have encountered it in working with people from other disciplines—history, say, or international relations. It often appears that in public speeches at interdisciplinary conferences during the day, everyone speaks with a voice of confidence that sounds impressive, especially for nonexperts. But then later on, in informal debates, perhaps after dinner and a glass or two, one begins to hear all this self-doubt, a confession that the discipline actually is in crisis, its basic elements intensely subjected to scholastic dispute. Confidence during the day, self-doubt at night.

David: How that kind of doubling operates is a fascinating aspect of the experience of field cohesion or plausibility. Contrast two quite similar moments—the 1980s world of two intertwined voices, repeatedly braided into some kind of resolution, and the contemporary situation of fragmentation *sans peur et sans reproche.* Just as you say, professional practices also cabin incompatible frames in different settings, "appropriate" for different roles. For senior and junior players, for public and private discussion, for the court and the client . . . on and on.

Just as a side note, UnitedStatesean international lawyers routinely stabilize the "international law speaks with two voices" dilemma in temporal and geographic terms: the traditional voice is old-fashioned and European, the other more modern and American. And that turns out to be a distinction that can put *either* romantic idealism *or* hard-boiled realism in the old-fashioned European past. Somehow the field works as a rotation between modern and traditional stories—less progress than self-perpetuating repetition.

Martti: I used to feel infuriated about the way people relied on such narratives; there were heaps of them, they shared a cliché-like quality, and they were cited for whatever contrary purposes. This was before I realized that it would wrong to think about international law in terms of logic or a philosophy. It was not about "truth" but persuasion.

David: Though remember what we said about *persuasion* when we talked about law's power.

Martti: Good point. I am thinking of *persuasion* in terms of what cannot be professionally dissented from. As I then explained in *To the Uttermost Parts of the Earth,* such narrations were part of professional legal bricolage, pieces of discourse that could be used imaginatively in an effort to persuade an audience. *From Apology to Utopia* helped explain why they were held only loosely, so that one could move between them with relative ease as the polemical context required. Utopias and apologies each carried their historical narratives—or, better, contained resources for framing any present moment within some moral history or an account of the inexorable laws of power.

Questioning these narratives has been part of the "turn to history" I mentioned earlier. Demonstrating contingency, showing ruptures, producing counternarratives, and drawing attention to what might have taken place (but did not) have all been used by people wishing to bring about change in the way we understand international law and what is possible to accomplish with it.

To produce a history of the European Convention on Human Rights, for example, as a project by European postwar conservative leaders fearful of communist takeover does make the treaty and the institutions set up by it seem less the bastion of liberal progressivism it has often been presented as. Analogous stories can be told about almost any postwar international legal institution; they were not products of historical laws but concrete struggles. Success might often involve luck—who would have guessed that the mundane facts of *Costa v. Enel* would enable the Luxembourg judges to stake a claim of subordinating the rest of Europe's courts?[17]

Each moment creates its own history that opens up a good access to that moment's law—Laurent's *longue durée* was perfectly appropriate for the founding moment of the late nineteenth century. Grewe and Schmitt both wrote their ultra-realistic histories as bombs were falling over Berlin at the end of World War II. And Samuel Moyn published his *Last Utopia* as a 2010 reframing of something that had been presented as timeless or originating in the French Revolution as having actually come into existence only by the globalization of themes in the US civil rights debates in the 1960s and 1970s.[18] The immediate response and proliferation of alternative histories of human rights has now opened a privileged access to today's ideological struggles.

Vattel has been a prolific source of historical imagining. Already as I was composing *From Apology to Utopia* I felt that his texts were in a strange way both old and new. You could extract from them a story about self-determination and the good government of the modern state; you could even read him as an early proponent of the welfare state, as Jouannet did.[19]

And you could read him as a cold realist at ease with the hypocrisies of eighteenth-century European diplomacy, advocate of colonial expansion and preemptive war—the way Allott reads him.[20] Such readings have their own coherence and their well-known weaknesses, of course. I now see them as perfectly legitimate narrations highlighting elements in a complex past that illuminate risks and opportunities in the present.

David: No question, elements for various interpretations are lying around in a text with as many words as Vattel's. And his preclassical sensibility was comfortable, including lots of elements that later came to seem heterogeneous. Periodizations—including my "primitive," "traditional," and "modern"—are ostentatiously constructed. I remember questioning a colleague's periodization with cases that didn't quite fit: he said, with a smile, "well, there are always precursors and lags."

For all the methodological sophistication in professional historical work, people nevertheless often imagine history as the discovery of facts or read historical work as if it were a description rather than as the presentation of interpretations which always have their aesthetic qualities and practical purposes—all the more so for intellectual history. A colleague of mine recently disparaged a brilliant work of intellectual history with the question, "Isn't this just a description of the ideas of some dead people? How could that be helpful?"

This takes us to your second theme: building a narrative unity for critique where the field seems all over the map or obtuse to its historical situation and development. Certainly the construction of continuities is as much a matter of interpretation as ruptures. We've talked about how disciplinary histories are so often constructed around enduring field-specific problems—"legal order among sovereigns," most prominently—reinforcing the idea that the world is a state system and order is the challenge. Rupture, the recovery of accident, are ways to push back. Others have constructed alternative red threads through the material—for example, it was all about dealing with and subordinating the culturally different, ultimately through colonial and neocolonial arrangements.

You've also pushed back by reframing what was continuous. In *From Apology to Utopia,* that enduring relationship between utopian and apologetic professional positions. In *To the Uttermost Parts of the Earth,* you trace the presence of "legal professionals," of "law" or "legal imagining," and of preoccupations with "property" and "sovereignty" across a huge span of European history. Could you speak to the critical strategy at work in the construction of this kind of continuity?

Martti: At the time of writing *From Apology to Utopia* I was quite uncertain about the status of the "grammar" of ascending/descending, the structure that I suggested in some sense controlled the effort to explain order among states. I was influenced by the critique of liberalism in Unger's *Knowledge and Politics* and saw the tension between the rhetorical elements of individualism and solidarity as really fundamental for the modern mindset;[21] state sovereignty and binding legal order were just an extrapolation, or transformation, of that basic contradiction. So, if it was not fully transhistorical, I imagined it at least as hugely important for modern—which I tended to collapse into "liberal"—framing of the world. You could only look for legal authority in the sovereign freedom of the state or in a binding international order; yet both alternatives produced conclusive critiques of the other. This was logically interminable, an argumentative prison house. It covered everything. What else could one hope?

David: Roberto's book—and course—were very compelling: something called "liberalism" (which sounded like everything at the time) had a deep structure of antinomies. That also got me going in the search for coherence (or I guess I should say incoherence) across time and topic. It worked as critique if the object (liberalism) claimed coherence and you found recurring contradiction. Or, in Roberto's telling, it just *was*, and the critic identified it in recurring antinomies and the (unsatisfactory or partial) efforts to elide or resolve them. I'm sure I was tempted to see this as more universal or unavoidable than I might now; Roberto made it sound not only like "liberalism" but like something closer to human nature.

Martti: At the time I thought it—your words—*universal* and *unavoidable*, at least in the sense that if you wanted to be a persuasive international lawyer, then you could not avoid entering a world where "ascending" arguments from sovereign freedom clash interminably with "descending" ones from some binding legal order. Even if you did not believe in them, you had to learn them so as to perform your job properly. And the texts and debates of international lawyers made sense only when read against that structure.

Remember, I thought of this as "grammar." So I would say, if you wanted to communicate something in that language, you had to do it with these argumentative rules. Otherwise, you would not sound professional. I think I would now wish to remain agnostic about the philosophical implications of this. I recognize that there may be people who extrapolate from that vocabulary itself also a transhistorical narrative about the plight of being a human; the conflicting pull for autonomy and community must always have been there. But I'm not interested in that.

David: That was obviously Chomsky's project, the structure of language as the structure of the mind and of man—an important essence of the human and of consciousness.[22]

Martti: Yes, that was Chomsky's project. But it was sufficient for me to use those tools in order to make sense of the present, of international law as a language. I know it's possible to slip from there into philosophy, sociology, ethnography, something like the "structure of the modern consciousness." And I may have occasionally slipped. But I now want to refrain from such extensions. Let's just think of it as a rather forceful sketch of a world of professional possibilities and practices as they had existed since the late nineteenth century. It frames a set of problems that most people have since then come to think of as enormously important but hard to resolve.

What I wanted to say is that a profession as a project is created precisely by imagining such vicious problems into existence; you cannot "resolve" them without at the same time doing away with the profession itself. We are impressed by the complex maneuvers whereby legal professionals appear to maintain a fragile equilibrium between sovereignty and order, say. That's precisely where its power lies, its ability to suggest an authoritative articulation to a relationship reflecting that tension. *Here is how far your right goes; from here on, you must yield.*

David: The discipline does seem to keep going by rolling an insoluble problem out in front of itself. My *International Legal Structures* made that kind of argument: the field sets itself a problem—legal order among equal (political) sovereigns—against which it throws itself repeatedly, in contradictory ways. Legal materials developed in the shadow of that challenge could then be harnessed to problem solving across all kinds of domains. But where did this "legal order among sovereigns" idea come from, and how was it experienced in earlier periods? Perhaps you can help me with that.

The twentieth-century folks I've studied saw the "legal order/sovereigns" framework as a late "classic" or "traditional" definition of their field. But Europeans had developed legal ideas, doctrines, and institutions with an eye on all sorts of other problems: consolidating mercantile trade networks, establishing plantation colonies, building and managing the slave trade, figuring out when to go to war and what to do afterward, and so on.

Do you have a sense for which came first? Did the pre-twentieth-century problem solvers start with the "legal order/sovereigns" definition of their field and have to find legal solutions consistent with that prime directive fit for various purposes—just like their twentieth-century progeny? Or did they find legal solutions to various problems, including those relating to property and the perquisites of various authorities, which were then organized and retold, after Austin, as responses to the "legal order/sovereigns" problem? Probably both, but how would you describe the animating driver of their practice?

Martti: I am not sure I have a definite answer to which came first. Perhaps I can offer some elements. As you know, I have always stressed the great debt that international law today owes to German public law. The issue of *Landeshoheit*/imperial order was the defining legal problem of the "constitution" of the Holy Roman Empire. By the nineteenth century, German lawyers had already developed an immensely sophisticated vocabulary to deal with it. After the demise of the empire (1806), they projected that frame to the international realm. As I discuss in *To the Uttermost Parts of the Earth*, lawyers from elsewhere—John Austin, for instance—were impressed.[23] As a result, this perspective became a central aspect of the field's professional thinking.

And what about those other problems, then—commerce and colonialism, war and peace? They came with eighteenth-century texts and vocabularies that had really little to do with the Holy Roman Empire. Commerce and colonization were very largely about projecting domestic regulatory systems and property rights onto foreign soil. War and peace was a topos in diplomacy, balance of power, security, and "glory." Vattel treated it in systemic terms, but it did not really catch on until a little later.

I would say that the "legal order among sovereigns" became the master problem of twentieth-century international law owing to the influence of German law. And then there was a set of separate legal discourses also dealing with international matters, such as "just war," royal prerogative, consular law, merchant law, diplomatic privileges that would then be pulled together toward the 1870s and 1880s as parts of a project to manage the "order among states" problem. That private international law was gradually and quite consciously regarded as a related but different field highlights the type of coherence sought after.

Finally, I want to say I am surprised that so few commentators have noticed what I felt most acutely when writing *To the Uttermost Parts of the Earth*—namely, that this was a legal history of *capitalism.* I dislike that word and did not use it. But the play between sovereignty and property, public law and private law, the king and the merchant—all of that came together, however tentatively and with different variations in different places as a narrative about the big C. Here was another coherence, hidden in plain sight for most of the historiography of our field. Why this would be so I hesitate to guess.

David: I hope we can explore *To the Uttermost Parts of the Earth* in just those terms when we turn to political economy. I do feel your unease in naming the thing you're chronicling "capitalism."

I asked about the origins of the "legal order among sovereigns" problem because there are stakes in framing some actors and their interaction as an enduring foundational reality and everything else as secondary: a practical problem to be solved, dispute to be settled, an aberration to be overcome, within the frame set by that reality.

Framing it as all about the "state system" makes some things global and some local—things like culture, religion, family, private law. It also occludes global patterns of hierarchy and domination beneath a formal equality. Economic matters fade from view altogether.

This takes me to *The Gentle Civilizer of Nations,* where you studied the folks who assembled what we inhabit as the "traditional." How did they manage to reinterpret everybody from Grotius and the Spanish forward through Pufendorf and Zouche and Gentili and Vattel as offering partial but ever better answers to their late nineteenth-century preoccupation with the possibility of an intersovereign legal order?

Martti: Well, I don't think that was so easy. These were mostly practical men, not academics, interested in assisting liberal legislative reforms across Europe and eventually also civilizing the colonies. They were quite alien to the eighteenth-century world of Vattel and the balance of power. When in their writings they sometimes referenced Grotius and—rarely—the Spanish scholastics, this was only in a loose and casual way. They had not studied those texts. The name of Grotius was easily available for educated Europeans, and they could simply assert that they were doing what Grotius had been doing three and a half centuries earlier. Later on, academic lawyers could seek to give historical substance to that assertion. That was helped by the fact there already existed a package of names—a story of the development of natural law. You could simply attach your project as a continuation or a mature version of theirs.

But as we are now discussing historical continuities, one of them must surely involve a religious struggle. It is useful to remember that not everything went smoothly in the late nineteenth century, either. There had long been a Catholic-Protestant rivalry regarding how to understand natural law. During the religious wars, it had been the Protestants—Gentili, Grotius, a whole host of German scholars—who had been inclined to insert their world-building projects in natural law. The Catholic side already had a powerful institution with universal authority, the church and impressive intellectuals—Dominicans and Jesuits—who specialized in *raison d'état* thinking. This often came surprisingly close to law—although it invariably presumed the supreme authority of representatives of faith.

In the late nineteenth and early twentieth centuries, Catholic jurists began to stress Vitoria and the Spanish Dominicans as the "real" fathers of international law, highlighting colonialism's place in the shared international narrative, while the Protestant side—Britain and the United States—kept colonial matters firmly in domestic hands. The standard narrative is about secularization; the reality was anything but.

David: That's super helpful—I think I've fallen for the "secularism" story. It was John Haskell's work on Protestantism in nineteenth-century international law that got me looking again at religion.[24]

Martti: Coherence was also at issue with the rise of "international relations" as a discipline on the basis of a critique of the lawyers' "harmony of interests" resolution of the sovereignty/order problem. People like E. H. Carr and Alfred Zimmern in the United Kingdom framed the lawyers' problem within a wholly different set of historical assumptions.[25]

David: They are much more familiar fellow travelers, certainly in the US context.

Martti: I mention this only because a few years ago there was much talk about a shared interdisciplinary agenda between lawyers and international relations (IR) people that I felt, in fact, was a struggle for policy-making influence.[26] If international law's project really was "order among states," then surely a hardheaded realist could do that job better—a move that pushed international law to a rather defensive posture of moral justification. But in the end, not much came of it. This was because both law and IR were already both split against themselves, each with their own moral and realist stories about the world, so that it was more about institutional than intellectual power, an ideological clash, framed as assumptions about human nature and history. Perhaps predictably, the push toward interdisciplinarity may have taught each side one thing or another, but it certainly did not diminish their sense of identity and distinctiveness—most likely, to the contrary.

David: Certainly. There is a pas de deux between the fields in which they are each able to stand for alternative things—power to my reason, reason to my virtue, and so on. The methodological call to embrace—or distinguish—the other field helps solidify these internal disputes. The international law of the PCIJ confronts the international relations/political science world of the League; the "spirit of Geneva" opposes—advances beyond—the "spirit of The Hague."

At the same time, it was Alvarez who I first found calling for international lawyers to embrace political science after World War I and in doing so eliminate the "irrational" in politics.[27] And then the fields are together, and then they're separate . . . and then . . . To whom does the balance of power—or the Concert of Europe, for that matter—belong? Are networks—all the rage at the turn of this century—legal constructions? IR alternatives to the "billiard balls" of political science? Are the two fields alternative channels for dispute resolution, or partners in a common endeavor? And so on.

This is the kind of continuity I've been intrigued by—repeated habits of professional identification and differentiation, of blurring and distinguishing arguments, of traditional and progressive voices. They are all familiar, once you point it out, but they aren't the continuities the discipline frames for itself. While they imagine they're solving problems or knitting a normative fabric from sovereign practice, what they are "really"—or, anyway, also—doing is flipping over cards in a deck of contradictions.

Martti: Now you sound as if there existed a logic of professionalism or logic of disciplinarity with the status of something like a metaphysic of an alienated form of human relationality. How might that relate to such large entities as capitalism, imperialism, nationalism?

David: Not a logic or necessity, but a pattern I keep encountering. Or, perhaps better, a useful tool for opening a field to new inquiries, recombining the elements to foreground patterns like this. You've called the structures of your structuralism a "grammar" of professional competence. I'm not sure the structure is there to be discovered rather than an interpretive tool to identify open-ended patterns in a set of performances that might otherwise seem either solid or chaotic.

Perhaps this takes us to your third theme for today: historical work that brings international law "down to earth," as you called it. I don't think you mean *putting it in context* as if there is the *it* and there is the *context,* still less identifying the larger thing—capitalism/imperialism—for which it is but a useful tool. You've called this identifying the "frame" within which professional practices unrolled. But you've also been telling a story about international law as the project of particular people, a provincial rather than a global endeavor, of an elite with the preoccupations, the larger sense of the situation, the trauma, the direction of travel of that elite at the time. So, your men of 1873 are also Victorian liberals who happen to take international law as their terrain of action and imagination.

Martti: Interpreting these people as inhabitants of a past world that's culturally familiar; that can be quite an effective mode to engage one's audience.

David: Perhaps in that spirit I've suggested broad preoccupations in generational terms, some of which are specific to the international legal profession, others of which bleed out into the preoccupations of their milieu. Students readily identify the succession of traumas and opportunities that have preoccupied international lawyers in the United States: World War I, isolation and League failure, the Depression, World War II, America's new global "responsibilities," worry about "totalitarianism," the Cold War, the Vietnam War, American empire, neoliberalism, 9/11, failed states, the Great Recession, inequality, populism.

As you can see, the continuities here are in the perceived situation of the (American) international lawyer as a participant in the American ruling elite. But they were also particular people with idiosyncratic debates and projects, role-specific possibilities. Some were European émigrés bringing normative cosmopolitanism to restrain American adventurism; others were enablers of American power. They pursued all this in a profession which in each period had its own favorite doctrines and problems worth solving, favorite modes of action: codification, then administration, conventions and rights, debate and adjudication, principles and standards, unilateralism and stakeholder engagement. And different heroic figures: the jurist/judge; the international institution, networks/nongovernmental organizations; then experts and national leaders—or maybe managers, advocates, and stakeholders.

If we are thinking in politico-economic terms, bringing international law "down to earth" in this way presents these people as participants in the projects of the elites of which they are part—sometimes usefully, sometimes not—rather than as part of a global "invisible college." This is how you get to human rights as *rulership* or international law as *interested governance,* acting to distribute things in the world, identifying the problems worth and not worth solving, consolidating powers here and not there. And, of course, they could also be marginal to the whole operation—a nice sinecure in an elite whose dominating players are elsewhere.

Martti: We have both focused on individual lawyers or groups of lawyers and interpreted the law as a part of their "projects," reading their universalist language as an aspect of their sensibilities, ambitions, and insecurities. What you say about my men of 1873 being part of the domestic elites and representatives of a certain liberal bourgeois mindset prevalent in

Europe at the time is certainly right. Whether they were leaders or followers, that is harder to say. I suspect their influence varied. Rolin, for example, was sometimes in, sometimes out of government in Belgium. But they were well represented as recipients of the Nobel Peace Prize. Perhaps one can say that they were quite skillful as translators of the moral idioms widely shared in their milieu into an idea about international legality. To speak about *their milieu* would also indicate that they were not the only project around but that there were others, such as pacifist, socialist, and feminist internationalisms, as well as to draw attention to the way the milieu itself was defined by distinctions of class and gender, for example.

Among other things, this milieu was characterized by the *moral* tone that people cast over what they were doing—quite irrespective of whether they were classed as naturalists or positivists, more or less idealists or realists. In one of your early texts, I remember, you reflected on how different the attitude of international lawyers was to their field from, say, that of banking lawyers. It was hard to imagine a banking law professor making arguments *for* banking law, that its existence was morally necessary and that there should therefore be *more* of it. But this is what modern international lawyers do. I suppose this anxiety reflects a certain bourgeois interpretation of the two world wars as a result of a *moral* failure—in contrast to some irreducible or systemic conflict. As a result, what seemed needed was not foundational rethinking but a firmer commitment to the principles that everyone was, anyway, touting: "If only there were no hypocrisy." One can see how hopeless such desire was.

In *The Gentle Civilizer of Nations* I wanted to examine in some depth that sensibility while avoiding generalizations about modernity, capitalism, or internationalization. I did not want to reduce my persons—their projects—to such frames. That would have been to share the world-historical perspective of my protagonists. Instead I wanted to make it concrete and relatable in view of their biographies and professional pursuits, their thinking and feeling, their wisdom and stupidity. I wanted to frame the idea of "modern international law" as a story about the ambitions, ideologies, and assumptions of a group of well-placed lawyers who had participated in all kinds of charity activities and debates on how to enlist social science in the service of modern government.

I wanted to enable readers to see the world of international law in view of a cultural milieu in which some truths and predispositions were included and excluded already, at the outset. I had shown in *From Apology to Utopia* that international law's coherence could not be derived from any logical or philosophical system. Instead I was now arguing that it could be understood to be coherent as a cultural or phenomenological entity. I took some pleasure in "provincializing Europe" in this way; far from emanating from some universal reason, international law emerged from an intellectual and practical world of a handful of late Victorian lawyers.[28]

Let me add that when I wrote about those lawyers, I felt I understood them and had things to say about them in a way that was only obscured and distorted by those grand frames. I had been working as a lawyer-diplomat in the UN and elsewhere, and the things they wrote and the assumptions they held did not seem that different from those current among my colleagues. I felt I was able to imagine how they came to their legal problems and what attitudes controlled how they dealt with those problems. I wanted to give them a human voice.

That's why I focused on Rolin, not only as a founding member of the Institut de Droit International but as an unlucky investor who went eventually bankrupt and migrated to the Orient to take up the position of legal adviser to the king of Siam. I was interested in Westlake's split with Gladstone and his evening courses at the Working Men's College. I recounted Lauterpacht's meetings with McNair and the impact of their joint activities to the way international lawyers would understand what their law really was about; I drew attention to Jean Monnet's League experience that counseled him to avoid precisely *those* lawyers in his work for European reconstruction. By focusing quite closely on the writings and doings of a certain group of individuals, I wanted to sketch the "rise of modern international law" so that it would appear both real and of human size, a reflection of the activity and thinking of people whom we can understand the way we understand those with whom we associate with on a daily basis.

David: And you could have some sympathy for them.

Martti: Yes. You could have sympathy with them.

David: I felt a similar sympathy for, and anger at, American international lawyers of the early to mid-twentieth century—largely, men my parents' or grandparents' age. I had my favorites—professional father figures, if you will—and I felt I could understand their intense investment in various intradisciplinary debates and rivalries. But, taken together, they were also part of a liberal ruling elite that had failed at home and abroad—racial injustice, Vietnam, the list was a long one. And the few international lawyers who tried to row in the other direction had such flimsy oars.

To compare with your men of 1873 story, I'd say that twentieth-century UnitedStatesean international law got going twice. First, somewhere between the 1906 establishment of the American Society of International Law and debates about American membership in the League of Nations, and then again in the decades after 1945. In both moments the leading voices understood themselves to be both inheriting and rejecting European international law traditions, setting in motion the field's distinctive drama of traditional and modern voices responding to the "legal order among sovereigns" problem while moving beyond or after it to a more pragmatic and functional focus on problem solving across a diffuse terrain of actors and procedures and normative inventions. It's the sensibility of the second postwar moment that became the professional style of American legal hegemony.

But let's stay with the interwar period for a moment. I do think we forget how unstuck everything seemed after World War I and how many competing innovations fought for space. Within the European international law world, you had the exuberance of the International Labour Organization in Geneva—remaking relations between capital and labor!—and the restoration ambiance of the PCIJ in The Hague. Nathaniel Berman was the first to point out the cultural and intellectual "modernism" of so many European international legal developments of the interwar period.[29]

And all the major revisionist movements of the twentieth century are also stirring: in the colonial world, in the new socialist world, in the rising fascist movement. All of them sought to remake international law to remake the world order. Looking back, probably the fascists got the furthest in building their ideas into the legal vernacular; the others all tended to build the legal vernacular into their projects.

The legal establishment of the League as an *institution* illustrated the complexity of the innovation in thinking about law's relationship with politics. As an institution, it was understood to inherit both a move from the failed (formal) law of The Hague to a constituted politics *and* from the catastrophic politics of Europe to an orderly problem-solving legal competence. This was an enormously inventive—even literary—achievement.[30] Through a diplomatic process that concluded with an agreed text, one could transform the global situation from something violent and sterile to something orderly and effective. Politics and law conjured into something with the virtues of both and the dark sides of neither. But the concoction was unstable. Percy Corbett—who ended his career as a more modern (and American) voice—in 1924 despaired of making legal sense of the League, only with great difficulty determining that although not sovereign, it had "legal personality."[31] An original modern something pulled back into the law—I've always thought it a terrible demotion.

Martti: Reinforced by readings of the Covenant of the League of Nations—awkwardly part of the Treaty of Versailles—as "higher law" in a constitutional vein; neutrality would be excluded if a member were to go to war in defiance of its obligations. But even the United States came on board, partly through the Kellogg-Briand Pact and its nonrecognition policy.

David: Well, you can get rid of "neutrality" both by constitutionalizing/centralizing the move to war and by relativizing the distinction between war and peace, replacing *war* with vaguer neologisms like *use of force* and proliferating principled justifications for coercive measures of all kinds. All that was at work in the postwar period. The Covenant/Kellog-Briand "outlawry" has to be understood in relation to these other—in my view, more significant—transformations.

Meanwhile, after World War I, American international lawyers were across a big ocean trying to get on with things—and figure out their relationship to developments in Europe. In their minds, the 1914–1918 war demonstrated the catastrophe that was European interstate politics. The League project seemed a vehicle for entanglement in exactly that. The leading figures were republican isolationists whose goal was to stay away. Elihu Root, founder of the American Society, was typical in his opposition to American membership.

In their defense of American neutrality they were as robustly positivist and formalist as any of their European counterparts. But their focus was international business and trade, long the priority for American statecraft. As commercial lawyers they were already in a world of law where a more pragmatic and private law-driven sensibility reigned. They were busy establishing businesses and resolving disputes and managing colonies in legal terms—at least until the Europeans interrupted things with their war. The "Can there be law among sovereigns?" question didn't arise or was easily answered by their daily professional work. Moreover, in transnational commercial affairs, as Philip Jessup framed things already in 1928, all those European doctrinal categories and distinctions were obstacles to pragmatic problem solving.[32] A "functional" and "realist" mode of legal analytics—being developed in American legal thought and practice—offered a sounder basis for international legal activity.

Martti: That does not sound so different from my first-generation men, prior to World War I. They, too, had all kinds of commercial operation going on; they were active as politicians, parliamentarians, even members of government, not because they were "international lawyers" but because they were part of their countries' liberal and professional elites. They resented the influence of religious peace activists and socialist agitators and saw the fact of things becoming more international as an opportunity for expanding cooperation between similarly minded elites; comparative studies with the Institut de Droit International would promote homogeneous legislative reform across Europe. The "legal order among sovereigns" problem would be disposed of quite naturally by the expansion of trade and communications, as well as cooperation in colonial matters.

As the Great War then destroyed that hope, the next generation—that of the 1920s and 1930s—would no longer detach its eyes from the "order" problem. Spontaneous cooperation would not suffice; the law needed to be institutionally and textually embedded. "Public" international law would assert its independence from "private" international law by trying to speak in a constitutional vocabulary.

David: Sounds right, and you can see why "order" seemed a European problem to work out. And why this "traditional" preoccupation—along with high positivism as a response—emerged with particular force *after* 1918 rather than, as I was taught, in the dim mists of premodernity. In trying to figure a way through the order problem, Europe's legal intellectuals—like the rest of the intelligentsia—were all over the place. I imagine a conventional European international law professor in 1920 thinking the nineteenth century was great—the Concert of Europe, balance of power, the Hague Conventions, lots of administrative and other cooperation in Europe and the colonial world. How do we get back there, given that we just had World War I? At the same time, everyone younger—and many of that professor's contemporaries—thought the war showed exactly why we *didn't* want to go back there. And, so, you get innovations in all directions.

Only after 1945 did global order become an American preoccupation—and again you got all kinds of innovation. By then there had been a wholesale replacement of personnel in the American international law establishment. A younger generation, Democrats and closer to the New Deal, to postwar reconstruction and to Washington, DC, than to the New York commercial law world, took the lead. Chantal Thomas once helped me trace this changeover in the membership of the *American Journal of International Law*'s board of editors.

For the immediate post-1945 crew, international organizations were part of the vision, public law their focus. Over the next decades, the field redefined its working methods and its history. Law and politics were less distinct, functional and pragmatic action on the world stage a matter of wise "policy." The world of international adjudication and normative "validity" seemed long ago and far away. Statecraft required a subtle blend of legal principle, institutional process, and political power. That legal norms were ambiguous, contradictory, and of uncertain provenance enhanced their usefulness for the likes of Dag Hammarskjöld.

Martti: The immediate postwar period really did see the United States take the lead. But I want to dwell a little more on the experimentation in Europe in the 1920s and 1930s. A permanent international institution and a court, collective security, the League's functional activities, minority rights, the mandate system, cooperation in the fields of trade and finance. The legal substance was extrapolated from domestic laws: from territorial rights to state responsibility, from treaty interpretation to the law of international institutions. As a result, Lauterpacht could argue that international law was a "legal system," functionally analogous to what you saw at home.[33]

What began as doctrinal speculation in his works and those of his interlocutors emerged as "international human rights law" and "international criminal law" in the 1960s and 1990s. Behind the quite superficial history and philosophizing was a deep suspicion about "sovereignty." Statehood represented the "politics" that had become the great enemy. But that was not the only game in town, as you pointed out. Innovation went in many directions. In the Anglophone world Brierly, Waldock, or Julius Stone were suspicious of Lauterpachtian legalism and perhaps more representative of the immediate postwar generation—people like Charles de Visscher or Paul Reuter—whose principal concern were the pragmatic problems of the Cold War and European reconstruction. But if everybody did remain obsessed by the "order among states" problem, it is no wonder that a new generation of political and legal historians have recently begun to reevaluate that period as engaged in much more than mere legalist excess.

But as innovation moved to the United States after 1945, the Europeans learned to think of most interwar activism as somehow naive and "formalistic." That did not prevent them from continuing pretty much in the same vein through the Cold War years. But instead of principled choice, it would now become a Cold War strategy, part of the techniques of peaceful coexistence between fundamentally suspicious adversaries. This did not mean there was no legal innovation in Europe, only that now it was directed toward reconstruction at home—the European Economic Community (EEC), the Western European Union (WEU), the European Convention on Human Rights.

I wanted to stress these interwar innovations to explain why so many people in the 1990s felt that with end of the Cold War they could reenter the diplomatic and legal game. It was—many made this point expressly—as if some intellectual obstacle had been lifted as the Berlin Wall fell; the march toward something like a Kantian peaceful federation could be picked up again. Fascism and communism were over. End of history. That sort of thing.

David: The 1990s were like that in the United States as well—the great restoration of something only dimly remembered. But was the UN suddenly really working? Legal norms really constraining? Or was it rather an opportunity for lots of new norms and players, new *techniques* of lawmaking and enforcing—normative "entrepreneurs" everywhere? Adjudication—or more complex modes of dispute resolution, national courts, arbitration, conciliation, mediation, negotiation.

The interwar projects later associated with the word *formalism* I certainly recognize—law come to domesticate, civilize, restrain politics. Law can do that, of course, as formal rules identified by jurists and brought to bear by judges and/or as pragmatic standards infiltrating the decision making of political actors. The postwar reinterpretation of the interwar as "formalist" is strange given the dynamic relationship between formal and sociological innovations that characterized the period—not to mention the optimism and horror of "politics." As you say, Europeans were also innovating to *overcome* the limits of a formalist positivism—norms validated by investigation of their "sources" pedigree, for example.

I think of that as the "no norms" problem—if norms have to pass through a positivist/formalist sieve of juristic validation, you won't end up with a lot of norms. So people like Lauterpacht have to look elsewhere—the principles common to private law, for example. And famous Latin maxims inherent in the idea of law itself—or in sovereignty, or community, or . . . and the normative terrain opens up. The period was remembered as "formalist" but it would be more accurate to say it was preoccupied with escaping the limits of a formalism it could not do without. Formalism was, just as you said, more a post-1950 Cold War strategy—in Europe—to constrain the hegemons, enable coexistence, and so forth.

These strands were also alive in the American postwar world, and most prominently in the efforts by international legal scholars—particularly those in New York who circled around the UN world, many of whom were European émigrés—to advocate legal restraints on American foreign policy adventurism in Vietnam, the Dominican Republic, and so forth. But even these guys were operating in a vocabulary quite different from that of Lauterpacht's world, in conversation with the world of *policy*, of international relations, of sociological conceptions of law. The American international lawyers of the 1950s hadn't been there in the 1920s and 1930s—their world was the late New Deal and the Marshall Plan. In their professional experience, law and institutions had *worked* both nationally and internationally. As they tried to settle everything down and stabilize the Cold War, they rethought international law on the models of that experience, which meant building institutions and rethinking law's relationship with policy.

You're right, though, that the post-1990 generation's renewed enthusiasm for a legality unbound echoed that Victorian/interwar world even as it fueled the expansion of the legal vocabulary, dispersed the functions of international legalism across the planet.

Martti: Europeans were furiously suspicious of what US lawyers were doing in the 1950s and 1960s. They were especially apprehensive about the dubious talk about policy; they could not detach themselves from the view of policy/politics as precisely the adversary to be chained by law and legal institutions. They did not understand US policy science and feared that it would contaminate the law. These people were mostly professors of international law, academic publicists whose view of international law focused on the "order among sovereigns" problem.

But there was also—one tends to forget—another group busily working to set up the institutions of the EEC and the WEU, negotiating arms control, the International Trade Organization and the General Agreement on Tariffs and Trade, as well as the Bretton Woods system; they had a very different mindset. They saw European legal reconstruction as an eminently pragmatic task and often collaborated with US lawyers—many of whom, like Eric Stein from Michigan, were, as you pointed out, refugees from Europe and had all the reason to keep a distance from what the interwar jurists had been doing. For these lawyers, policy was part of daily work.

Postwar European lawyers working with European integration, trade, and development policy had little to do with UN law, the UN Security Council, codification of the law of the sea, and so forth. They were pragmatic technicians, often not academics, and rarely expected to explain their projects to their international law colleagues or the general public.

I make this point especially in view of my own experience in a public international law division in a foreign ministry from the late 1970s to early 1990s. In the course of those years, most of what we did was either connected to the UN, had to do with treaty law or general interstate relations. None of us was, as far as I know, ever consulted by the commercial or development assistance divisions. I once participated, almost by accident, in a meeting of the lawyers of the "Paris group" within the Organisation for Economic Co-operation and Development, discussing nuclear liability issues—a visit among a tribe whose existence had been previously undiscovered (by me). Already, early on, European law became the stuff of lawyers with a different mindset—indeed, they were quite expressive about the need to keep a distance from public international law and lawyers practicing it.

It was the same with trade and development. They had their own lawyers to conclude development assistance contracts or bilateral investment treaties. International commercial arbitration was carried out by experts from private law firms. I suppose a stigma inherited from League legalism—real and imagined—hovered over public international law in Europe as well, strengthened by the intensity of attention on the UN—the stasis in the Security Council and the political oddness of decolonization. By 1960, the year at which I ended *The Gentle Civilizer of Nations*, international law in Europe had become cocooned as a project to support legally oriented multilateralism—the UN and the International Court of Justice—and techniques for treaty making. Bits and pieces of substantive law would soon separate from it through specialization and "fragmentation."

David: You could see that kind of disciplinary specialization in the United States as well, but I think their shared inheritance from American legal thought and the sensibility of "good lawyering" prevented so stark a divide. Still, international commercial law, trade law, international economic law—specialists in all these fields—could look on international law as a pathetic cousin. In law faculties, everybody who did something vaguely international might feel a bond, work more closely with foreign students than their colleagues, but international law—with its debates about "is it really law?"—could seem a recipe for career exclusion from the real action of foreign policy, military affairs, economic, and commercial work.

Nevertheless, I was struck by the continuities across these fields for all their division of intellectual—and practical—labor. That's what got me to the "international style" shared by people like John Jackson, probably the leading international economic law voice of the late twentieth century, and the postwar Hans Kelsen.[34] Then, within public international law, people were of two minds about how to rework the legal ideas of the prewar—largely European—tradition, positions which I associated with leading international law scholars of the Yale and Manhattan schools who remained in dialogue with one another for four or five decades.[35] The leading Manhattan voices were those European émigrés. They hewed closer to the European tradition, although they represented critical and sociological strands of prewar European legal thinking that were extremely rare in the postwar European international law establishment.

They had a doubled commitment to international law's ethical liberalism and realist practicality and were acutely aware of the conflicting demands made upon the legal materials and the contradictory principles those materials reflected. Managing these tensions was a matter of sound professional judgment and inspired statecraft, epitomized by people like Dag Hammarskjöld.

The Yale school associated with Myres McDougal came to a similar professional synthesis from a different direction, building on the traditions of prewar American social science rejecting the image of "law come to politics." "World public order" was at once ethical, political, and legal. Politics operated only though legal institutions and vocabularies while law was known only as it was made real though social and political processes. Crucially, any world public order expressed an ethics. Values were not added in later or brought to world order by law.

As they all struggled to guide American hegemony in a divided world, the ethical and practical were equally in play. For Yale, that tended to mean a hard-boiled commitment to a world public order advancing the forces of democracy and liberalism against totalitarianism. For the Manhattan school, this meant holding the American hegemon to its international law commitments.

Between them they occupied the field of possibility in the discipline for sixty years. Their technical arguments and doctrinal positions were often close but seemed to express radically alternative ideas about law and politics and value. By 1980 the continuity in the field lay in this interminable debate: Was everything out of Yale ideological, if usefully realist? Was everything out of New York just liberal moralizing, if noble in its commitment to a universal law? And so on. It seemed a dead end. Meanwhile, however, between them they had built an astonishingly plastic legal vocabulary, able to transform pretty much any political project or position into a matter of legal principle and institutional prerogative.

Martti: That sounds to me like another transformation of apology / utopia, enacted as a series of disciplinary positions and moves at US law schools. We in Europe, of course, associated with the Manhattan people and felt very alienated by the Yale ones whom we saw as egregious specimens of US imperialism, infecting the legal language with incomprehensible neologisms. But although attention on the "policy-oriented" approach has been altogether out of proportion to its influence on the ground, it continues to be used as a bête noir for Europeans ever keen to stress the virtuous nature of their version of international law. But you are right that the ensuing debate had the potential to fill the whole world of the "international."

David: All the Yale neologisms failed to catch on, certainly, but their sensibility did become dominant "on the ground."

Martti: Perhaps. But let me just nuance a bit your grim image of the absence of critical or sociological thinking in Europe. There were Marxist lawyers in the academy in the 1960s and 1970s, and although many of them dismissed international law, some did not—especially not in France where Chaumont and his Reims school cooperated with many North African jurists. Germans were busy purifying their ranks, but Schmitt and his type of realism were not that far under the surface. Jurists who had courted variants of fascism in the interwar period often took "realist" positions that their adversaries regarded as cynical. Although realists were never hegemonic, they did have a presence as an intellectual and political counterpoint to the rather dull mainstream.

David: That sounds right. But I was always surprised that the interwar innovations in European legal science made their way into the postwar international legal world so rarely. Where were the "free law" voices in the German international law academy? Yes, there were "sociological" voices (with a serious leftist orientation) in the French scene, but my sense was that they were profoundly marginalized. Beyond that? In comparative law, certainly in Italy. Were there Scandinavian realists in Scandinavia? Perhaps—but quite muted, don't you think? More what we'd call law and society types; at least that was my experience among the Danish and Norwegian international law professors I encountered. Perhaps I'm wrong, but it seemed like a commitment to legality, to normativity, was everywhere, even among the UN enthusiasts.

Martti: *Especially* among the UN enthusiasts, I would say. But you're right, international law remained, generally speaking, a bastion of old-fashioned normativism and idealism. It still is in many German and French universities, for example, as well as Italy and Spain—although here and there signs have arisen of interest in feminist and postcolonial scholarship. In any case, the privileged form of engagement has been with human rights, into which 1970s and 1980s Marxists and "law and society types" largely converted. Philosophically serious realism—and normativism for that matter—remain confined to the jurisprudence class.

David: To get at the limits of this wall-to-wall legality in the United States, I tried to contrast it to parallel work in adjacent fields. For international economic law, for example, the historic trauma was the Smoot-Hawley Tariff Act and the Depression, not World War II and the Holocaust. Their world was one of (potential) buyers and sellers rather than a legal order of equal sovereigns. For comparative law, the axes of differentiation were culture and stages of industrial development, not law and politics.[36] By working out the entailments of these contrasts, I aimed to shed light on the foundational assumptions of each about the problems that mattered, the responses that were possible, the actors who counted. For all the plasticity—and field-occupying comprehensiveness—of each discipline, they were also quite narrow in their field of vision.

But the upshot was a set of differences which seemed to express *all of the possible differences,* making it difficult to get at or question the underlying foundations. When I entered the field in the late 1970s and early 1980s, this was surprising given the ways in which the foundations of global order *were* being questioned all over the place after 1968. The prevailing style of international legal work had lived through those ruptures and somehow accommodated them.

Martti: Hold on, let me interject that I think we in Europe began feeling the entry of what you call the "international style" of US lawyers sometime in the mid-1960s. Friedmann's *Changing Structures,* which you mentioned earlier, came out in 1964 and was a real watershed book.[37] It preached the need to move from Cold War formalism to the many functional tasks that seemed waiting in the international world: integrating law into development projects; conceiving new, specialized fields to deal with specific problems; international administrative law; international labor law; international corporation law; international antitrust law; and so on. Law was to become an instrument of change. It would deal with environmental problems and individual rights. It would begin imagining corporations as subjects of international law. Friedmann was, of course, European by origin, but taught at Columbia—in an excellent position to articulate your "international style" so that it was acceptable to the Europeans.

But, in fact, although Friedmann's invitation to move from what he called a law of coexistence to a law of cooperation was endlessly repeated in Europe, very little happened. There was no foundational rethinking. This was not from lack of reasons for it: the 1972 UN Conference on the Human Environment in Stockholm; all the noise about self-determination and the New International Economic Order (NIEO); the plan for the International Seabed Authority, which would distribute the proceeds from seabed mining to the developing states—all that had the potential of bringing about something new. But in fact, the "European style" remained. Mind you, lawyers from the third world were also apprehensive about the US way of doing things. There was Vietnam and being trained in Paris or Cambridge; their cultural outlook, or at least their sense of the professionally possible, was closer to Europe. Even the debate on state succession in the aftermath of decolonization—pressing for the "clean slate"—was conducted in a wholly traditional vocabulary. Whatever innovative thinking there was in Europe in the 1970s and 1980 was directed to integration and human rights.

David: I remember being told that Friedmann's book was the bee's knees. Already in the 1970s it seemed astonishingly tame—even obvious, describing a functional specialization long underway. Jessup had called for functionalism and pragmatism already in the early 1920s. Friedmann's was the voice of "the social"—interdependence, duties rather than rights, recognizing the new conditions of modern life as demanding solidaristic norms and institutions. Alvarez had said much the same, drawing on the same European intellectual traditions, in the 1920s. Robert Meagher, a friend and follower of Friedmann—and my PhD supervisor—wrote a book about the NIEO as a New Deal or Marshall Plan for the world.[38] Just as confidence in the "welfare state" was collapsing. Nevertheless, you're right—that was the sensibility, at least of the Manhattan people. It was innovative, but most American international law experts in the 1980s were not into foundational rethinking. McDougal's break with the European tradition—and the "realism" of some postwar political science—was the sharpest, but it was in service of the new foundations, not of their rethinking.

When they looked back, moreover, when had foundational rethinking helped? The whole European order fell apart between 1914 and 1945 and they had put it back together. In the late 1950s, nuclear weapons and the Cold War had the West on edge. In both cases, more law—better law, more sophisticated law—was part of the solution, foundational rethinking unnecessary. Who had tried to think foundationally? The Bolsheviks—but they just ended up as positivists in a rather old-fashioned way. The colonial world—and now they were eager UN members. My colleague, Detlev Vagts, wrote a terrific article on the foundational rethinking by the Nazi international law elite which read equally as a caution against foundation rethinking.[39] The Vietnam trauma and the various other American misadventures could have been avoided with more attention to international law as it *was*—or as they renarrated it. And then you get 1989, and the law takes off as the instrument and expression of American political, economic, and ethical self-confidence.

Martti: Combined with institutional innovations borrowed from the interwar thinkers.

David: Precisely—the whole project takes off again as renewal and reform. The interesting thing is how brief a period that post–Cold War period was. It didn't take ten years before it started to fall apart.

Martti: I now think of it as strangely significant that there was no historical reflection on international law in Europe between the 1960s and the end of the Cold War—none. It was a kind of "Don't ask, don't tell." The hot war was still too close, the cold one loomed over everything. Asking historical questions would have been inconvenient for many. Everyone was needed in the work of construction. This would mean keep building these institutions—especially the UN. Let's keep expanding a "law of cooperation." The ideal would be—the 1980 title of the Hague lectures by Hermann Mosler, the doyen of a purified cadre of German international lawyers—*International Society as a Legal Community*.[40]

And then came the 1990s. A back-to-the-future moment. Political obstacles toward a more integrated, more democratic, more legally oriented world had vanished it seemed. During the First Iraq War in 1990, I was among other lawyer-diplomats sitting in the UN Security Council intensely scrutinizing the UN Charter provisions on the right—legal—way to take measures when a member state had been invaded. Could one engage in military action already before economic sanctions had been tried? Would the Military Staff Committee have to direct any action? What did Articles 39, 41, and 42 of the UN Charter *really* mean? Even the US legal advisers asked such questions. The secretary-general, Boutros Boutros-Ghali, would soon come out with his *Agenda for Peace* and the negotiations for the International Criminal Court and the WTO were underway.[41] And there was Kosovo and the "responsibility to protect." It was astonishing to see questions about war and peace, about sovereignty, debated as if their solutions could be found in legal rules and principles.

David: It did seem strange, preposterous even, to be debating war that way—but meanwhile, war was being *waged* that way. While you were in the Security Council, I flew out to an aircraft carrier in the Persian Gulf enforcing the no-fly zone in Iraq, which led me on a long exploration of law in what has been a twenty-first century of nonstop American war. The neologism *lawfare* says it all: law as a tactic, a strategy, a terrain, an ally in war. Pretty much what Clausewitz called "policy."[42]

But we should stop here for today, I think, no?

Notes

1. Koskenniemi, "A History of International Law Histories."

2. Koskenniemi, *The Gentle Civilizer of Nations;* François Laurent, *Histoire du droit des gens et des relations internationales,* 18 vols. (Ghent: L. Hebbelynck, J.-B. Merry/Brussels: A. Lacroix, Verboeckhoven, 1850–1870).

3. Carl Schmitt, *Der Nomos der Erde im Völkerrecht des Jus publicum europaeum* (Berlin: Duncker und Humblot 1950); Wilhelm G. Grewe, *The Epochs of International Law,* trans. Michael Byers (Berlin: De Gruyter, 2000).

4. Koskenniemi, "Between Coordination and Constitution."

5. Henry Wheaton, *Histoire des progrès du droit des gens en Europe depuis la paix de Westphalie jusqu'à nos jours,* 3rd ed., 2 vols. (Leipzig: Brockhaus, 1853); Ernest Nys, *Les origines du droit international* (Brussels: Castaigne, 1894).

6. Koskenniemi, *To The Uttermost Parts of the Earth.*

7. Wolfgang Friedmann, *The Changing Structure of International Law* (London: Steven and Sons, 1964).

8. Koskenniemi, *From Apology to Utopia.*

9. Kennedy, "Primitive Legal Scholarship."

10. Michel Foucault, "Nietzsche, Genealogy, History," in *Aesthetics, Method and Epistemology* 369, James D. Faubion ed., Robert Hurley et al., trans. (New York: New Press, 1988).

11. Thomas Kuhn, *The Structure of Scientific Revolutions* (Chicago: University of Chicago Press, [1962] 2012).

12. Duncan Kennedy, *A Critique of Adjudication (Fin de Siècle)* (Cambridge MA: Harvard University Press, 1997).

13. Emer de Vattel, *Le droit des gens, ou principes de la loi naturelle appliqués à la conduite et aux affaires des nations et des souverains* (Washington, DC: Carnegie Institution of Washington, 1916).

14. Nathaniel Berman, "Modernism, Nationalism, and the Rhetoric of Reconstruction," 4 *Yale Journal of Law and the Humanities* 351 (1992).

15. Kennedy, *International Legal Structures.*

16. Kennedy, "The 'Rule of Law.'"

17. Case 6/64 Costa v. ENEL [1964] ECR 587.

18. Samuel Moyn, *The Last Utopia: Human Rights in History* (Cambridge, MA: Harvard University Press, 2010).

19. Emmanuelle Jouannet, *The Liberal-Welfarist Law of Nations. A History of International Law*, trans. Christopher Sutcliffe (Cambridge: Cambridge University Press 2012), 17–20, 64–70.

20. Philip Allott, *The Health of Nations: Society and Law beyond the State* (Cambridge: Cambridge University Press, 2002), 56–62, 413–416.

21. Roberto Mangabeira Unger, *Knowledge and Politics* (New York: Free Press, 1975).

22. Noam Chomsky, *Language and Mind* (Cambridge: Cambridge University Press, [1968] 2006); Noam Chomsky, *Reflections on Language* (New York: Pantheon Books, 1975).

23. Koskenniemi, *To the Uttermost Parts of the Earth*, 938–939.

24. John Haskell, "Hugo Grotius in the Contemporary Memory of International Law: Secularism, Liberalism, and the Politics of Restatement and Denial," 25 *Emory International Law Review* 269 (2012); John Haskell, "Divine Immanence: The Evangelical Foundations of Modern Anglo-American Approaches to International Law," 11 *Chinese Journal of International Law* 429 (2012).

25. E. H. Carr, *The Twenty Years' Crisis 1919–1939* (London: Palgrave Macmillan, [1939] 2016); Alfred Eckhard Zimmern, *The League of Nations and the Rule of Law, 1918–1935* (London: Macmillan, 1936).

26. Koskenniemi, "Miserable Comforters."

27. Alejandro Alvarez, "The New International Law," 15 *Grotius Society Transactions* 35 (1930).

28. Dipesh Chakrabarty, *Provincializing Europe: Postcolonial Thought and Historical Difference* (Princeton, NJ: Princeton University Press, [2000] 2008).

29. Nathaniel Berman, "Modernism, Nationalism, and the Rhetoric of Reconstruction," 4 *Yale Journal of Law and the Humanities* 351 (1992).

30. Kennedy, "The Move to Institutions," 8 *Cardozo Law Review* 841 (1987).

31. P. E. Corbett, "What Is the League of Nations?," 5 *British Yearbook of International Law* 119, (1924).

32. Philip Jessup, "The Functional Approach as Applied to International Law," in *Proceedings of the Third Conference of Teachers of International Law* 1 (Washington, DC: Carnegie Endowment for International Law, 1928).

33. Koskenniemi, "Lauterpacht."

34. Kennedy, "The International Style."

35. Kennedy, "When Renewal Repeats"; Kennedy, "Tom Franck and the Manhattan School."

36. Kennedy, "The Methods and Politics of Comparative Law"; Kennedy, "New Approaches to Comparative Law."

37. Friedmann, *The Changing Structure of International Law*.

38. Robert F. Meagher, *An International Redistribution of Wealth and Power: A Study of the Charter of Economic Rights and Duties of States* (New York: Pergamon, 1979).

39. Detlev F. Vagts, "International Law in the Third Reich," 84 *American Journal of International Law* 661 (1990).

40. Hermann Mosler, *The International Society as a Legal Community* (Alphen aan den Rijn, Netherlands: Sijthoff en Noordhoff, 1980).

41. Boutros Boutros-Ghali, *An Agenda for Peace: Preventive Diplomacy, Peacemaking and Peace-Keeping; Report of the Secretary-General Pursuant to the Statement Adopted by the Summit Meeting of the Security Council on 31 January 1992* (New York: United Nations Department of Public Information, 1992).

42. Kennedy, *Of War and Law.*

CONVERSATION SIX

Law in the Political Economy of the World

David: Law's role in "political economy"—that's our topic today. We've both thought about law's role in constituting and managing what we know as "politics" and "economics."

Legal arrangements certainly lie at the foundations of things we see as "economic" and "political." Credit, labor, capital, like citizenship and authority—or exit, voice, and loyalty, for that matter—are put together legally, in one way rather than another. Uncovering those foundations and stressing their contingency has been a staple in recent progressive scholarship on law and political economy. I'm thinking, for example, of Chris Desan or Katerina Pistor's work on money and finance.[1] Both stress the role of legal minds and lawyers doing legal work in both conceptualizing and managing what it means to be money or credit.

On the one hand, legal work contributes to commonsense notions about what politics and economics *are* and how they relate. On the other hand—and simultaneously—legal work takes this world as its oyster, serving as a professional managerial practice linking and separating what "politics" and "the economy" have become. You've thought about this historically. Perhaps we could start by tracing these two constitutive functions—one imaginative, one managerial—of legal ideas and legal people, beginning with the story you tell in *To the Uttermost Parts of the Earth*,[2] which focuses on the big picture over a long stretch of time.

Along the way I hope we can think about whether legal elites see themselves building and managing an *order* in the political and economic realms rather than—or more significantly than—managing a hierarchy or engaging in distribution. That distinction so divides mainstream and critical thinking today. A sense of managing an ordered world of equal entitlement to representation and participation in exchange is so characteristic of today's elites for whom inequality—or too much visible inequality—is a kind of surprise and scandal.

You know the picture: traders exchanging and notionally equal sovereigns relating in a legal order which is thought to be realistic, practical, and virtuous. And without alternative. Contrast this with heterodox and critical traditions of "political economy" that focus on conflict among groups, hierarchy and inequality rather than order or equilibrium. Were our legal analysis to begin there, we would see professional constitutive and managerial practices as integral to the reproduction of global inequality and useful as terrains of struggle to alter those hierarchies.

Political economy and law is a relatively new focal point for me, so this may be a bit speculative.[3] But that gives us a couple of themes: a deeper focus on the constitutive and managerial role of law in the ongoing pas de deux of politics and economics, and a reframing of both as first about conflict, distribution, and domination rather than balance or good order.

In an earlier conversation you described *To the Uttermost Parts of the Earth* as a legal history of *capitalism,* although I'm not sure that word appears in the book. By tracing the *entanglement* of sovereignty and property in the legal imagination, you must have intended the book as a sharp critique of those who focus *either* on the political (and public law) history of sovereignty *or* on the economic (and, largely, private law) history of property. But, say more. What were you writing *against*?

Martti: *To the Uttermost Parts of the Earth* is precisely about the way legal vocabularies have helped ambitious people to imagine and manage the worlds of power around themselves. It's a very long trajectory I examined there—from late medieval times to the nineteenth century. But I wanted to use a *longue durée* perspective to get far enough from the present so as to examine the present as "strange" and to find longer trajectories where contexts arise and fade away so as to make visible both what persists and what changes—or, in terms of this conversation, how things are imagined into existence and then how focus moves into the pragmatic management of those things.

For example, what this history immediately showed as "strange" in the present was the way some people could rule over others in such natural seeming ways or exclude others from things or practices that they thought self-evidently belonged to them. There has always been hierarchy and possession. But most of the time, they were supported by complex normative systems that, when we now examine them, seem awkward and hard to fit with the values or preferences we profess to share today. I am struck by how firmly those justifications arise from religious concepts and categories.

Christians interpreted Genesis as an invitation to think of each other as equal before God, who donated the world to them in common. In that thinking, power is always corrupt and profit translates as usury. Looked at from that angle, the present world is weird and incomprehensible. It took a long and convoluted history of conceptual innovation—predominantly carried out by theologians—for Europeans eventually to find a justification for *public* power to rule over them and a system of *private* property to distribute material values among them.

We are both interested in law as performance and a linguistic practice, the competent employment of a professional vocabulary. In *To the Uttermost Parts of the Earth* I examined the imagining and managing, order building and value distribution carried out by a series of professional vocabularies in a legal idiom that followed each other in the space of a half millennium. The first and, I often think, the most important was precisely *theology:* throughout 1300–1870 theology helped Europeans to balance between their ideals and the world they saw around themselves.

I was struck by the skill with which the Spanish scholastics—Vitoria and others—employed the partly Roman, partly biblical vocabulary of *dominium* to imagine into existence a world of sovereign rulership and global commerce, two domains that in time came to rely on other. They brought this secular world under a morality of Christian perfection by describing it in terms of a law of nations, *ius gentium,* consisting of pragmatic accommodations of the natural law based on Genesis so as to adapt it in a real world of sinners. That presumed a two-level world where daily life would always nostalgically look back into the ideals of moral perfection while going about its business. That's how we still live.

David: Let me stop you there. You say *theology* provided the material for imagining and managing both sovereign *rulership* and *commerce*. How do you see the status of theology? As a shared intellectual context for working out the parameters of power, should we see that as a kind of elite ideology, increasingly in struggle with ideological alternatives until it is finally deposed?

And were *rulership* and *commerce* what we now mean by *politics* and *economics*? Or did those come later with the advent of alternative elite vernaculars? How was a theologically imagined *sovereign* different from the *sovereignty* of 1880—or, again, 1980? Same for *commerce.*

Martti: I think of languages such as *theology* as pretty autonomous, capable of being semantically grasped by elites and nonelites alike, and being used both to work out parameters of power and as depositories of fighting words—a distinction that may often be hard to keep. I saw elite theology managing a legally articulated frame within which Christians would orient their lives and distinguish actions as virtuous or base. Its status in that sense was somewhat comparable to vocabularies such as *politics, science,* or *economics* in later periods.

Are *rulership* and *commerce* our *politics* and *economy*? A family resemblance, surely, and a structurally significant pairing. But I would not collapse, say, divinely ordained kingship in the sixteenth century with the US Congress. A trade fair in sixteenth-century Antwerp may look surprisingly similar to the New York Stock Exchange, but not as lived experiences—nobody in the latter worries about whether they are engaged in usury and seeks a churchman's counsel on that point.

David: Right—hard to imagine.

Martti: For a very long time, theologians were the leading intellectuals and royal counsel; their mission was to reconcile both royal power and an extensive commerce with biblical faith. How to explain the distance between the freedom and common ownership as explained in Genesis, and the ubiquitous claim of princes to rule, by bankers to raise interest and merchants to buy cheap and to sell dear? What about serfdom and slavery?

The theologians devised a two-step procedure: first, they explained that humans used their very freedom—their *dominium*—to create two types of authority: sovereignty (*dominium iurisdictionis*) and property (*dominium proprietatis*). This they imagined to take place through law—namely, a process they labeled *ius gentium,* law of nations. Then they had things to say about how both types of authority were to be employed. How was the king to act in relationship to landowners or to the indigenous? How to relate virtue and profit? When to wage war? What was just price? From Salamanca, this looked like a global order of divinely controlled imperial power;

for the rest of the world, it operated as an expanding process of distributing power and material values.

David: So, for each form of *dominium,* if I understand you, the key issue was its relationship with the divine; this wasn't a world divided between public and private, sovereignty and property, but between sacred and profane. That puts rulership and commerce in the same boat: secular modes of *dominium* to be reconciled with Christian ethics.

How comprehensively did these theologians imagine what they were putting together? I imagine they thought they were figuring out—describing or building or authorizing—an "order." Were they? This is a very presentist question, but did they understand that "rulership" was, as we might now say, "distributive"? That their work was about building or authorizing domination, in effect, more significantly than order? Or that a world of commerce would have a center and a periphery which they were self-consciously trying to distinguish?

Martti: That's exactly what I am arguing. The powers embodied in rulership and property were essentially of the same character, two aspects of a single, teleologically ordained cosmos where everything has its hierarchically determined place. Rulership would be "distributive" in that the king was to act as the secular sword of faith. Distributing rights over land at home and in the colonies was utterly mixed with the power to order hierarchical relations between humans. Colonial companies were just one—but a good—example of the persistence of this: private capital authorized by royal decree to extract resources from and exercise jurisdiction in pagan lands.

Order and distribution, vertical and horizontal forms of power came hand in hand. If the attention of theologians was perhaps more on order, they also counseled the king against excessive differences of wealth, the sin of avarice. They did worry over constant peasant uprisings. Aristotelians or not, these early modern elites were keen on all things being in a proper "balance." Of course, they had no sense of an "economy" as distinct from good royal household. But the virtues of prudence and the golden middle still created a political economy of sorts.

David: That sure sounds familiar—inequality becomes a problem when it threatens the status quo order. Another way of asking, "Was it order or was it domination/distribution?" would be to ask what groups were in struggle with one another and what conflicts were they managing or pursuing? Where were the stakes that could be distributed, as they saw it—material stakes, ideological stakes, authority stakes? And among whom?

Throughout *To the Uttermost Parts of the Earth* we see struggles here and there—the merchants and the landed aristocracy, the king and everyone else, the pope and the king—although you don't thematize these struggles as the central armature. Your central focal points are the vocabularies that get consolidated in each period through the management of these struggles. Could you say more about the struggles? In particular, were the terms of theological interpretation *tools* or *stakes* in struggle? Or perhaps both?

Martti: There is struggle everywhere—church rulers and secular rulers, rulers and nobles—especially over taxes, nobles with peasants about enclosures, nobles and a rising merchant class, merchants among themselves over monopolies. In the colonial world, struggles between metropolitan actors and "men on place," between settlers and merchants, settlers and indigenous, slaves and masters. And then, of course, struggles between the innumerable factions between and within the Catholic and Protestant groups, Christians and non-Christians.

A lot has been written about these and other struggles; but I am more interested in struggles over meaning—especially legal meaning. How a legal ideology—say, of "good kingship" or "nobility"—becomes a platform for struggle: how their meanings consolidate and change. "Free trade," for example, was propagated both by the British East India Company and its competitors. Or "civilized nation," to take another banal example. This is not so much about the ways of struggle between existing adversaries as about how adversity emerges within a camp.

David: The significance of struggle about meaning is easily overlooked when the word *struggle* brings to mind only material stakes—money, land, authority. But there are these other ideological stakes in the struggle between groups—not just being right in order to claim material stakes but advancing your group's vision of what means what, what right *is*. By focusing there, you help us get away from thinking the meaning is always a means rather than an end.

I also like your focus on the ways a shared idea we might think decides the issue—"free trade," say—becomes a terrain for opposed interests with alternative notions of what it ought to mean. That is so much the way today's legal vocabulary accommodates alternatives, becoming both a terrain and a stake in struggle.

You have argued that this theologically saturated professional world gave way to one in which *politics* became the coin of professional practice. Again, if I understand you, a vocabulary of meaning, in which different positions were associated with different interests and served both as a tool of struggle and as at stake in the struggle. Could you spell that out a bit? And perhaps say a bit more about what you mean by *politics* here. Was this the period in which the *political* in *political economy* is invented? And if the vocabulary was *politics,* was this what legal people were doing and thinking they were doing?

Martti: The power of theology was eventually undermined by its collapse into casuistry, "probabilism," "Jesuit morality." And then replaced by a more direct culture of political advice. Security and welfare of the community became independent objectives of government. The story of the rise of a new raison d'état literature under Richelieu in France is well known—Naudé, Rohan, others. Even Grotius pleaded with King James not to let the British onto the Moluccas, as that would undermine the investments of the Dutch East India Company. And the company form itself was chosen so as to deal with transaction costs: a commercial-military enterprise governed by representatives of the provinces but economically autonomous. If one thinks of *politics* as deciding on the distribution of power or material values, then one can see a move from normative to increasingly more technical vocabularies to achieve this.

A self-conscious political economy appeared only once concern moved *from teleology to causality*—with empirical science, Hobbes, Pufendorf, Smith. Security and welfare remained the principal objectives, but attention was now with the technical means and the cost whereby they could be attained. The emergence of the protection/obedience nexus was important: allegiance was to be conditional on the ability of the ruler to protect a people. The first question now was how to gain and maintain power. A second step was the reconception of power as the wealth of the realm. This was mercantilism, of course, and the topic of the first generation of "political economists" of the early seventeenth century, such as Malynes and Molloy—lawyers and practical writers who framed their instructions for merchants within a natural law idiom.

Mercantilism presupposed an absolutist political theory—but that was pure abstraction. It enabled Louis XIV to say, and maybe even believe, "L'état c'est moi" at a moment when the state apparatus was wholly in the hands of over fifty thousand venal officeholders as private property, inheritable by their sons; the king could not move a finger without consulting his financiers. The way European order was *imagined* had utterly separated from the way it was *managed*. Statehood would be a system for distributing power at home and opportunities for enrichment abroad.

David: An imagined world sharply split from the real world is also very familiar—"global governance in a world of equal states and free trade" is certainly like that.

You tell the story as a vocabulary that starts relatively coherently and then "collapses" into casuistry—rather than one defeated by rivals. In *The Gentle Civilizer of Nations*, the rise and fall of the vocabulary of 1873 is entangled in the battles of your little group of professionals with a whole series of alternatives.[4] I've also used the "paradigm falls apart" metaphor to talk about the fall of theology into political reason and political virtue; I credited the increasing recognition of contradictory possibilities within the international law vocabulary as Protestants and Catholics had at it among themselves and with one another. Elites sometimes do lose confidence in their vocabulary—something like that happened to Washington Consensus economists—but usually there are also robust contending alternatives. Perhaps part of reframing our stories as "political economy" might be placing these rise and fall narratives in the context of an elite's retreat or defeat.

Martti: Self-marginalization or defeat: isn't that the same thing looked at from two perspectives? I admit that I have a tendency to think in rather deterministic "rise and fall" terms. I mean the world changes, an ideological vocabulary becomes stale—and then somewhere somebody comes who proposes a new meaning for the old vocabulary, or develops another idiom, and that begins to enchant.

David: Okay, and what of "politics" and "economics"—or "rulership" and "commerce"—in the mercantile period? It sounds as if they are still part of the same soup in the mercantile imagination, not both secular in relationship to the divine, but both—well, *what,* exactly? Sovereign responsibilities?

What happened to the two modes of *dominium*—sovereignty and property—in the mercantile period?

Martti: Mercantilism joined with absolutism as a coherent legal order—though, of course, many merchants resented it and had to fight in order to gain the sovereign's good graces; they had to yield. In England, all foreign trade came under the royal prerogative (i.e., sovereignty) because the common law (i.e., property) "did not travel abroad," as Coke put it. But if the colonial companies also ruled the lands where they operated, where was formal sovereignty? Constant quarrels over this question ended only in 1806 when Parliament finally decreed that sovereignty over the Indian principalities lay with Britain and not with the British East India Company. It is good to remember that the whole plantation economy in the Caribbean was based on slavery—a power that mixed the right of property and sovereignty. It was precisely because Bodin thought that in France there could be only one sovereign that he thought it legally impossible for there to be master-slave relations in the French realm.

Many people suggest that today's transnational companies are successors to the large colonial companies; I think that is also a useful way to characterize the investment law system that transforms the owner of foreign capital into a participant—even a privileged participant—in the domestic legislative process.

David: As I recall, you described the role of *lex mercatoria* in that assertion of royal prerogative, importing, in effect, an imagined transnational merchant legality to push against the common law. Perhaps I have that wrong, but what interested me was the way the legal imagination established a mode of absolutism—which wasn't very absolute, as you say—by legally managing the relationship between sovereignty and commerce, here by positing an alternative legal order to place the king in command of foreign commerce.

Martti: Absolutely.

David: Would I be on the right track to say that, for these guys, thinking of sovereignty and property as distinct—if not yet absolute—pushed the action toward a kind of boundary work, managing their relations, asserting authority over the limits of each with respect to the other, qualifying each by the other, and so on? That sounds very modern: politics and economics are imagined as different and distinct realms, but everyone also knows they are not distinct and may not be that different; all the legal work is about their relationship.

Martti: In contrast to sovereignty, property was imagined as absolute only with Locke and what began to happen in the Anglosphere after 1688. On the continent, the physiocrats in the 1760s expressly equated the need to hold both sovereignty and property rights absolute. Only an *absolute* sovereign could guarantee that the contractual relations between the three relevant groups in society—farmers, merchants, and landowners—would bring about the growth of profit provided by what they called the "natural order" of the economy.

But you ask about boundary work between sovereignty and property; well, the very road to the English revolution was paved with an intense legally articulated struggle over where the limits of the king's taxation powers lay—his ability to think of all properties in the realm as his. The *Ship Money* case (1637) is a wonderful example of sophisticated legal boundary work precisely on this issue.[5] I like this term, *boundary work;* it highlights the way an experienced internal actor would rarely think of themselves as pushing for an absolute claim; instead, the claim would be to find a reasonable way to "reconcile" the countervailing considerations—and thereby to maintain control. A standard piece of early modern royal counseling!

A really significant split between imagining sovereign rulership in contrast to the techniques for managing the territory took place in Germany in the late eighteenth century with the rise of *Policeywissenschaft.* Here, now, a new generation of legal experts were no longer concerned to justify the prince's authority. It was solid. Now the task was to say something about how to manage his realm. With Smith in Britain and Justi in Germany, good management would no longer be just fiscal policy but helping to create the conditions of something like "civil society" that had its own laws to which the ruler should pay much attention. This would now be a recognizable "political economy"—as explained by men such as Petty and Davenant. With this, distribution could emerge as an independent concern. No longer just crumbs to the nobles but dividing profits between farmers, merchants, and landowners—the three groups that physiocrat theory used to replace the traditional distinction between nobles, clergy, and the third estate. Here there would arise an apparently autonomous "system" of economic relations.

But one needed a new kind of *philosophy* to give expression to this. The French revolution coincided (to put it no stronger) with the revolt of the peasant masses, tired of the extreme injustice of the old regime's patterns of distribution. This never put the absolutism of sovereignty into question. Instead its holder would now be the totally virtuous nation. But when that effort failed, it was replaced by a historical, a gradualist view: the title of Kant's famous essay from 1784 says it all: "Universal History with a Cosmopolitan Purpose." Sovereignty would eventually become compatible with a binding international order: individuals across the earth would enjoy human rights while everyone's looking after their own profit would end up in benefiting all. Nationalism and liberalism, virtue and profit.

David: That Kantian turn to a virtuous history has an almost religious feel—a philosophy a legal professional can inhabit in the mode of "This I believe."

Martti: I was struck by the way nineteenth-century jurists sounded like the scholastic theologians—although they were far behind in their sense of the needs of pragmatic management. Lawyers were influential in imagining a world divided into two horizontally parallel realms: sovereignty and property. Having imagined them, they had little to say about *how* they should be used!

Not that they did not try. The transformation of policy science into *economics* at the turn of the nineteenth century was the result. Smith thought of himself as a natural lawyer, and *The Wealth of Nations* emerged from years of lecturing on historical jurisprudence. The legal technique of distinguishing between the state and civil society—sovereign power and binding contracts—brought into visibility a whole world of relations that could be called "economic." On the one hand, liberal philosophy would imagine a world of profit-seeking individuals situated in a universal history moving from separation to unity. On the other, the management of this world, both at the level of nations constantly moving closer and individuals busily contracting with each other, would be the task of economics, the nuts and bolts about how to exercise public power in the general interest and how to enable the production of wealth by contracting on the basis of property rights.

David: Meanwhile, what about the order versus distribution/domination frame in the "political" era? Were these legal minds thinking they were devising and building an order? Or, as we sometimes remember this period of absolutism, were they precisely consolidating a hierarchy?

Martti: I find it striking that all those thinkers framed the political world in terms of *law*—namely, natural law. From Grotius to Kant, with Hobbes, Rousseau, and Adam Smith in between, it was natural law that provided their idiom of politics. And natural law was, first of all, about *order,* which they derived sometimes from God, sometimes from human nature, the nature of the community, or some logic of moral words. Its *distributive* role was eventually expressed in the way it identified this or that set of interests or preferences as the natural *rights* of those who held them.

In other words, law intervened in history precisely for framing our ideas about order and distribution. It first helped imagine and juxtapose the worlds of sovereigns and of commerce. It would then manage that interface with constant boundary drawing, allocating rights, powers and vulnerabilities for groups on both sides of the boundary, thus creating the worlds of public and private law as platforms for the struggle between those groups. This was my story of the *longue durée* of European law; operating always inside a new professional-ideological vocabulary to replace an older one. *Theology—politics—philosophy—economy.*

David: Before we leave the story, I want to focus on your phrase "ideological vocabulary." My last book, *A World of Struggle,*[6] aimed in part to illustrate a path for analyzing the role of "ideological vocabularies"—which I called "expertise" in that book—in the political economy of the contemporary world.

To me, the word *ideological* brings with it a suspicion, in Mannheim's sense, that the constellation of attitudes has its foundation elsewhere, in the social position of the intellectuals who developed the vocabulary, their psychological or political formation.[7] Not a coherent totalization to be believed arising from their particulars, but more like a direction of travel, a tendency in their argumentative choices or positions with a genealogy beyond their reasoning. Presumably, they just *had* or *developed* a vocabulary which they thought of as absolute and which *we* label *ideological.* Or were they already aware of the invented or tendentious nature of their vocabulary, understood to be in contention with alternatives they could see were also "merely" ideological in this sense? Back at the start of your story, I imagine the Spanish scholastics seeing their Protestant counterparts as something like ideological—but not themselves.

Martti: I think the moment people listened to theologians and heard "Jesuit morality," they identified a vocabulary as ideological. A really important disenchantment moment and an opportunity for "organic intellectuals." Was not Luther in some ways such? Were they aware of the fabricated nature of their vocabulary? The emphasis Montesquieu lay on what he called the *moeurs* of a people presupposed that the vocabularies of people of temperate zones or hot climates were reaction formations to their environments; they were historical and thus necessary only in a limited sense. But English political economists and French revolutionaries both believed that their ideas were *scientific*—so, not fabricated but true. And they would think that the ideas of other people—their adversaries, typically—were ideological in the sense of wrong and maybe even created in bad faith. That is, of course, a familiar pattern in modern political discourse: my views are true and proven a million times, while yours are an ideology. I don't use ideological in that sense; I merely want to highlight the instrumental rule of a discourse—its order-creating and distributional effects, you might say—while remaining agnostic about its truth value.

David: That takes us into questions of method: How should progressive people think about law in political economy? *To the Uttermost Parts of the Earth* puts some markers on the table that we've touched on already: law as a constitutive imaginative and managerial practice reflecting and bringing into being what we treat as the facts and the objectives of political and economic life. Law caught between the aspiration for order and the practices of distribution and domination. Legal arrangements as the nuts and bolts beneath political and economic practice.

A critical *legal* dimension can be hard to find in the contemporary literature on world political economy. That's unfortunate because—in American policy circles, at least—the term *political economy*, rather than denoting any direct inheritance from the canonical texts of classical political economy, has become a mark of progressive and reformist aspirations. It suggests that markets and governments are part of a larger whole whose structure and functioning can be studied and opened for revision and that economic arrangements are somehow political, contestable, revisable.

The phrase "*law and* political economy" signals the aspiration for a new style of legal analysis, more progressive, more willing to regulate, more skeptical of markets, more comprehensive in descriptive and analytic ambition. To study "law and political economy" indicates a resistance to the complacent and technocratic specialization so common in the contemporary American legal academy. All this is to the good. I think we both share the progressive ambition to consider law's role in the political and economic arrangements of society and to identify points of useful contestation. I think you do too.

Martti: Indeed, that's one of the things I wanted to examine in *To the Uttermost Parts of the Earth.*

David: But as I read the American literature, it is somewhat cramped by its focus on the *nation* and on what a right-thinking American government could do in real political time. In this, the literature is situated *within* rather than against the dominant ideology of the establishment, although the authors probably wouldn't see it that way. At a minimum, the focus on the governing state makes it difficult to extend the analysis transnationally where other arrangements—global value chains, for example—are the predominant organizational form.

No surprise to you, the image of a society overlaid with an effective government undertaking policy in the public interest has no global parallel. Even as a national idea, this is pretty optimistic about the United States. Few societies and few governments, including my own, are really like that. But if you start out focused on what might be done by a progressive government, it is harder to think of inequality or injustice as a quotidian feature of political economic life or the sought outcome of successful struggle. You are likely to see sites of inequality and domination as aberrational—in need of reformist attention—in an otherwise well-organized society.

It seems to go with framing politics nationally and vertically—a government and a polity—that the nation seems a place for action by policy while economics gets framed differently, inertly and, particularly at the global level, as a horizontal field of flows and forces impinging on national political life. All of which makes it harder to get under the hood and see how political economic life is put together legally—although this might be the goal of the inquiry. When law comes into it, the focus has been on law as a regulatory tool of national government rather than as we've been discussing it, a matter of foundations, a mode of imagining, a practice of managing, and so on. All of which raises the question, how could progressive voices get outside these limitations?

So that's what brings me back to method—how to reframe the inquiry with a critical legal sensibility. Let me ask you, is there a mainstream contemporary literature about law and political economy in Europe with parallel aspirations and limitations?

Martti: I am afraid the new critical interest in law and political economy is largely an Anglophone phenomenon, though—like other such things—perhaps spreading. In Europe the same concern—the situatedness of the economy in a "system" or a "society"—has a more well-established place in various Marxist, neo-Marxist, structuralist, and systems theory approaches (Luhmann would be a big name), as well as constructivist legal and political thought. I have been interested in a debate among historians of political thought about the relations between a "juridical" history of statehood (Bodin, Hobbes, Kant) and a more governance-oriented history on virtue, commerce, and the national debt (Montesquieu, Hume, Smith). Reading those two together would be very useful for developing a critical, historically oriented perspective on law and political economy.

I agree that as conventionally rehearsed, the topic presumes the state and a civil society—two entities existing side by side and whose relationship then forms the theme for political debate. And this is supplemented by a whole body of works in "international political economy" written in a political realist vein that operates in a kind of neomercantilist mindset—powerful nation-states plan their economic policies with a view to exercising hegemony, that sort of thing. There may be some little constructivist variation, but it rarely departs from the standpoint of the state. And of course, by far most of this literature thinks of the "economy" or the "market" as natural features of the world, operating under their own (natural) laws—this is the physiocrat legacy. In this world, economic actors have stable identities and utilize law as an instrument of their "will." If the theme of struggle emerges, there is little awareness of how assumptions about legal entitlement affect it. The three styles of modern law—formalism, the social, and pragmatism—make what seem pretty random entries and exits in these texts.

David: Well, that's what we're up against. Let me put some elements out there that I've drawn from the legacies of critical legal studies and the heterodox social theory we were exposed to in the 1970s and 1980s that suggest alternative paths and see if they resonate for you.

A starting point would be a conception of "the society"—whether global or national or local—as an ongoing struggle among groups with different material or ideological interests rather than a society of individuals engaging in economic activity and ruled by a governance system in which they participate. So the dynamics of group interaction—winners and losers, dominators and dominated—would be at the center of the story. Not that groups are always fighting, but the analytic focus would be intergroup conflict over the distribution of stakes.

A focus on groups helps avoid treating the legal jurisdictional units—states, but equally corporations or cities—as the main actors. Groups of people with loosely or tightly shared material or ideological interests can emerge across all these political and economic formations. The vague term *groups* helps avoid the *developing/developed nation* or *international/national* oppositions which otherwise dominate the discussion. Then one can imagine stakes divided among groups that have roots across those lines—sectors in various "nations" who benefit from patterns of oil extraction, for example. Not that groups are organic or primary. They get constituted, come into and fall out of self-awareness as a group, might well map on to more conventional divisions like *developed/developing*. And the analysis that identifies them probably also contributes to their construction. But starting here provides an entry point orthogonal to the more familiar world of nations.

And then one would ask about law's role in the construction of the groups, the production and distribution of stakes among them, the consolidation of gains, and so on. Law as both the rules of the game and open to contestation as stakes in struggle. At the microlevel, one would analyze particular legal ideas and arrangements for their impact on the distribution of stakes among groups with differing interests. At the macrolevel, law's role in constituting the imaginary and factual terrain on which struggle takes place, who the agents are, what their authority is, what the structure is, and so on. At the ideational level, where you were working in *To the Uttermost Parts of the Earth*, the role of law as an "ideological vocabulary" framing and managing the contours of "politics" and "economics," where and when they are separated and related and to whose benefit.

Part of what I found compelling in *To the Uttermost Parts of the Earth* and *The Gentle Civilizer of Nations* was your presentation of law as a kind of knowledge work by an intelligentsia with one or another axe to grind, self-consciously building the system in such a way as to privilege these interests over those, throwing off almost as a by-product a sense for what "society" and "politics" and "economics" are and how they work.

Martti: Yes. But I also like to stress the limits of their building work, the way even when they feel most in control, their minds are actually operating within intellectual vocabularies that enable them to think only some things and not other things. I have always admired how you, David, have written precisely about the way law operates to distribute resources between human groups—but how it does this not instrumentally, through biased decision-making, in ostensibly "neutral" institutions but by structuring the very world of assumptions within which those institutions work. This is what I tried in *To the Uttermost Parts of the Earth* by situating the legal performers in larger ideological frames connected to specific institutions—theology / Counter-Reformation church; politics / absolutist statehood; law / constitutional governance; economy / civil society. Within each moment, law would both participate in setting up the institutional terrain and provide initial entitlements for operating within it.

For critical legal thought it would be methodologically quite fruitful to do as you propose. I mean to abstract from the world image communicated by present idioms (e.g., sovereignty / property) and instead produce a description of the world less infected by some existing interpretation—for example, by using your category *groups* or perhaps the more structural *relations*. This would then enable framing the relations of group members and between different groups by alternative idioms that might bring to the surface relations of hierarchy and subordination that the ruling description makes invisible. Some of such stuff is quite familiar—for instance, framing religious worldviews in political terms—that is, as systems for distributing authority—or political ones as systems for distributing material resources, and so on.

David: It is that terrain-setting role that is so often overlooked. But, of course, it is both—or all of the above. Whether you're thinking of material or more ideological stakes, law's distributional significance is more familiar, certainly to lobbyists and other participants in everyday struggles. People readily understand that legal arrangements distribute when they affect the bargaining power of people or groups struggling with one another, or when they mark the line where coercion will enforce an allocation, excluding others from political authority or economic gain. Because struggle is an iterative affair, people fight for an improved starting position in the next round by locking in gains and defending their dominance as entitlements. In this sense, legal entitlements do mark the fault lines between winners and losers in past struggles and affect the alliances and trajectories for the next round.

And there is a dynamic element. Over time, gains and losses compound as legal entitlements and authority, sparking dynamics of inequality between groups, sectors, regions, and nations. From colonial governance to modern trade and investment, for example, legal arrangements have consolidated the distribution of rents from global economic activity and the political authority of those committed to the stability of that outcome. The challenge is that in thinking about these overt distributional effects, it is easy to lose sight of law's role in commonsense frame setting or world making.

Martti: I suppose one example of this is the consolidation of investment law in recent years—I mean the way it has been constructed so as to define and oppose the rights of the investor against what it defines as the regulatory powers of the state. The way investors are entitled to bring states to account for their domestic laws and administrative decisions has strengthened their bargaining power in a truly remarkable way. And while people usually look at the case law—and note that some cases do go in favor of the state—the real effect of this law is its chilling effect among politicians and government officials—an effect hard to measure—who refrain from enacting some pieces of legislation out of fear for cases or their costs. The vocabularies of "fairness" and the "rule of law" have brought international investors as powerful participants into the domestic legislative and political process. How did those utterly open-ended words receive the meanings they did? Here critical thinking can help a lot.

David: I think that's right. There's the frame "investors can engage governments" and then there are all the tools of struggle between them. Within that frame, certainly, governments (both developing and developed) and investors (local and foreign) have sometimes played for "rules" or for institutional procedures which tend to advantage their material and ideological interests: consolidating or relativizing contract and property rights, strengthening or eroding sovereign powers. But it is often quite difficult to identify the kind of bias that would result had foreign investors consistently outplayed developing governments in the doctrines or institutional procedures.

Amr Shalakany and Svitlana Starosvit have argued, if in different ways, that it is rather a kind of professional background consciousness among arbitrators—their assumptions about what is public and what private, what the remit of arbitration is, and so on—which privileges investor interests over those of host states.[8] For them it is the "ideological vocabulary" of the profession—to use your phrase from earlier—that does the distributing. They identify the arbitral professionals as participants in struggle with an ideological position rather than as "neutral" professional dispute resolvers interested only in their own authority or "legitimacy." Because the key ideas framing things toward these outcomes are background common sense, arbitral professionals may not think of themselves this way at all.

Their point is not that arbitrators reify the *private* or the *political*, elevating one above the other, but, strangely, that they do not. That would be a clear, identifiable bias: public policy over or under private rights. Rather, they understand their vocabulary to be all about managing the boundary and the relationship between *the economy* and *politics*, or *the international* and *the national*, or *the public* and *the private*. And yet, the way they understand these terms frames how those relations come to be managed over time.

Andrew Lang makes a similar point about the professional sensibility of the international trade law bar.[9] They know they are all about managing a set of extremely vague and contradictory boundary conditions between legal arrangements that are "market supporting" or "fair" or "normal" and those that are not. Yet their management activity consolidates a sense for the appropriate differences between these domains which makes their current forms seem both adjustable and inevitable. As lawyers distinguish *market-supporting* from *market-distorting* regulations—or *private rights*, which travel, from *public policies*, which typically do not—they solidify the conceptual and institutional arrangements which keep the global economy and national politics at a distance from one another.

Martti: Indeed, it is precisely that apparent sophistication of modern modes of governance—their "pragmatic" effort to take into account *all* circumstances and provide a hearing to every stakeholder group—that creates its invulnerability to critique, allows it to perpetuate itself.

David: And yet, for all that, foundational things *are* sometimes changed—*To the Uttermost Parts of the Earth* is a story of just that, as is *The Gentle Civilizer of Nations*. There were seemingly small shifts, and then, somehow, while I was driving my Chevy to the levee, my ideological vocabulary died.

Martti: Absolutely. Why I left the structuralist world of *From Apology to Utopia* (though always only in part) to these historical works was precisely to focus on the mystery that even foundations do sometimes change.[10] The succession of vocabularies—religion, politics, philosophy, economics—was for me the visible surface from which to survey that change. Take the eighteenth-century transformation of "freedom": from the old freedom of equal citizens deciding on the fate of the polis to the new one, where everyone is busily making themselves rich and ruling is left to governmental experts; struggles over distribution move from the chancellery to the market. Foundations change as struggles for wealth and happiness move—in eighteenth-century German public law, for example—from a concern about the scientific techniques of sovereign rule to liberating actors imagined to exist in a "civil society," or when Jean-Baptiste Say writes that "foundations of prosperity are independent from purely political considerations" and sketches a number of social "laws" for the study of which he proposes a new science.[11] Instead of nobles, clerics, and peasants, we now see farmers, merchants, and "workers," as well as "producers" and "consumers."

Foundations move when an imperial economy refrains from annexing foreign territory but instead helps it into independence so as to become the principal investor in its infrastructure projects. In every such move law is not only implicated but the very sense of the transformation is given by law. How is public credit organized? Is it possible to imagine a "state" as something ruled by a king? But it is often way more enlightening to see it as an oligarchic arrangement between ruling families for extracting wealth.

David: Focusing on shifts like that could help strengthen our reformist imagination and our ability to rethink the foundations. Existing legal arrangements offer a red thread to identify the effects of (legal) power in global political economy—a map of winners and losers, gains and losses. Once you identify a legal something that allocates a surplus among individuals or groups in political or economic struggle with one another, you can start looking for the other legal arrangements that made this possible, reproducible. If it appears the allocation is a function of a "fact" or "power" you can look for the legal arrangements, ideas, and practices that enabled that fact or power.

The goal would be to identify law's background role in the foundations of political and economic life, in the shape of credit, property, money, capital, labor, citizenship, sovereignty. As you said, law's distributional significance is most pronounced in the way it puts the pieces together in the first place rather than in the way it "regulates" or "administers."

Martti: The principal stakes are determined in setting the conditions of access to the market—or whatever the terrain of distributive struggle (state, corporation, family . . .). A big question in eighteenth-century France was, May nobles engage in mercantile activity without losing their privileges? It took the European powers until the mid-nineteenth century to agree to give up the use of privateers in marine warfare; without a letter of *marque* there might not have been any British Empire.

David: Absolutely. Who gets to play and on what terms? And what's a *who* for this purpose—a merchant, a privateer, a bank, a sovereign? Once you have a map of law's constitutive and instrumental significance for contending forces, you can think about how this works dynamically—once you turn the engine on, if you will. Perhaps we should talk a bit more about the dynamics of political economy. On these legal foundations, how does it roll?

Thinking dynamically takes us to political economy as a "system." Not the conventional system—how the relevant institutions work, and so forth—but a picture that is not obvious or familiar: a system that needs to be discovered, analyzed, and illuminated by intellectual work. In this critical framework, the system is the way things *really* work, beneath the system we imagine around us every day. The *capitalist system* or the *world system* or *financial capitalism* or *racial capitalism* or *structural racism* or *patriarchy* or *neocolonialism* are thought to be underlying systems with their dynamics, lead actors, and plot lines. You and I have both been skeptical about this kind of system thinking, particularly when it becomes dogmatic. I wrote *A World of Struggle* to get away from this kind of structure/agent thinking—seeing claims about "the system" and the "agents" as just that: *claims* made for a reason by a person with a project. Still, taken with enough grains of salt, this kind of system picture can help us say something about how the struggle unfolds—and where to look for the legal enablers.

Martti: So, what you are saying, if I understand you rightly, is that there is a lot of critical power in the effort to think what is conventionally presumed as the "underlying system" as not underlying at all. It could instead be presented as a product of a specific set of political, cultural, or legal assumptions that this type of thinking would project as "merely" parts of the determined surface. In this way it would be easier to abandon the instrumental view of law in favor of a "framing" approach. Once the ruling system explanation has been set aside, at least for a moment, it will become possible to focus on the people or the groups who struggle at the "surface" so as to *redescribe* the conditions that frame their struggle. Such a redescription might then make visible some alternative set of systemic relations. And it would allow asking questions about the nature and significance of that earlier systemic account: How did it operate as "claim," as you put it, intervening in that struggle itself?

David: Yes, that's the idea: to take the "system" notion as an interpretation rather than a fact, a kind of heuristic or alternative framing to help shift from visions of order or equilibrium to foreground struggle and dynamically reproduced hierarchy.

System ideas I've toyed with start by identifying divisions which cross a society characterized by unequal distribution or hierarchy. That gives us a couple of groups to start with that we can imagine to be struggling over their relative power or wealth or authority. They may or may not be groups that see *themselves* this way—the old question of "class consciousness" arises here, similarly for "the center" and "the periphery" or "northern and southern somewhere." But the analyst identifies them and locates the institutional, cultural, or political arrangements that structure their interaction and diagnoses the (unjust) consequences that emerge from these dynamics.

This kind of system analytics usually identifies a default dynamic pattern that is less of balance or equilibrium midwifed by reform and cushioned by guardrails than of enduring conflict generating predictable patterns of inequality. The goal is to identify changes that could alter these underlying system dynamics. Sadly, most of these system theories pretty much leave law out of the account; that's where critical legal thinking can be helpful.

So, to take an obvious example, Marx had a theory like that. To simplify drastically: where capitalists own the means of production, competition among workers allocates the gains from production to the capitalist, alienating the laborer from the product of their labor. Remedy: empower the proletariat to own the means of production. Expropriating the capitalists won't lead to a decline in production; their gain is all surplus resulting from their "ownership." But "ownership of the means of production" turns out to be a complex regime. If we bring a constitutive law into the story, we'd look for the legal arrangements that placed laborers in competition with one another for access to capital more than capitalists for access to labor, for example.

Ricardo also had a theory like that: as the population grows, increasing demand for food brings ever more unproductive land into cultivation, raising the price of food and enriching landlords who hold the most productive land at the cost of consumers facing ever higher prices. Remedy: repeal the corn laws, reduce the price of food, and impoverish those landlords. Impoverishing the landlords won't lead to a decline in production, because their gain is all surplus resulting from their ownership of the productive land. Again here, the legal constructions, both ideological and institutional, which enable this pattern are complex: ownership of the land, the authority of tenant farmers, the market for grain, access to credit, patterns of trade, and on and on—all legally constructed.

Martti: Just to interject, I have been especially interested in the way even earlier theories like that employed nature and natural sciences as their paradigm to speak about a natural or "underlying" system of human relationships—to which lawyers then had better conform. I am especially thinking of the algorithm extending from Pufendorf to Smith that used the optics of natural human weakness and egoism to make cooperation seem compelling as an analytical, and not moral, truth. Nevertheless, when translated into institutional or legal terms, we could see that it was compatible with a wide variety of schemes for distributing rights and liabilities. The idea of a natural or true response to the requirements of nature (or of the economy) was proven an illusion. There were decisions to be made whatever the "underlying" seemed to be. Or, indeed, in eighteenth-century balance-of-power thinking—you can see the naturalist metaphor quite at the surface—that was used by Mably and Vattel to ground a "public law of Europe" with scientific pretensions. And the whole construction was based on assumptions about groups organized in "states" and oriented toward specific types of gain as they entered a world with other such states in purportedly equal terms. Here, like in so many other instances, the explanation of the "underlying system" is received from elements—many of them legal—that the underlying system is presumed to have produced.

David: Certainly, identifying the "underlying system" has a long pedigree—and is often about balance or equilibrium or progressive development. The key, as you say, is opening up the alternative modes of organization—legal arrangements—which give the "system" its shape. The system theories I'm focused on are of the narrower subtype that start with an animating antagonism and don't lead to stability or balance; rather, you get heightened injustice and/or instability.

For global political economy, Wallerstein's "world system" analytics and the tradition of "dependency" thinking in development economics are examples of this type. Both see the world divided between a center and a periphery and identify patterns in the interaction between them which rest on legal arrangements—including patterns of sovereignty and property—that generate and reinforce hierarchy and inequality.

So, conventionally, the global trading "system" is thought to have been put together in a spirit of universal benefit. Liberating trade from national protectionist tendencies is said to enable "gains from trade" vaguely imagined to accrue to all parties. No struggle here other than against the temptation of predatory politics. In that light, it would be in everyone's interest to arrange a legal regime to promote (relatively) free movement while restricting "unfair" or "market-distorting" activity by territorial authorities. There is a critical legal story to be told about the transformation of these ideas into doctrines, institutional procedures, and professional practices to manage that relatively and give meaning to intellectually incoherent distinctions like "market distorting"/"market supporting." Dan Tarullo and Andrew Lang have probably told it best: a professional interpretive practice resting on common sense images of the "normal" regulatory regime that turn indeterminate materials into a regime biased toward the practices of leading players.[12]

Wallerstein and the dependency folks develop a range of hypotheses about the institutional, doctrinal, and ideological arrangements which encourage the consolidation of gains in the center—from legally enabled relative monopoly to elite dependence in the developing world on economic activities benefiting the center. This opens a different door for critical legal analysis: unraveling law's role in the relationships brought to light by this kind of system story—in the constitution of the actors; their relative situation; their animations, powers, and vulnerabilities. The rules that encourage monopoly here, competition there, that enable *these* flows (finance) and impede *those* (people).

Martti: We have seen this in the context of COVID-19, haven't we? The intellectual property system has been constructed in the course of the decades so that the wish to reward "private" and "innovative" solutions led to the medical industries concentrating in the West and the banning of the production of generic drugs in the South under all but the most stringent conditions. As a result, we have come to feel as natural and inevitable a system of distributing health and sickness that is really the product of contingent ideas about public and private, ownership and political jurisdiction. To what extent HIV or COVID-19 has been seen as a health or an economic issue, or public benefits or private rights, has come to wholly dictate the present imagination of what can be done. If there are reforms, they remain marginal and often serve to support the basic background arrangement.

David: Exactly. Or take the European Union (EU). It is easy to see that the EU's legal arrangements set up various unequal dynamics between the financial and industrial centers and the regions at the peripheries. Yet if you ask someone in Brussels, they'll talk about unity—a Europe of citizens with equal rights to engage. And they'll highlight the efforts being made to redress inequalities through various transfer payments, the agricultural policy first and foremost. But they have little to say about the role of European law in creating and sustaining those inequalities. All the capital flows into the center fade from view; that's the result of private action, not government policy.

That is where a critical picture of law's role in European political economy should put in the shovel. How is "free movement" legally designed and managed to encourage dynamics that enrich some regions and impoverish or deindustrialize others? How is a single currency legally constructed to enable some and constrain others? And so on. Rather than seeing these as (unfortunate) natural results of all that freedom, reframe them as legal institutions, the institutionalization of inequality.

Martti: As you have said, it is really hard to work with such general terms as *capitalism, systems theory,* or *neoliberalism,* for example. They tend to obstruct meaningful critical work. I think we are both rather extreme as nominalists—breaking things down to their elements, such as your "groups in struggle." That is one way critique of petrified general terms can go. On the other hand, we do need some such terms to be able to generalize about history and structure, to get away from the trap that it is all about individuals strategizing or group psychologies. I try to remember that language plays a huge role here in mediating between the individual actor and the ideological conditions where that person—the expert—works. After all, it is language—a professional idiom—that often defines the groups and highlights their opposition. But I have also used notions such as *imagination* and *sensibility* to speak in a vocabulary that would encompass both individuals acting and the conditions of their action but would leave a sufficient amount of fluidity for explanatory purposes.

David: I see these system narratives as hypothesis generators: accounts that foreground relationships whose legal foundations may be altered. But they are all stories, after all, told for a reason: to highlight patterns of domination and distributional injustice, linking them to legal and institutional arrangements. They are told *against* other narratives that frame things more benignly—as universally beneficial, lifting all boats, as a benevolent order in which all can participate, and so forth. Told with the aim of identifying constitutive arrangements that might—at least in principle—be changed, even if there is no clear mechanism now to do so. To say "It's a legal arrangement, a legal story, and it could be different, even has been different" is not a policy proposal. There may be no place, no vocabulary, to contest it. But we know that, over time, it could be vulnerable.

Martti: One often-used way to seek to realize what you call law's "progressive and reformist aspirations" has been to insist on the "political" character of the object of one's critique. The new interest, "Let's think about the economy politically," is yet another example. But I am a little dubious about the force or even the sense of this (leftist) gesture. As if there were an authentic realm of "politics"—outside legal technocracy, for example—and as if going to that "place" would solve our problems, we could see what really goes on there. The move seems to follow from a disappointment about older political slogans such as "socialism" that petrify into a series of propositions that were often incoherent, unrealistic, or plainly absurd from the perspective of the original progressive intent. The reference to "politics" seeks to correct that by adding open-endedness and revisability, I know, but I would hope to be able to find some other way to articulate it.

David: I'm on the same page, but I can see how people come to that vocabulary. Feminists, for example, who raised the slogan "the personal is political" *against* a dominant cultural narrative that the personal is precisely not that. The slogan expressed an opposition to the idea that "politics" was the specialized province of people in government with the narrow range of ideological and material interests recognized as "political." In today's technocratic world it can seem that a politics of clashing ideologies and interests has disappeared into expertise and science and the consensus of an elite condominium that stretches from center right to center left, dominating the commanding heights of cultural production, business, and government. Against all that I can imagine thinking it useful to shout "Politics!"

Our field has certainly had its ambivalence on this score. A century ago, I can see why many international lawyers felt one should keep "politics" at bay—there'd been too much of that, and "law" offered something quite different. But I can see how others went the opposite direction: time to rebuild the political, legalize it, civilize it, and so forth. We've both seen the oscillation back and forth as a driver of developments in the field. Where are we right now? I can see how someone might say the problem now is the absence of something called "politics" in a technocratic world—made that way in part by the legalization of everything.

Martti: I can see that. But I still think it often acts like the reference to the underlying system—a stopgap—and induces paralysis, or then acts as an invitation for party hacks to take over.

David: For sure. The key, I guess, is how people imagine "politics." I share your sense that it can be an unhelpful and misleading shorthand. For example, people do use the term to turn from professional expertise to engagement with the clash of interests or ideologies as if one could figure out what is in the interests of, say, "labor" or what the "progressive" position should be without finding oneself back in the soup of expertise. Or, in our field, they treat "politics" as if it were different in kind from a legal professional activity that turns choices into technical and factual necessities—as if statesmen had not come to speak a kind of legal patois.

This explains, I think, part of the appeal of people like Schmitt or Weber and the whole decisionist tradition—Kierkegaard, Nietzsche, Sartre, and so on—for critical voices. In different ways, they frame the political as a personal experience of commitment in uncertainty, even irrationality. For Schmitt, of course, in us/them terms, a taking of sides. Just the opposite of adhering to a preexisting program of action, be it "socialism" or whatever that could be embraced and implemented directly by state power using law. A moment outside, against, agnostic, skeptical—all that.

Martti: I note that you use here the adjective "the political," and I agree with that. The semantics is really important. I know and appreciate the tradition you reference. It points to the way various different things can become "political" in the sense of involving strong feelings, struggle and open-endedness. The need for "decision" is highlighted. But that's quite different from trying to sketch a realm or a space for "politics" that would be juxtaposed to something that isn't it. Statements like "This is law and not politics," "One should keep distinct the realms of economy and politics," "Don't bring politics into the classroom," and so forth. Such statements assume that there is a specific time and place for politics—the parliament, elections, or a town meeting in the evening—where it is okay to act in accordance with feelings and "subjective values." "Struggle" and "decision" would be appropriate there, but bringing it to places where facts and reason should operate—science and technology for example, or law or economics—would be quite inappropriate. When I say that I am dubious about the call for politicizing something, I am rejecting this latter assumption. And I am rejecting it so as to bring to light the ways in which power and hierarchy operate within regimes of knowledge and expertise, the way they are also realms of the irrational, of uncertainty and decision. But I think you would agree.

David: I do; not "the political" as a separate domain but as an experience of conflict, choice, responsibility in uncertainty, which could or should be available in all domains—and certainly in the worlds of *facts* and *reason* and *science*—and, of course, *law*. But the idea that politics is a separate domain, separate language, does shift things—different players, different modes of expertise, adjacent to law or science or whatever. A disciplinary difference that can harden or soften.

In a way, for example, the language of "politics" versus "what's otherwise going on" operates a bit like "reform" versus "more foundational change." There is a relationship between foundational rethinking and the details of everyday struggles, but it is an obscure one. It is difficult, in advance, to know which shifts point the way to more foundational changes. Advocacy muddles the picture when the vernacular encourages hyperbole and a narcissism of small differences: choices that differ only marginally framed as embodying diametrically opposed ideological positions. The opposition "reform"/"real change" functions as a language of contestation—the other guy's project can pretty much always be stigmatized as one or the other. Negotiating drug prices would be socialism, resisting a mask mandate replaces science with superstition—that kind of thing. Paradoxically, this practice also reduces the sense that any reform could actually be foundational.

But one can make progress in unraveling the moments when foundational shifts are forged in more prosaic struggles. Your *To the Uttermost Parts of the Earth* demonstrates exactly this: the knowledge class is inventing this or that to solve something, please someone, advance a project, and a new vocabulary arises conditioning the possibilities for this kind of activity going forward. New foundations then open avenues for new strategies and new conflicts. New players can consolidate a different ideological hegemony, arrange things to reinforce different winners—all sometimes within a relatively short period.

A couple of more recent examples it is easy to forget: the international financial institutions started off supporting capital controls and import substitution industrialization before they became the voice of free movement and austerity. The human rights movement, led by Amnesty International, started off, as its name implied, favoring *amnesty* before it embraced criminal justice as the first response to deviation from its purportedly global standards. Although the EU has always been an ordoliberal affair of free movement, the *how*, the space for local arrangements, the meaning and strategy for social policy has shifted wildly with broader changes in membership and elite ideology.

In our lifetime, the world political economy promoted by the North Atlantic powers has shifted markedly from efforts to stabilize national regulatory capacities and the terms of interstate commerce through governmental and intergovernmental institutions to a global economy stabilized, if at all, by private actors and financial institutions reinforced by the regulatory power of leading national states. If we call any of these foundational shifts, they were made in a thousand identifiable legal and institutional changes.

Martti: I did try to draw attention to change in *To the Uttermost Parts of the Earth*—as you say, both small-scale and larger—but refrained from providing a theory to explain it. A redescription had to suffice. I suppose that we both feel that the frame that conditions international political economy tends to allow only small-scale reforms; I recall you having an article that described endless reform as the very heart of conventional expert work at international institutions. But even without a theory of the larger changes, those that affect the "frame," we do know that they nevertheless—policies of financial institutions or of human rights elites, for example—sometimes do take place.

A notorious example from recent years is the framing of an increasing number of items as matters of "security," with the result of empowering people with military and policing backgrounds and directing resources to their preferred projects. Such "politics of redefinition" is common enough as part of the way expert regimes struggle to expand their authority.

Sometimes when I read your *World of Struggle* I detect a behavioralist or rational choice element that you obviously complicate with social theory and sharp psychological insight. I know you do not believe in the economist idea of reason—nor do I—but once we express our doubts about large systemic propositions, socialism, or Wallersteinian world systems theory, say, the temptation to fall into strategic action formulas may make frame thinking more difficult. This, I think, is where I am led to a historicism that thematizes frame thinking by focusing directly on the performative role of ideological languages.

A consequence of this is that I have come to think more about how social problems or social actors are defined and redefined in the context of legal practice. Surely there is an everyday frame thinking taking place in global governance as lawyers, economists, various technical experts reimagine and redefine what it is they are doing and expand their jurisdiction as they are doing it. But this rarely takes place consciously; more as an automatic effect of their attachment to their field. "A man with a hammer thinks every problem is a nail," as you often say. Perhaps if redefinition were thematized as a technique of influencing the jurisdiction of governance bodies and distributing resources, the political stakes of expert speech could be made more obviously visible. I wonder if something like this could be taught at law schools as an aspect of how law and legal practitioners engage in their social milieus.

This might also be useful to recalibrate the relations between expert bodies and classically privileged political institutions: parliaments, parties, governmental coalitions. Every politically appointed representative today relies on their experts. But expertise is the way of small-scale reform. From education, experts receive attitudes, predispositions, biases. Thinking of experts as the final managers of conceptual systems, operating within learned frames but never really "bound" by the official materials, suggests the need for some intervention in expert training and the production of professional self-image—to make them see themselves as also carriers of ideological projects, normative programs, makers of choice. Studies critical of rational choice type of governance have, since Weber, focused on the concept of "virtue" that I suppose would involve that kind of self-inspection. I am afraid it might not lead to frame thinking but a bland form of professional ethics.

David: Like you, I've been a writer and teacher my whole career, so I guess I do think minds can be opened to other possibilities that way. I'm pretty skeptical, though, about education reform or curricular reform as the royal road to change. Universities are complex, overly administered bureaucracies that cleave to the established wisdom like sunflowers to the sun. Intellectual inquiry goes in and out of fashion in disciplines with real speed, perhaps particularly in law faculties which default now to narrowcasting technical knowledge. On the demand side, open minds are not what most students seek. They come preloaded with the ideology of the establishment, acquired somehow with their mother's milk, and generally want to get better at it. I suppose I've taught more students who have gone on to sustain the status quo—or make it worse—than otherwise.

You mention the endless waves of reform so common in today's global regimes. It is a curious practice. Whether it is the human rights movement, the United Nations (UN), or the EU, this self-regarding impulse to reform is a strange foundation for professional work—constantly adjusting and rebuilding themselves, somehow as if that *were* to engage a problem in the world. That's a different sense of reform from the adjustments in legal arrangements contending forces seek to consolidate their position and defeat their rivals. Those become interesting when they change distributive patterns or shift the foundational premises of the regime. That's why people fight for them. Although I suppose one could say the endless internal reforms are part of a struggle by the global technocratic class to consolidate and insulate their authority.

In any event, that takes us back to the purpose of critical reflection. The kind of critical or heterodox notions we've been talking about in these conversations aim to empower people who do want to go after the foundations, change the society's direction of travel in what they feel would be a more progressive direction. It is exciting to think about—and seductive to promise—to change the world, but mostly I think one walks down this path to understand, to service an internal itch or express an animus. Who knows if it will work, or just be an amusing footnote in some future history of how everything stayed the same.

Martti: Let's say a few more words about "struggle." Both of us have, of course, always stressed the importance of examining the work of legal and other experts—knowledge work, boundary work as you call it—as taking place in a logically (though not sociologically) indeterminate milieu where knowledge systems clash. Many people have seen your use of the term *struggle* as overly dramatic, and not really true—we do see experts negotiate and talk to each other. This is their managerial mode. In a sense, I have always thought that consensus can be understood as a kind of "truce" in the struggle; we negotiate and make ad hoc compromises when we know we cannot win. But as soon as we have developed the capacity for winning . . . Do you think that an expert that views his or her work as "struggle" works differently from the one who does not?

David: I'm not sure. I do think lots of knowledge workers think of their work *both* as struggling for this or that outcome or interest *and* as contributing to an overall beneficial order. It is an odd split-screen sense of what is being done. It is less common for strugglers to see themselves acting on behalf of an ideological commitment or expressing the ideological convictions of a group. Some do, but the professional managerial classes and government types tend only to see *others* as ideological and to frame their own work precisely as *substituting* for struggle.

A footnote on boundary work: what I have in mind is the expert practice of managing the relationship between domains, like public and private or the economic and the political, rather than policing a moat between them. Is trade expertise about free trade? Well, yes, but far more it is about managing the boundaries between free and fair trade, between market-supporting and market-distorting measures, and so forth. So the search for "bias" in the expertise—favoring free trade, for example—is harder to make out.

But back to struggle. You're right that I have tried to reframe the international situation as struggle rather than order—hence the title of that book, *A World of Struggle*. I hoped readers would find it both plausible and useful to see the world as a variegated terrain shaped by past victories and defeats, populated by potential friends and foes engaging one another through a ruthless practice of assertion, at once coercive and persuasive, undertaken in loose vocabularies shared among the world's political and commercial elites and among the citizens and shareholders with whom they are in conversation about priorities and strategies. A mouthful, but there it is.

It's a common opening gambit in critical work, reframing stability as the consequence of struggle and open to revision in struggle. The "truce" idea is key—Foucault titled one of his annual courses "War in the Filigree of Peace."[13] Clausewitz came at it from the other end, in a way—it was the "pause in war" that needed explaining and where all the interesting insights resided. Theoretically, he said, war is like a duel—an absolute opposition in which the action will never stop since it will always be in one party's interest to advance. But there is "friction" and irrationality and the intrusion of "policy." So not all wars need to be fought to be won.

The conventional social sciences also often start with conflict—a Hobbesian state of nature or the competitive market of Adam Smith—and then work to explain how things nevertheless turn out well ordered, through a "balance of power" or "invisible hand." In the more critical picture, struggle and conflict remain constitutive of our everyday world. The result may be stable not as equilibrium or balance, but as hegemony. A truce, if you like.

Martti: We said we'd turn to law in contemporary global political economy before we finished—the postwar order and the legacy of neoliberalism.

David: Right, let's do that. When I started teaching a course on political economy, I looked at the many textbooks on "international political economy." There's a whole field devoted to explaining how the order works, surveying the institutions through which political economic issues are said to be managed on a global basis, from the Bretton Woods institutions down and out to important national players—the "role of central banks," that kind of thing.

This textbook view of the order "from the top" encourages an overestimation of the orderliness of things. Nor is law much in evidence—presumably it's what lawyers do in these settings after the economists and political scientists figure out what is to be done. You get simplifications like "the World Trade Organization (WTO) regulates world trade" when commerce is actually overwhelmingly "regulated" by local and national law, private ordering, business custom, political deals, informal networks, criminal gangs, and so on.

When you try to draw all the intersecting legal regimes that touch on global economic affairs on the blackboard—national, international, transnational, public and private, and so forth—you quickly get something very Jackson Pollack, which suggests that the "order," if it is one, is held together in a far more disaggregated and chaotic way than these books suggest. How did that happen?

In retrospect, the postwar period does seem a moment of self-conscious "political-economic" reinvention—the ordoliberalism of the emerging European Economic Community (EEC), macroeconomic stabilization through the International Monetary Fund, and so on. And then the institutions quickly took different paths, spawned different professions and legal arrangements. The "UN system" for politics and humanitarian projects, the economic/trade institutions separate—as separate as the League of Nations had been from the Permanent Court of International Justice (PCIJ), but not politics against law, but economics (in Washington, DC) against politics (in New York). And all the legal inventions we've talked about in national, private, and commercial law.

Martti: I think there is more than one experience of the postwar era. People came to it from different angles, and the European story is right now subject to intense redescriptions. But it seems clear that the project of the men of 1873, the idea of a world ordered by something like the principles of the domestic conservative-liberal world, was increasingly limited to a UN-oriented public international law that did not really have much to say about the perceived needs of postwar reconstruction. There was a tension between law and politics, received techniques and what were seen as the needs of a changed world.

David: And between the economic and the political: different institutions, professional cultures to manage each; different roles for the legal in each.

Martti: As you say, the International Trade Organization negotiations failed, and from early on the General Agreement on Tariffs and Trade (GATT) took a different direction; still, when the WTO negotiations were finally concluded in the early 1990s, the negotiators tried as best they could to steer away from a *legal* understanding of the result—thus "reports" and an "appellate body." They were scandalized when lawyers nevertheless treated these like judgments and an appeals court.

The oddest thing was, it was only a decade after I had become one of my government's UN lawyers in 1978 that I found out that the government had a wholly different group of lawyers dealing with trade law and, eventually, legal issues on development cooperation. The training and the whole outlook of these people—including political alignments—were totally different from mine. In my whole career as a Finnish UN guy, dealing with General Assembly issues, law of the sea, and so on, I was never invited to give any opinion on a trade or investment treaty or a legal development problem. This was the situation in other European countries too. It has been only in the more recent years that the power struggle between those groups has come to the surface.

David: You can tell so much from that kind of professional specialization. I'm recalling the struggles over the UN's role in development—was development international or national? Political or economic? Well, both and both. So, where to put it institutionally? I've always interpreted the big institutional story as a move from a vision of law and politics as distinct (the League in Geneva, the PCIJ in The Hague) to a more fluid integration of the two in postwar administration and policy—followed after 1989 by the legalization of everything.

Where "economics" stood in that story is less clear.

Martti: I certainly agree that—at least in retrospect—the great move would be from "law" in the League to various more pragmatic and technical, self-consciously innovative institutional projects. This was something that UN lawyers saw as more "political" or "economic" than work within the UN system was for them. More recently the Millennium Development Goals (MDGs) have pushed the UN General Assembly to closer cooperation with the economic and financial governance institutions. Still, lawyers stay aloof from that—in this year's almost four-hundred-page report of the International Law Commission (ILC) there is not one reference to the MDGs.

David: My interpretation has been that in the first half of the last century, North Atlantic legal elites more often seemed to feel it important to distinguish law and politics—there was a case for their separation, for building separate institutions devoted to each. In the second half they more often bled into one another, there was more self-consciousness about their interactions. And then, after 1989, perhaps law became triumphant, as if global politics had ended (along with history). Certainly the rise of technocratic "problem solving" in the postwar period is part of the story, but the post-1989 enthusiasm for adjudication and normative invention, law as universal ethics, and so on, was something different. It is striking how "specialization" in the sense you notice when the ILC disregards the UN's ongoing normative project continues despite this sense of interconnection or fluidity.

Martti: Yes. I think that is the *global* story. But I am interested in the complexity in its European variant that links postwar legal formalism with the very political work of institutional reconstruction: the debate on military organization from the Western European Union to the North Atlantic Treaty Organization, the Council of Europe, the European Convention on Human Rights, the Organisation for Economic Co-operation and Development (OECD), the process toward the EEC. And the fantastic project by the institutions of the EEC to imagine it as a supranational legal system. It was neither "law" in the old League mode nor pure "politics" because it aimed at rather fixed institutional structures. As you say, it was fluid mix of law and political instrumentality.

Many countries—mine, for example—arose from the war with little perspective on the global reorganization. The interest of lawbooks from the 1950s and 1960s was on consolidating the European legal-political frame. Erik Castrén's canonical textbook *Finland's International Law* from 1957 was all about Finland's sovereignty, Finnish boundaries to the east and west, the regime of frontier waters, the legal organization of the peace with the Soviet Union, incipient cooperation with the Nordic countries, legal position of the Åland Islands. If one was not in the European core, then it was national sovereignty, including what role to adopt in global organizations as a neutral country—and the legal status of various forms of neutrality (Austrian, Swedish, Swiss)—that dictated one's perspective.

The Cold War compelled a certain realist conservatism that was also, paradoxically, intensely legal-formalist. Until very recently, I used to repeat the statement of the first postwar Finnish president, Paasikivi: "The Kremlin is not a court of law." You did not reference legal principles when negotiating with the Soviets. But once the contracts had been made, and Cold War policy took its institutional course, everything would be interpreted in strictly formal terms. I had no problem with that mixture of law and politics in 1978 when I joined the foreign ministry's legal department. By the time I left, in 1994, everyone had begun to speak of the "the rule of law" in a way that would have been inconceivable twenty years earlier. That had its merits. But I regretted, and still do, that a certain political wisdom fell aside.

Legal principles articulated political doctrines, so it's hard to say which one was on top. But economics was utterly subordinated. Finland could not even contemplate membership in the EEC; neutrality dictated a balance in the commercial relations between Western and Eastern Europe; trade with the Soviet Union was carried out through a bilateral clearing trade system. Even the plan for a Nordic free zone, NORDEK, was ultimately overrun by Soviet veto in 1970. And yet, this did not mean that the Cold War world would have been all politics. A hard-headed realism required complex legal techniques.

David: It is interesting that a kind of legal/political realism took hold, formalism subordinated to a more eclectic policy assessment, in Finland, within the EEC/EU world, and on our side of the Atlantic—if in quite different ways.

I can see their distinctiveness. Political realism + formalism ≠ McDougal + Manhattan. But still, they are all styles of thought that push your Victorian figures back in time. Linking hard-boiled realism—the Kremlin is not a court of law—with dogmatic legal formalism, in Finland as, I think, in the USSR, is nevertheless different from placing political reinvention and legal reinvention in distinct institutional universes—the League and the PCIJ, for example. As you tell it, they were partners rather than alternatives, and that is akin to the blending of law and politics in the American style.

Over here, there was parallel play across the disciplinary divides. Back to the postwar Hans Kelsen and the John Jackson of the 1970s and 1980s I mentioned the other day. Two quite different characters with different maps of the world and their place in it; I called them "metropolitan" and "cosmopolitan." Yet together they represented a distinctive postwar style that incorporated both a division of labor and a partnership that crossed the lines between public/political and private/economic ordering.

All of that was shifting in the 1990s, to be sure—more confidence in norms and adjudication, less in government/administration, and all the changes we associate with the word *neoliberalism.*

Martti: I think that may be true for the EEC/EU world, but not for the world where I come from. My "postwar mode of reasoning" did not adopt your "international style"; that would have sounded like the "American style" or the "Western style," and quite problematic as such. A part of the elite was drawn toward it, for sure, but a large part, including the official part, was against, for reasons both principled and strategic. Remember, with us, communists occupied a third of the seats in parliament—not that rare in non-Soviet Europe—and often in government. Social democrats were divided (the "great tent"), but many were closer to the Left than the Right.

Your cosmopolitan/metropolitan combination might have existed in some Western European contexts—though it must have collided with *Ordoliberalism* and Christian democracy—but in the "neutral zone" only public law cosmopolitanism was available. A Finnish translation of Kelsen's *The Pure Theory of Law* was compulsory first-year reading in my law school in 1972. Still, in the foreign ministry's entry course in 1978 we were taught—this was really self-evident—that there were three contexts for Finland's foreign affairs: the regional Nordic context, the global UN context, and bilateral relations with the Soviet Union. Trade did not have an independent role, and any idea of economically drawn global governance outside the UN frame sounded like US imperialism.

David: The differences you describe also tell us something about the late lamented *postwar order.* That term—that assertion—unifies quite a range of divergent situations and self-evident propositions about how and where the world is "ordered." And what we now call order was, anyway, quite uncertain at the time. The world was more unequal than it is today, with nonstop proxy wars around the periphery. Elites worried constantly about the uncertainties of nuclear weapons in the wrong hands, feared Soviet plans and capabilities. European empires were in fast retreat, a quite a disorderly experience and uneasy feeling as they were transformed into the center/periphery hierarchies we live with today. The "thirty glorious years" was more a domestic story in the North Atlantic than a world event.

But I can see how all this would be remembered with nostalgia, at least in our worlds. Partly because of the ruptures that hit the "order" in the 1970s and the whiplash of the quick post-1989 rise and fall of Western self-confidence. And, of course, all the wrong turns and disappointments of this century—failed wars, security pursued in all the wrong places, the 2008–2009 economic crisis, collapse of confidence in Western elite rulership. It's a long list. It is hard for anyone in the North Atlantic elite not to be nostalgic for *the idea* of a global order, centered in the North Atlantic, which could be effectively mobilized by bankers and generals, diplomats and businessmen, bureaucrats and citizen activists. Even if we know it was never really like that, the idea is intoxicating—the sort of dream that makes you sorry you woke up.

In the dream, everything seemed promisingly open-ended: anyone could join, participate, and then catch up. Development was available to any country with the right policy, just as liberal democracy might come to any nation with the right constitution. The global consensus and the institutional arrangements it underwrote were open to anyone with the right values. If outsiders could not be assimilated, it was only because they presented existential threats and could be kept at bay through an ever expanding surveillance and security establishment.

I'm sure you can remember how *natural* and *stable* things seemed—even, I would have thought, in Finnish-Soviet relations. The postwar settlements felt *hard won*—the global market rescued from national protectionism; a legal order wrung from intersovereign competition. For political stability to replace war and great power conflict, particularly in Europe, required enormous commitment and effort. There was *no going back*—and lots of ways to move forward, strengthen and deepen and expand and reform. Going back would mean returning to World War II, to the economic catastrophes of the Great Depression, to colonialism or even further back to a world of religious wars. And the order seemed remarkably *resilient*. It had gotten through the Soviet era, absorbed decolonization, the 1960s, the oil shock. It had underwritten and survived repeated global economic crises and wars all around the periphery, as well as dramatic changes in technology, communication, the structure of manufacturing and finance. Why wouldn't it also survive today's challenges?

Martti: I suppose the populist surge and the cliché about "taking back control" is indeed based on a skewed nostalgia; but it, too, must pick its romantic objects differently in different places. (Isn't everyone nostalgic for the time and place of their youth?) There are many memories in Europe, not to say anything about the rest of the world, about which it is hard to generalize. The clichés about the hard work of postwar reconstruction, solidarity with the nation, remembering the sacrifices of the war cover some of that terrain. Social democracy was still strong; a world so well described in Eribon's *Returning to Reims.*[14]

Taking a global view would come only slowly; Finland became a member of the OECD only in 1969, joined the European Convention on Human Rights in 1990 and the EU in 1995. Until that time, it was the UN and the Helsinki Accords of 1975 that consecrated the politico-legal frame within which a non-EU Europe imagined its place in the international world. The focus of today's nostalgia, I suppose, is to the way concern for survival transformed gradually into a concern for welfare—*les trente glorieuses,* as you put it, where one hardly saw much beyond the nation.

You speak in such global terms—Washington, London, Brussels—whereas in my Europe we lived in a much smaller world, getting on with neighbors, thinking about local or regional integration, teaching monism and dualism to students who came to international law; only the UN stood visibly for something wider. Wider and good. People were proud of the Finnish and Nordic role in UN peacekeeping forces and commented eagerly on the new UN convention on treaty law, the law of the sea, and on various territorial questions. The legal status of the Conference on Security and Co-operation in Europe (CSCE) Final Act and proposals for nuclear weapon free zones inspired intense commentary. But the legal system and legal training remained domestic; as it reached toward the international, legal practice was understood in view of a "Nordic tradition"—after all, much of the public law as I began law school still referred back to 1772, the period when Sweden had been a great power. No wonder that when they broached the international, Nordics would always try to coordinate among themselves—bearing in mind the need to remain within the frame of Cold War neutrality.

David: You're right, I have focused on the global—a kind of imperial—vision of world management, world ordering, world legalization. That's how your men of 1873 were thinking in their cosmopolitan European and colonial projects. So also the League people, the PCIJ people—and certainly the postwar American folks. But, of course, these are strange people—Davos people—and most elites were finding their way in relationship to them, oblivious to them, ignoring them, engaging them, joining them, and so on. We're back to our discussion of Arnulf Becker Lorca's focus on the borderlands, the legal intelligentsias of the semiperiphery.[15] He'd include Finland, I expect.

Martti: I suppose so. But it was—it *is*—characteristic of the legal argument that, even when it was made most directly in the "national interest," it was always believed to be in the "international interest" as well. In the semiperiphery of the Nordics, but not only there, one always encounters the sense that there is no discrepancy between the rightly understood domestic interest and the interest of the "international community." But I think the intensity of this feeling is greatest in small countries—Belgium, Netherlands, Sweden, Finland—while in larger ones it tends to collapse into imperial desire.

David: That sounds right for the Nordics, but I wonder if that sense of continuity between the national and the global interest, that pride in being in some way at the forefront of internationalism, characterizes small powers elsewhere. Thailand? Peru?

Martti: The key, I think, is in the assertion "rightly understood" that applies both to the proposed domestic policy and the asserted global interest. For an elite member in any country, including Thailand and Peru, it cannot be useful to stress the degree to which there is a clash between the two. Even a Brexiteer likes to think that theirs is the right policy for every other European people, too.

David: I do think some elites experience a sharper split between their national and their international engagements, as if they were operating in two vocabularies, two cultures of rulership. For others, as you say, there is a continuity—a scaling up of national vocabularies to the world. And, I suppose, often also the reverse—the elite experience of one's local world penetrated by global rulership styles. After all, global institutional and ideological arrangements have always been more significant for the political economy of nations outside the North Atlantic than for the North Atlantic powers which put them in motion. Maybe that's why they so easily evoke nostalgia here. The specialized agencies, the humanitarian and development programs, the peacekeeping—it all takes place outside the North Atlantic. If it is a governance regime, it's not governing the UN's Permanent 5 and the major donor states.

And the regime came to the (nonsocialist) world outside the North Atlantic with *law* more than money or troops. The impact, obviously, of rules promulgated in Washington, London, and Brussels and by the corporations and banks established there. But also legal recommendations for development; legal requirements for receiving funding; legal controls and monitoring and compliance machinery emanating from donors, from investors, from international banks, aid agencies, military suppliers—on and on. I did some work on Haitian reconstruction a decade or so ago and it was the law of "donor states" that mattered, prime among them the Nordics.

And the law that infiltrated so many places in the 1950s and 1960s differed radically from the law of the 1980s and 1990s, which was different again from the law of the early 2000s and 2010s. It differed not only in its doctrinal and institutional details—high tariffs/low tariffs, public law licenses/private law entitlements, legislative supremacy/judicial review—but in *the ideas* about law as an instrument of policy and a repository of rights.

In the first postwar decades a pragmatic and social conception of law's purpose linked with an expansion of administrative and regulatory law, a willingness to reshuffle private entitlements to a greater or lesser extent and a sensibility that combined legislative supremacy/positivism with legal realism. By the 1970s, rights thinking had become more central—earlier legislative and administrative arrangements now experienced as entitlements to be balanced against other interests and objectives. A social conception of law's purpose drifted into entitlements for "basic needs," social and economic rights. In the 1980s the legal vocabulary shifted massively from enabling public power to enforcing a neoformalist conception of private rights combined with a legal policy vocabulary borrowed from second-best welfare economics.

This kind of change in priorities and consciousness—in ideas about what law is and is for—was the work of elites both in the global institutions and across the developing world as generational changes empowered experts versed in new vocabularies they experienced as "modern" and realistic rather than ideological. In the last decades, the shift in "legal thought," if we can call it that, was as important as changes in the economic field, which are usually foregrounded in accounts of the rise of neoliberalism. Neoliberalism—like its predecessor—was an "ideological vocabulary" of governance as much as of economics. Indeed, I'd go further—the short-lived hegemony of neoliberal economic and policy ideas free rode on a foundation of legal ideas which were also in contention with alternatives. Their consolidation as common sense about law in the professional classes was rapid but fragile.

Martti: In much of postwar Europe, the pragmatic and social ideals of law you mention had to grapple also with a traditional type of public law formalism. The "neoliberal" moment affected different legal fields differently, showing the internal contradictions and the flexibility of that vocabulary itself. At home, constitutional law changed from contemplating the formal relationships between the highest state organs into a quasi-philosophical rivalry about preferences to be listed among fundamental rights. A new generation that had followed summer courses on the European Convention on Human Rights or the work of the UN human rights treaty bodies were entering those debates with a wholly different set of ideas about what a constitution is or should be. At the same time, a parallel debate took place about transplanting those lists across polities imagined to exist in a transitional phase in the newly found—but actually quite old—script about societal development. The civilizing mission again. As the Rome Statute for the International Criminal Court (ICC) was being negotiated, diplomat-lawyers honed in UN practices and experts in domestic criminal law found themselves on opposite sides. What were the objectives of the process—peace, or justice? The suspicion between those two groups of lawyers was palpable. Hardheaded professionals were invited to enter a debate on "moral" principles. How could they do that? And, which type of moralities?

New fields such as the law of sustainable development and climate change law were penetrated by economic calculations in a way that made it impossible to deal with them in a meaningful way in public international law processes in institutions such as the ILC, for example.

I remember sitting as a commission member in the early 2000s in one of the screening rooms of the Palais des Nations, listening to geologists and economists lecture on the situation of the transboundary aquifers in Northern Africa and central Latin America. Was the global use of underground water reservoirs really something that could be legislated by generalist experts in Geneva? How meaningful was a global rule that invited its addressees to follow the principle of "equitable utilization" and then listed a dozen potential uses and asked the local regulator to "take them into account"—with the caveat that any other uses or interests might also seem contextually important? Important to whom? And, how was it to be measured?

There is a deeper question here, I think. The conventional reforms usually listed under "neoliberalism" came in the 1990s in two modes: an administrative or managerial mode, which imported various functional techniques, often of a law-and-economics type into law schools and legal practices, and a rights mode that brought with it, as you said, a neoformalism hard to square with that managerial ethos. Neoliberalism was an *Ordoliberalism,* too. Although we now tend to think of that post–Cold War moment in a relatively uniform way, as if it stood clearly for something, I doubt that there was much of a coherent legal project with it. Because it did open up the possibility of legal innovation—rethinking the public/private boundary became easier, for example—its open-endedness consolidated and expanded an already existing global hierarchy. Merely glancing at the inequality statistics of the early 2000s surely confirms this.

David: That's certainly right—far more an open vocabulary of invention than dogmatic program.

Martti: I think—and we discussed this earlier—that the recent turn to history among critical lawyers has to do with trying to liberate oneself from the terms of the reform debate that predominated the post-1989 moment. It became important to think about what preceded it. What other avenues might have been available? Hence the new readings of the New International Economic Order, for example, though I fear that involves too much nostalgia. New studies on the early formation of European law and the European Convention on Human Rights.

I recall how it seemed just a small concession when the "third basket" was introduced in the 1975 CSCE Final Act—and how ridiculous it sounded when the United States and its allies called this a human rights arrangement. Wasn't it about the intangibility of European boundaries? Anyway, Sam Moyn and Jessica Whyte have said what has to be said about the way "rights" broke the way for the neoliberal moment—the move from state-drawn development in the 1980s, the connected instrumentalism of social law to structural adjustment and the market on the one hand, the transport of "light" democracy (the "IKEA model")—everywhere.[16] A neoformalist moment, as you say, but one not averse to pragmatic adjustments, teleology, and managerial balancing. *Neo-* and *Ordo-*. Frankly, the liberal hubris seemed able to suck everything in.

David: A quick anecdote on that. Clyde Ferguson had just initiated a course on human rights at Harvard when he passed away in late 1983, and I took over the spring version he had planned to coteach with a Canadian activist on Jewish emigration from the Soviet Union. As they saw it, rights—and the Helsinki Final Act—were all about the Cold War, pressure on the USSR, what would become the Reagan demand, "Mr. Gorbachev, tear down this wall," although I don't think anyone I knew thought that would ever happen (in our lifetimes, at least). Still, human rights were to be a weapon in asymmetric warfare—along with American television. The struggle to reorient American affiliations in Latin America and then to discipline third world governments alongside basic needs and development programs were just getting going. Of course, the ambition after 1989 was far more robust and universal—democracy was on the march.

Martti: But again, I want to nuance the Western story a little. You tell it as the succession of interwar formalism: dynamic policy orientation in the postwar era; neoformalism with rights, rule of law, and the primacy of the private. This rings true for Brussels, but again, in my little world a public law formalism of German origin reigned until the Anglo-Americans began suggesting that civilized people should be "taking rights seriously." Policy and social law existed in trade and labor law, as well as in the margins of the academy—though surprisingly few had an interest in Scandinavian realism. Until they were taken over by that odd combination of pragmatic managerialism and the neoformalism of rights in the 1990s.

From that moment on, I think it possible to speak of a rather uniform Western legal world. The WTO and the ICC, the increasing activity of the human rights organs, the Security Council "finally working as it should."

The legalistic debate about the Belgrade bombing in 1999. Law and the rule of law everywhere, and the old view that democracy and the market are inseparable and that both are created and maintained by rules.

Now it was also possible to imagine that one was part of "globalization" and, as an international lawyer, a participant in "global governance" that would be something other than state-drawn modernization of national economies. "Transnational law" would focus on boundary work to coordinate international markets with locally preferred social, environmental, or labor policies. Investor protection would check excessively ambitious local regulators. Struggles over distribution channeled into the hyperlegal proceedings of the WTO's Appellate Body and investment arbitration. Alignment of domestic laws by international human rights standards. How closely all this was watched! Trade and human rights, trade and environment, intellectual property rights, and the developing world.

David: In the world of law—as much as politics or economics—we forget how different the "ideological vocabularies" of the postwar period and those of 1980–2000 were. There were continuities, of course—the same institutions, the same ruling professions, many of the same background ideas: on the whole, private rights travel and public policies don't; international trade is arranged among "normal" traders with institutional machinery to enable trade with "abnormals"; governments ought to support, but not distort, "the market" at home and abroad; states are territorial (and cultural/political) while the economy is global (and technocratic).

But a new generation of players shifted the direction of travel, reversed priorities, flipped exceptions into rules. It's a familiar story. After the oil crisis, private banks were in the driving seat for global finance, the relative power of governments and global financiers to influence exchange rates shifted dramatically toward finance, and the exposure of national economies to the trade volatility increased as economies everywhere became "globalized" to a greater extent. Economies were increasingly globalized and "disembedded," to use Polanyi's term. National regulatory power in most states became constrained by internal ideological shifts in the ruling elites and external pressures of various kinds.

In the North Atlantic, it is easy to forget that these changes didn't happen equally for everyone. The expansion of global credit and the erosion of the tax base bound sovereigns in the service of those global investors who benefited—along with the jurisdictions that serviced the massively expanded global financial industry or worked in partnership with it. Enabling the free movement of goods and services weakened the territorial regulatory maneuver room for many public authorities—but not all. Some found their regulatory influence expanded exponentially, newly able to extend the impact of their local arrangements across the world. The transnational impact of public and private rule making by leading firms, nations, cities facilitated the construction of dispersed global value chains depressing returns to labor and leeching the gains from productive activity toward the center.

These things were all victories over alternatives. How much credit goes to foundational shifts in economic, political, and legal thinking and how much to specific regulatory changes is an open question. It seems right, though, that they proceeded in a relationship with one another.

Martti: To be part of all that, in whatever form, as a domestic regulator, financial expert, or trade diplomat, possessing a "gentle civilizing" ethos, was useless. In the new world of law and political economy one needed to specialize: investment arbitrator or human rights expert? Once you had found your place in those terms, you would possess a vocabulary suitable for the new institutional regimes: trade, environment, investment, human rights, security. The "global" character of these regimes meant that they penetrated deep into domestic bureaucracies. To get a job in government, you needed to have taken an Erasmus course or to have an LLM degree from the London School of Economics! And that course would have been given by a succession of specialists delivering a dynamic, specialist consciousness among the upcoming elite. The most ambitious law students would no longer be found in domestic constitutional law—unless, of course, they were prepared to discuss it in terms of global vocabularies of rule of law, good government, and human rights.

International lawyers spoke of the collapse of the old center as "fragmentation," but there was also a transformation of the platform for struggle and the stakes. The specialist regimes were as much about distribution of resources and priorities—political projects—as cognitive structures. The official idea was that they would wage their distributive struggles in the open platform of globalization, while the acceptability of the process would be guaranteed by liberal rule of law principles: openness, legitimacy, accountability. This then would be not just globalization, but "global governance." This, it now seems to me, is the Western—or North Atlantic, as you say—international legal sensibility in nutshell.

But this way of thinking was to imagine these new regimes or institutions as billiard balls, identifiable clusters of preferences, to be sent to the arena to clash against each other: trade versus environment; security versus human rights; investment versus domestic regulation. In fact, none was ever quite that stable inside. Each has its orthodoxy and its heterodoxy: the regimes themselves are places of struggle between differently thinking specialists in a field. Here is where basic assumptions and the fuzziness of the cognitive world of today's law and political economy becomes obvious.

Some of this is, I suppose, captured by the reemergence of the vocabulary of "transnational law" that would extract legal professionalism from its chains in old public law and sovereign statehood. It would enjoy authority both inside and outside territorial boundaries and give specialist expression to the economic, social, and technological "processes" we call globalization. The notions of property and contract, for example, would have to be made compatible with the requirements of security, digital technology, private-public networks, production chains, and other aspects of a "transnational arena." This has had a huge impact on views of what it was to be a legal professional.

Was this still neoformalism, or neoliberalism, or something else? Both of these transformations have clearly benefited the Global North, which houses the places where these kinds of expertise are transmitted and the centers of the many networks lie. I think this post-1990s moment is much less conscious of any ideological program than its earlier version was. It presents itself as science and knowledge. And yet, it is heterogeneous, the experts clash, and the clashes are the visible surface of the way we are governed—one result is the "populist" outrage. Instead of homogeneous knowledge, there is struggle, but the terms of that struggle exclude as incompetent most of those who are affected by its results.[17]

David: That's a crucial observation: the professional project and sensibility of the contemporary moment is inhabited more as expertise than as ideology or program. What followed the chastening of the neoliberal vocabulary is self-consciously nonideological—*professional, scientific, expert,* although those terms mean different things and are institutionalized differently in various regimes, as Sheila Jasanoff has chronicled.[18]

Looking back, people also overestimate the continuity, rigidity, and comprehensiveness of "neoliberalism," treating it as an enormous institutional and ideological wet blanket over things from 1980 to the present. They tend to ignore the legal/governance dimension and underestimate the open-ended and conflicted managerial practices through which political and economic life took shape during this period. Quinn Slobodian's work is helpful here, demonstrating how extensively the original Mont Pelerin Society intellectuals who "invented" neoliberalism were invested in governance.[19]

Martti: Well, Hayek's three-volume *Law, Legislation and Liberty* was an important reminder of the centrality that law plays in that world of assumptions and proposals.

David: We've been talking, if in our own elusive way, about the role of ideas—particularly legal ideas—in the global political economy. I think we've been trying to avoid the tendency, so common now in progressive discussions, to frame the global political economy in ideological and world-structural rather than institutional and legal terms or by reference to the professional sensibilities you're describing. "It's a world system run by an ideology"—that kind of thing. If there is a world system—Wallerstein was quite clear—it is *institutional.* The structural mechanisms are legal. If there was an "ideology," it was expressed in legal—as well as economic, political, and so on—terms and it shaped and was shaped by legal ideas.

So, what was "neoliberalism" anyway? Maybe we could conclude this conversation with that. People lump together policy preferences; economic, political, or legal verities; and rules of thumb that became hegemonic. If you are outside looking in, the "ideology" seems like a cult of zombies. But in this technocratic world of professional management, it's not lived like that. What are the indicia of a lived ideology? Or the grounds for asserting that someone else is in the grip of an ideology?

We've talked about the blind spots and biases of professional good sense—things that are not seen, costs not noticed, arguments one can't make in the accepted vernacular—and the consciously held, widely shared attitudes, analytic moves, favorite arguments that seem decisive or need no refutation, accepted starting points for debate, all of which could be contested but turned out not to be. Beyond that, a group will typically share some foreground commitments or default position they'll argue for even when their opponents think they're falsifiable or being held too tenaciously. Their "ideology" is relational—a taking of positions on a shifting terrain against opponents, real or imagined, whose "ideology" is understood to pull in the opposite direction. Both they and their opponents will call one another "ideological" but they won't see themselves that way. They'll each think it right thinking.

The terms of differentiation might be alternate policies or rules—or more abstract positions or commitments. They may be things everyone thinks are "naturally" distinct but that turn out to be distinguished through judgment or political choice that could go in various ways—like public and private, or "market-supporting" and "market-distorting." Again, they'll each think their judgment is soundly based on a natural difference; their opponents won't. We could add abstract principles and magic formulas—general propositions asserted to defend more specific policies or choices through lengthy, but weak, deductive chains—and enchanted tools, those favorite policies promoted absent evidence or clear analytic connection to expected benefit.

People talk about neoliberalism in all these ways. There was a lot of coherence in the original ordoliberal/neoliberal vision. Those first theorists waxed nostalgic about a nineteenth-century global spirit of free trade and the commercial arrangements of the hands-off central European empires—a rulership consciousness before the rise of a sense that governments were responsible for and ought to manage national economic affairs, which the neoliberals associated with the word *social.* They meant to reestablish that (imagined) nineteenth-century sensibility *institutionally* at the international, as well as the national, level. That's how you get the GATT or the EEC.

But an institutional and professionally managed idea is different from a historical interpretation; it has to be operationalized in a thousand details and struggles. If we turn to the operation of law within a "neoliberal" governance variant, we find all these complex managerial practices. So, not a legal wall between national regulation and transnational commerce but a profession that understands every economic activity to require a governance foundation. Which takes us back to things like the legal distinction "market-supporting"/"market distorting," understood as a plastic vocabulary of advocacy and compromise—like "free trade" and "fair trade." You end up with law as both a plastic managerial tool and a neoformalist counter-project to uphold the entitlements of particular groups. And as a hyperbolic vocabulary of assertion and resistance in both directions.

So you get these strong statements by some that the GATT or the WTO or the EU won't permit us to regulate this or that, *alongside* a professional awareness that the texts of these treaties and their adjudicative practices are—or might be said to be—far more open-ended. Alvaro Santos traces this in Mexican government trade law practice, crediting a combination of professional incompetence and ideological commitment with a marked tendency to exaggerate the constraints on Mexican regulatory power.[20]

I guess you could say the approach we've been talking about starts here, with the professional practices and institutional details through which struggles over political and economic advantage are waged, won, and lost. You need to start with a sense for the winners and losers you care about and look for the mechanisms and practices that aid or retard their gains. A map of the many institutions and the managerial practices that structure the terrain is a guide, the legal details a red thread for tracing moments of domination, exclusion, or empowerment. Anyway, that's how I come at "law and the political economy of the world."

Final thoughts? Or shall we stop and have some coffee?

Martti: Maybe just to remind ourselves that "neoliberalism" employed a few rather nineteenth-century assumptions about the economy and the role of law. The values that bound together Austrians such as Hayek, Mises, and Schumpeter, for example, were broad enough to underwrite very heterogeneous policy proposals that often worked on rather "gentle civilizing" assumptions about decency and the rule of law—often of natural law.[21] The more the scientific urge took over, the less policy relevance would professional economics have. In the end, it became part of the polemic about distributing rights and status and competences and vulnerabilities where the language of law often framed the available alternatives.

Throughout these conversations we've been examining the role of law as a profession and as a language in the complex struggles of order creation and critique, distribution, and imagining pasts and futures. We have agreed that there is no space uninfected by "ideology," or by background rules and assumptions that create the sense of what can and what cannot be asserted and provide legal arguments their direction and power. My own historical studies have suggested that while the profession has had its ups and down, and its perspective has shifted internally, law is likely to continue as a tempting vocabulary for asserting authority and consolidating—and, hopefully, critiquing—established hierarchy as well. An "economic way of thinking," just like a theological or a political way of thinking, embodies more or less well-articulated ideas about rights and duties, powers, and liabilities in a way that highlights the resources available in legal thought and experience for the processes of governance. A critical view of law, it seems to me, to take on your two points, comes in handy to reveal those blind spots and biases that frame "the professional good sense" under each such way of thinking and reveal the constructed and contestable nature of what they bring forth as simply natural. At least that's the assumption that keeps me doing the stuff we do.

And now let's have that coffee.

Notes

1. Christine Desan, *Making Money: Coin, Currency and the Coming of Capitalism* (Oxford: Oxford University Press, [2014] 2015); Katharina Pistor, *The Code of Capital: How the Law Creates Wealth and Inequality* (Princeton, NJ: Princeton University Press, 2019).

2. Koskenniemi, *To the Uttermost Parts of the Earth.*

3. See, for example, Kennedy, "Law and the Political Economy of the World"; and Kennedy, "Law in Global Political Economy."

4. Koskenniemi, *The Gentle Civilizer of Nations.*

5. "Case of Ship Money," *Cobbett's Complete Collection of State Trials,* vol. III, T.B. Howell ed. (33 vols), (London, Hansard: 1809), 826; see also Koskenniemi, *To the Uttermost Parts,* 608–611.

6. Kennedy, *A World of Struggle.*

7. Karl Mannheim, *Ideology and Utopia: An Introduction to the Sociology of Knowledge* (Louis Wirth and Edward Shils, trans., Mansfield Center, CT: Martino Fine Books, [1936] 2015).

8. Amr A. Shalakany, "Arbitration and the Third World: A Plea for Reassessing Bias under the Specter of Neoliberalism," 41 *Harvard International Law Journal* 419 (2000); Svitlana Starosvit, "Managing the International Investment Law Regime in the 21st Century," SJD diss., Harvard Law School, 2022, on file with the authors.

9. Andrew Lang, *World Trade Law after Neoliberalism: Re-imagining the Global Economic Order* (Oxford: Oxford University Press, 2011); Andrew Lang, "International Lawyers and the Study of Expertise: Representationalism and Performativity," in *Research Handbook on the Sociology of International Law* 122 (Moshe Hirsch and Andrew Lang, eds., Cheltenham, UK: Edward Elgar, 2018).

10. Koskenniemi, *From Apology to Utopia.*

11. Jean-Baptiste Say, *Traité d'économie politique,* vol. 1 (Paris: Crapellet, 1803), ii.

12. Daniel K. Tarullo, "Beyond Normalcy in the Regulation of International Trade," 100 *Harvard Law Review* 546 (1987); Lang, *World Trade Law after Neoliberalism;* Lang, "International Lawyers."

13. Michel Foucault, "War in the Filigree of Peace: Course Summary" (Ian Mcleod, trans.), 4 *Oxford Literacy Review* 15 (1980).

14. Didier Eribon, *Returning to Reims,* intro. George Chauncey, trans. Michael Lucey (Los Angeles: Semiotextes, 2019).

15. Arnulf Becker Lorca, *Mestizo International Law: A Global Intellectual History 1842–1933* (Cambridge: Cambridge University Press, 2015).

16. Samuel Moyn, *The Last Utopia: Human Rights in History* (Cambridge, MA: Belknap Press of Harvard University Press, 2010); Jessica Whyte, *The Morals of the Market: Human Rights and the Rise of Neoliberalism* (London: Verso, 2019); Günter Frankenberg, "Constitutional Transfer: The IKEA Theory Revisited," 8 *I-Con* 563 (2010).

17. See, for example, Koskenniemi, *International Law and the Far Right.*

18. Sheila Jasanoff, *Science and Public Reason* (Abingdon, UK: Routledge, 2013).

19. Quinn Slobodian, *Globalists: The End of Empire and the Birth of Neoliberalism* (Cambridge, MA: Harvard University Press, 2018).

20. Alvaro Santos, "Carving Out Policy Autonomy for Developing Countries in the World Trade Organization: The Experience of Brazil and Mexico," 52 *Virginia Journal of International Law* 551 (2012).

21. Janek Wasserman, *The Marginal Revolutionaries: How Austrian Economists Fought the War of Ideas* (New Haven, CT: Yale University Press, 2019).

CONVERSATION SEVEN

Concluding Thoughts, Open Questions

David: We've come to the end of our conversations. Looking back, I'm struck by how much remains to be figured out. Four decades of work, and somehow we've just scratched the surface. Meanwhile, the world has changed and those with a critical impulse aim at different targets, draw on different intellectual resources.

Martti: You are right. Although the critiques we learned in the 1970s and 1980s still have a bite in a general sense, they often fail to illuminate the stakes in the present global struggles or offer pointers to where—in which themes—critical attention would be most needed today.

David: In my experience, many people who come to "law in global affairs" with a critical impulse now have more substantive or subject-matter-specific concerns than we did, or concerns more rooted in an identity they experience as outside or under the way the world is run. There are those whose critical animus was lit by a general disillusionment with contemporary governance or a leftist/progressive politics, as we were, but those things are also quite different today. Governance is different, the leftist/progressive intellectual world is different. Overall, the mismanagement of particular issues—the environment, development, even war—has been secondary to our general interest in legal rulership. And we are, after all, white men in the North Atlantic center, critical of mainstream legal reasoning and management from somewhere inside. I know that where I've tried to contribute to feminist and third world critical projects, for example, it has been from within that perspective.

It might be useful, by way of conclusion, to revisit our six themes and quickly sketch what looks different, what we don't yet understand, what work remains to be done. We probably won't be so adept at seeing what we don't see, but let's give it a try.

Martti: And maybe express along the way some tentative preferences of our own. That makes sense, so let's do that.

David: *Okay, our first question: What is critical practice?*

We said at the start that the critical impulse arises and takes form through intellectual influences—particular literatures or teachers—and out of a generational situation, as well as from personal experiences, identities, commitments. So an obvious question would be, aren't the influences and the generational situation different now? We'd probably be the last to know, but it's important, I think, to affirm the obvious: nobody today is starting where we started; it's exciting to see what new influences and critical animosities can generate.

For example, I know a lot of people who are drawing on science and technology studies to understand technocracy and the practices of expert power, a literature that wasn't around when we got going—although we both felt Kuhn had been important. I'm sure there are others, people taking their cue from queer theory or racial capitalism or "world histories." And then, what is the generational problem now, at least for people in our transnational and North Atlantic elite world? Is it economic insecurity? The poverty of public power, big questions like that? Or are there particular things, like Vietnam was for me, that get people going? Global warming? War in Europe? And what is the thing that people are tilting against here? What do you think?

Martti: Well, as you said, we began these conversations by contemplating how elusive our methods were at the time when we came in, and stayed on. Nevertheless, the political and intellectual situation was pretty clearly divided into left and right. And both of us went with the leftist critical canon, the Frankfurt school, Foucault, poststructuralism. Plus, at least for me, the linguistic turn.

David: Absolutely, for me as well.

Martti: Now I am not sure one can say the same of today's critical innovators. It seems to me that the Left and the Right are much more mixed up today; themes that used to belong firmly to one or the other move across that divide. "Rights," for example; "identity" or the environment. Each has its left and right version so that it seems hard just to commit to a theme and to rest assured that it is not captured by the opposite side. The blurring of class is another example. In the 1970s one tended to hear the call for a united front between students and workers. Nothing of the kind would make sense today.

David: I do think left/right remains pretty central, if in different forms. Of course, there are lots of political cultures which have a completely different set of poles—rural/urban, North/South, or religious differences, or "modern" and everyone else, that kind of thing. I suppose one might say that the "center versus everyone else" or "elite/establishment versus outside identification" is more salient. And obviously, the question of identity and its role, so national identity, gender identity, and so forth—both to champion, in the mode of "gay," and to interrogate, in the mode of "queer"—has become far more central.

Still, in our worlds and in the global world, something like left/center/right does seem orienting, orients the choices within these different positions, just as you say. So there's a left and right "human rights" or "populist"/"progressivism" or "gay identity." For example, you have both the Left and the Right divided between identity *as* the critical practice and the *critique* of identity as the critical practice. And on the right you have the critique of nationalism and the idea of nationalism as the orienting idea of what is to be conserved. All of these big divides, on what culture is, what cosmopolitanism can be, and so on, also do somehow track something like left/center/right.

Martti: I was thinking of left/right as the rhetoric of the "socialism"/"freedom" dichotomy. That seems to have no purchase today—a welcome development, surely. But although I agree that the left/right distinction still usefully indicates general sensibilities or attitudes towards the world, it is blurred by what I find is a novel *ambiance* among the new generation. I came across a study recently in which some youth group in Europe was interviewed about its expectations about the future. Twenty-five percent expressed the opinion that they don't think that humankind will survive. One-half had a generally really negative view on the future. Now that's really different from the 1970s and 1980s. I grew up in a hyperpoliticized environment; everything was political and much was possible. As students we were all the time on strike, and with quite radical demands. I am not idealizing it; the atmosphere was quite oppressive, too, and there was little space for neutrality. But at least the privileged critics thought that change was possible. But if the new generation really has such a pessimistic view, that must have a huge effect on the view of what they think law *can do* or what it can mean to be a critic. One may have to give up hope that conventional vocabularies could ever be used to push fundamental change; I suppose Europe's "extinction rebellion" captures this sentiment. But it involves only a very small group of activists. How could it not become just another Occupy story?

David: Yeah, I think the students I teach, even though they're very elite students who are destined for rulership, seem to have internalized that there's nothing they can do about the situation. That foundational change is needed but impossible, and what they need to do is find a good job and a house on higher ground in the suburbs somewhere. That is, they need a career, not a critique. I understand that impulse.

But, of course, there are others who have the critical itch—it's always interesting to talk with them about how it arose. Part of what opens a door to critical thinking is disillusionment with reform, with the available channels for oppositional energy in available institutions. From that perspective, one would think that generational negativity, as you called it, would yield platoons of critical folk. I remember Derrick Bell saying you could only begin acting when you'd abandoned hope; as long as there was hope, well, let's wait and see . . .

You do find that activist critical animus, of course—particularly in folks who come at, or into, the elite culture of rulership with a sense that their identity position is or has been marginalized, ignored, oppressed. Perhaps because they have something to affirm beyond fitting in. And also among those who think of themselves as some version of "progressive" or "on the left," or those whose experiences *in* rulership have left a bitter taste.

Martti: Identity was always a troublesome issue for the Left, the way it tended to look away from structures of inequality. I remember Dan Danielsen and Karen Engle inviting us to move "after identity" already early in the mid-1990s.[1] Sure, race and gender are powerful leftist themes; but the Left never had a monopoly on *whose* identity would be the cultural focus. This was a much more slippery terrain that human rights people, for example, originally believed. Nobody shouts louder about rights violations than far-right pundits about how their right of free speech has been curtailed by political correctness at universities, at companies, and in the public media. Maybe this is one aspect of what we spoke about earlier, that different vocabularies tend to be split against themselves. It's not the case that simply by enlisting as a member in a rights project you can be certain of advancing a critical project. Almost any vocabulary can be hijacked for contrary purposes; one has to be constantly alert to the real effects of the actions of one's group.

David: In one of our conversations, you said that there is an "embedded conservatism" in the situation, against which both the Right and the Left are tilting, both in their mainstream understanding of things and in their critique of that. It's just that the embedded conservatism they see is quite different. At least in the United States, from one angle, what's embedded looks like liberal cultural and political hegemony, while from another it looks like a gridlock of economic and political forces impeding wise rulership.

When I looked back at our conversation on critical methods, I was struck that we had relatively little to say about the whole domain of the irrational and passion, their role in animating critique and empowering that embedded conservatism, if you will. We kept coming to it by dismantling the rationality of the operation, but what is actually the structure of the unconscious? And then completely the opposite idea: What is the structure of, you know, racial capitalism or financial capitalism or global inequality and so forth? So, a very material kind of thing, a nuts-and-bolts object to try to unpick which would be supported and engaged by the ideational surround we were primarily discussing, but which also had its more material side.

In some way we've been strung between these two stools, creeping up to the irrational, creeping up to the material, but keeping our distance. There was certainly something to be gained by keeping them at bay, but perhaps it would be good to spend some time there.

Martti: The root of the critical lies surely in a passionate reaction to injustice, and the intuition that conventional vocabularies fail to deal with it, may even assist to perpetuate it. But I wonder to what extent we have any definitely legal—or critical legal—contribution to make to dissect it. A psychological or psychoanalytical analysis of professional vocabularies, for example; what would that look like? I suppose it is possible to imagine or assess performative techniques designed to awaken that sense of injustice, the way a passion opens up once the critique of reason has done its work. But how, then, to engage with it—beyond the acknowledgment of its presence—is what I find hard to imagine. Translating something into critique tends to rationalize that something. We once debated the issue of the "killing of the innocent" by nuclear weapons in these terms; I then suggested that law is powerless to touch that theme beneficially because if it tries, it makes such killing seem somehow rational and thus thinkable—while you were arguing *against* the view that there could be any alternative vocabulary to maintain such taboo.[2]

David: I remember that debate. I still default to suspicion of "outside" positions beyond rationality or legality, invocations of something more real, ineffable, sacred, or whatever. But I wasn't for legally reinforcing the taboo either. As I recall, I urged lawyers not to develop normative arguments to restrain nuclear powers but to engage in relentless critique of the strategies of justification that are developed—all the ways such killing is brought within the plausible.

Martti: But my fear is that entering the justification game will not work, that it will always make some killing appear the justified thing to do. On the other hand, to come to your second point, I agree that material or empirical analysis of the nuts and bolts of capitalism, and so on, is surely needed, and that the kinds of critical avenues we have followed do not lead there. Perhaps leaving them aside is the cost we pay for concentrating on the framing aspect of legal analysis. This leads into formal, abstract, and conceptual maneuvers that stop at the door of the empirical. Though it does not, of course, prevent us from using empirical materials others have produced and being suspicious of materials that purport to present themselves as "real" because that is how they are asserted, so that other people will yield to the conclusions they suggest.

David: Certainly, on the material side, law plays a big role. You know, like turtles, it's law all the way down. I think we could say something similar on the irrational side. Isn't the unconscious "structured like a legal regime," to adjust the Lacanian aphorism? Lots of postmodern feminists thought so—thought the body was as well. The machine of desire doesn't just "use" law to achieve its ends, but attaches itself to legal forms and forces. I mean, "sovereignty" is also a passion, a desire, a fetish. I remember Nathaniel Berman saying that even formalists had a fantasy life—which was integral to their "rationality." He has continued to place the irrational, the passionate, at the center of his research.[3]

Even the textual surface of law, if we can call it that, is a pretty irrational terrain. I remember trying to figure out how a text—the League of Nations Covenant, as they called it—could "constitute" an institution; what were the workings of progress and transformation that were operating there. What work elisions and chronologies and allegory and so on perform. A pretty mysterious alchemy.

Many years ago, I taught a course on sex, violence, and religion—things which were excluded from law in one or another way, the erotic, the sacred, the violent. And the further we got into the literatures of their difference, the more there was a deeper relationship with law to be explored and a kind of reciprocal patterning between those aspects of the human situation and the legal world, so I'm not so confident that we lack what is needed to explore the irrational a little bit more.

Martti: I do understand that important elements in the legal vocabulary come with an ethical overload that then incites both passion and taboo as they are broached. You mention "sovereignty"; one could add things from the rights repertory as well as from international criminal law. We both resent it when legal performance takes the emotional turn. And I often wonder about the strategic sense or value of such performance, often hovering between the defensive and the cynical. I have a hard time imagining what other way there might be to approach the moment when the legal turns into the passionate or the irrational . . . Sex, violence, and religion sounds a little bit too 1990s to my taste, maybe . . .

David: Well, actually the 1980s—so maybe I was ahead of my time! Anyway, I didn't follow up. Perhaps it felt too hot to touch—or too far afield to repay a dilettante's attention.

But let's turn to our second theme: What is "international law" as the object of critique? Here's a first thought: it was a lot easier to imagine international law as a discrete field with a particular canon forty years ago. The "classics" are really gone. Building a canon to tilt against now is more about identifying a professional world—arbitration, say—and its modes of analysis than picking up a well-thumbed set of classic texts. Or perhaps starting with a technology or a situation and working out from there.

I also find it harder now to think of the professional projects of "international lawyers" as worthy objects for critical reflection. Law in global affairs has exploded—just mapping it is quite a challenge—and the little world of "international lawyers" seems less useful as a doorway into global rulership practices. What do you think?

Martti: I am not sure if you can say the classics are really "gone." It may look like that from US law schools. But in the German and French context, "classical" names like Kelsen and Lauterpacht, and Scelle and others, are still intensely debated and students are expected to read the Collected Courses of the Hague Academy. The same goes for many Latin American academic institutions I am aware of. Which means that critique must go there, too. But you are right that alongside that cultural tradition, a number of new legal vocabularies have surged in the recent years that are much more attuned to the technology of governance without similarly big names for others to follow. Nor do terms like *transnational law* and *global law* associate with philosophical systems.

A couple of years ago I took part in a project sponsored by the European Union (EU) on "cyberdiplomacy." In the United Nations (UN), sovereignty had emerged as a major theme in the debates, and the initiators felt that one needed to begin by examining how the laws of sovereign statehood would be relevant in the cyberspace. But after a couple of meetings no progress had been attained in operationalizing the word meaningfully. It was a stopgap. There emerged no practical way in which the variety of interests involved in the global management of information and communication technology (ICT) could be meaningfully framed within international law.

My sense is that in this matter, as in many others, lawyers will eventually learn to coordinate their work in pragmatic terms. They cannot be identified as "international lawyers" in the sense of the 1960s. But as they will seek to further their different projects, significant allocations of power will once again sink into invisibility as aspects of technocratic governance, invulnerable to political contestation. "Cyberlaw" will be an offshoot of the business of security because that's how the hegemonic actors view it—and not of, say, part of project of bringing ICT capabilities to the Global South.

David: You're right, of course, that the traditional and conventional world of "international law" also survives, offers jobs, innovates in the way it or they grapple with things—coming up with frames like "fragmentation" or "specialization" and so on. But where to place it on the canvas of global legality? I was taught that it was a relatively distinct field, foundational for all the others. That was delusional even then, but more so now. Some terms from the vocabulary do seem foundational—*sovereignty,* for example—but as you've shown, only if understood in a relationship with property and as given meaning by a range of adjacent vernaculars—economic, political, theological, and more. It is even less plausible now that international law per se should be the whole rather than the part.

I suppose one could argue that the field retains, perhaps at least in Europe, a semipermeable boundary and the self-constituting procedures that make it one system in a greater plurality, but that also seems too neat. Often "international law" is a *position* in larger debates, one pole on one or another axis of differentiation.

Nevertheless, you're doubtless right that there is still something to be gained by looking at legal rulership through that porthole. I imagine it more like finding one pot or iron belt buckle in an archeological dig and trying to imagine a culture. You know you're starting with a fragment and your analysis is a creative interpretation. I know we sensed that as well, but forty years ago it did seem plausible to pretend otherwise—to hold up "international law" as if it were a discipline, a distinct field.

Over the years, you've been more faithful to the international law tradition. I've been more the dilettante, I think, coming at legal rulership from various fields, institutional practices, and projects. More jumping around than comprehensive picture. There's still a lot to be explored in that style: other adjacent professional worlds, other strange artifacts in the dig.

We also both worked from texts and from our own professional experiences. Others are finding different starting points, often more "material" or "technological" than textual. Maybe rather than starting with professions or canons, one should begin with an arrangement that brings them together—a "project," say—as the foundational unit for analysis. Or perhaps more attention to what international law—or legality in global affairs—has to do with *culture:* culture as an idea, as a practice, and so on.

Martti: So many things that remain open, or obscure, things we believe we know only because we can pin a label on them—*sovereignty, fragmentation, problem solving.* I suppose I see them as introductory gambits in some language game, perhaps as platforms on which certain themes can be foregrounded at the expense of other themes. *Legal imagination, legal consciousness,* too, or *culture.* I see some value in the way the vagueness of the world is met by the vagueness of the analytical vocabulary. Both of us have examined law not as a "thing," out there to be discovered, analyzed, and resolved, but from a phenomenological perspective, an experience that people encounter—especially an experience of power or weakness.

A word on "fragmentation." I want to stress that the little functional balloons are never sealed against each other or coherent in themselves but rather themes or platforms over which centers and peripheries get formed. Nor are they "things" as much as vocabularies and contexts for asserting and yielding to claims. As you say, we do not have a good sense of how they work as such. But it does seem to me that a lot of what used to be political politics nowadays takes place within and between those, as a politics of knowledge. It's not that there are coherent islands in some sea of single ideology; the islands themselves are experienced as places of contestation in a way we'll find familiar from past contestations. A "regime," after all, is like a "state" with its external boundaries and internal divisions and hierarchies.

David: Yes, and there are various contenders for the role of ideological sea. Every expert field I looked into was internally divided; mainstream and heterodox tendencies are just the beginning. For all these internal struggles—or maybe precisely *because* of them—they also all had difficulty opening foundational questions. That's another puzzle that remains to be explored: how foundational issues are kept off the table in so expansive and diverse a set of vocabularies, most all of which claim to have "taken everything into account."

So you know, take UN Security Council reform, not particularly foundational, but, "Oh my God, it would be impossible!" If Security Council reform is always on the table and never undertaken, that does something to the idea that we should get rid of our preoccupation with states, with sovereignty, with self-determination, all of which are pretty recent inventions—or obsessions. They get turned into enduring realities. Far outside the domain of the revisable, however recent their origin and form.

We've both called attention to the relationship between issues at the edge of possibility and what I think of as foundational, but we haven't really explored it other than to note that people have reshuffled the frame before and lots of people coming to study law would like it again to be possible.

Martti: I am constantly asked the question, "How would you reform the world of global governance?" I bet you are, too. And I feel that the prevailing reform debate is most certainly not the answer—tinkering with investment arbitration, say. But going at anything more basic sounds ridiculously utopian. How do things freeze so as to seem "fundamental" and therefore immovable? Surely there's also a difference: for some, the UN is fundamental; for others, free trade. Surely this is—once again—an experiential question: How does the *feeling* of fixedness emerge? How can one make the feeling dilute? A million-dollar question.

For some, issues about territorial sovereignty, self-determination, diplomatic immunity—"classical" questions like that—may seem quite "fundamental." Russia or China, say, or large parts of the Global South. For the EU, nothing outside its internal structure may seem that fundamental. Maybe the feeling is more a projection from one's insecurity than an objective datum about the way the world is. If so, then perhaps it can be addressed in all those ways that make "hot" things turn "cold," and the other way around. Dissolve a taboo, create one.

Take global warming, for instance—surely a question you'd like people to think of as "fundamental." Law treats it now through the old compromise, negotiated among state representatives, framing it as an incident of "sustainable development." The perspectives of ecocide, future generations or the "tipping point" have a hard time pressing against the conventional toolbox, and people who try tend to end up in the margin. Diplomats sometimes draw attention to the way the prohibition of the use of chemical weapons has attained taboo status. It has become somehow "unthinkable" to use them. Is there something to be learned from that? Or does it necessitate a crisis to create a sense of necessity to break conventional resistance?

David: A changing climate may yet yield that kind of crisis. For now, it is striking how the problem has been imagined in the image of the technical and governance machinery brought to bear on it, just as you say. Even thinking of climate change as "global" when we know the causes and consequences will be intensely local, differentiated, distributed. Although many people do see "global warming" as a big deal, the most pressing, intractable of "global problems," I'm thinking of *foundational* in a different sense—the structuring foundations which seem impossible to change even when facing something like global warming. *Foundational* almost as a synonym for "what can't be changed," even while others claim that precisely that will have to change.

Martti: As a question of perception, you mean—a false necessity, as we used to say?

David: Yes. In this sense, "foundations" are in the eye of the beholder. It would be great to understand more fully how intellectual and political forces mobilize around a claim to shift the foundations—from Brexit to Pan-Africanism—and what their destiny is. It is astonishing how effectively challenges claiming to be "foundational" have been metabolized by the way things are. How to make "foundational" legal realities seem open to change? What sorts of intellectual work might shift the balance between those sitting on the foundations and those wishing to alter them?

We've tried a couple of strategies along these lines which could surely be pushed further. Looking to the historical backstory has been one. Take the centrality of "states." Although "states" have been many different things, they've become an oddly compulsory form—you need an airline and art museum, and so forth. If they once seemed "foundational" as the institutional expression of something organic—ethnicity or language or "nation"—all that cultural stuff somehow got left in Europe when sovereignty exploded as the default format for public power. Even in their European heyday, they were as much project as foundation. In the last century or so, instead of the form seeming to arise from the society, searching constantly to intensify its representational veracity, the form descended over it, a construct, an arrangement of public power at some remove from the polity. There is every variety of "state" between these extremes and yet the state is treated as a universal foundation. Perhaps if we could map the legal and cultural relationship between these statehood "styles," their diverse histories, we'd understand their construction and perhaps their alterability. There's also been some good work starting somewhere else and working back to states, relativizing them while starting with cities or corporations or global value chains, and so forth.

Martti: We have indeed tried both strategies; in *To the Uttermost Parts of the Earth* I examined the origins of claims of property to make them seem open and revisable, instead of fundamental.[4] And we have showed how the structures of the "global economy" can be broken into small-scale activities with legal techniques and concepts that seem quite questionable and even random when detached from the veneer of governance in which we meet them. And we have done the same innumerable times to the invitation to commit to the "rule of law" in the first place. Being enchanted by the tools is a process familiar to both of us; but it is much easier to call for disenchantment than to figure out the exact process whereby it can be attained.[5]

You suggest that "culture" might be one direction in which such debates could be pursued; well, maybe. Not just the comparative study of legal cultures, surely, but of the cultural conditions that make the call for more law or legality or the legal form sometimes conservative, even reactionary, sometimes progressive. An earlier generation took on philosophy, and in the 1950s and 1960s US lawyers brought sociological tools to the field. Postmodernism, Marxism, feminism and postcolonialism offer their own perspectives and many seem to think—indeed I have suggested as much—that history might enlighten us of the character and role of international law in the world. But it seems to me that an agreed access point to the fundamentals is lacking, everything is moving.

David: You point to *foundational* in a different and important sense: focusing on the professional tribes and vocabularies that are understood to be asking "foundational" questions.

Claiming your vocabulary is queen of the sciences, the royal road back to basics, is a move—just like claiming your competence is not that, you're just mopping up, implementing. I certainly saw that between economics and law in the history of "development" expertise. There one wouldn't expect to find an "appropriate" vocabulary to touch the foundations, but a contested terrain. Perhaps one way to get at this would be to focus—at various historical moments—on the adjacent discipline that international law was both feeding from and contrasting itself against. Or follow patterns of 'foundation claiming.'

Shall we look at what we had to say about power, theme three?

Martti: Yes, we both made the move in our discussion from a kind of traditional realist notion of power, as great power politics, into what we've called *articulative power,* the power of asserting something as authority and having other people yield to that, which is typically something that lawyers have. A lawyer articulates something as a *true* statement about law, and then other people yield to that because of its very "truth." So that's a really broad understanding of law's power, and I wonder if it's too broad. It still leaves open the question as to the *conditions* within which legal authority emerges as "true" statements about the law are distinguished. Again, performativity appears crucial. But we do not really have a theory about the authority of legal performance, do we?

David: I think the articulation/performance idea goes pretty far, certainly deep into what you're calling *conditions,* which also have to be asserted—at least if one includes things that don't need to be articulated to be articulated. And there's not much difference between norms and facts when they are articulated as reasons. The world-making power to frame, the power of the grammar of international affairs more than the language performed: all those things open the aperture a lot, within the "articulative"/"performative power" framework.

After all, even "great power" practice is pretty articulative. I can imagine someone saying, "There's a great power conflict in the middle of Europe right now and you guys are talking about the power of articulation? I mean, the tanks are back!" Yet, both Russia and the United States are busy drawing lines about what's war, what's not, what's defense, what's offense. What's a country, a nationality, a state.

The idea of war as articulative performance—legalized—that I tried out a while back still has a lot of running room, although I'm sure the idea would have to get refined. Anyway, what we think of as *real power* turns out also to have this *articulative dimension*—I still think one loses more than one gains by imagining some aspect of all that as "real." There's so much more to be figured out about how that "reality effect" is generated, sustained, undermined, how it functions as authority, whom it empowers and subordinates.

Martti: One interesting legal feature in this recent great power conflict in Europe is the discrepancy between the articulations on the Russian side and on the Western side. The Russian texts, speeches by President Putin and the Russian representative in the Security Council, are full of legal articulations that are really weak as forms of professional performance, even ridiculous; whereas on the EU and US side, the law is apparently taken with great seriousness as a complicated mélange of rules and principles regarding the use of force and jurisdictional questions, questions of authority and division of power.

What is one to make of that discrepancy—on the one side, something that a recent blog post called "bullshit" and, on another, what appears as deadly formalist seriousness?[6] Is it possible in a great power crisis such as this also to perform *ironically*—I mean, to have the others yield owing to the demonstration that one simply has no serious regard for their ideas about good behavior and decent language? That can be a powerful performance, especially if one can show that the adversary's formalist seriousness actually hides a deep hypocrisy. It is also a way to put the existing rule-system, relied upon earlier by the adversary, into question. But Russia has not been very efficient in this regard. Beyond occasionally pointing to the Western violations in Iraq, Afghanistan, and elsewhere, it has refrained from asserting the substance of its preferred geopolitics. That may not be so important, however, as most of the Global South seems now to have noticed that something that used to be fixed, may no longer be so.

There is one related question we haven't really broached, which is the relationship between academic articulations of the law, and legal performances in the contexts of "practice." It has been my experience that the relationship is often badly understood, and also that on both sides there is a lot of suspicion. It is a very different thing to perform in these contexts—the standards of excellence vary—but, as the Russian case may demonstrate, also the very significance of one's idea of "excellence" may be contested in another. You noted earlier the interest in seeking to match elite perceptions and cultural legal biases to each other in some way; surely the same interest relates to matching ideas about elite legal training and practice.

David: Nathaniel has also placed irony front and center.[7] It certainly is one of the articulative modes or styles we could study further. It's hard to get a grip on the levels of seriousness which characterize professional work, and the misjudgments or reinterpretations that abound. So, who is being ironic here? I can imagine a Russian diplomat performing on a "global" stage in that spirit, which communicates so effectively that they are anyway *against* all that, that a clever fellow needn't take it as it seems. Didn't you write about the Milosevic trial in this way? Wasn't he also saying "Its all bullshit" in a way, all that professionally serious formal mumbo jumbo about treaties and principles, and so on, when the history of their invocation traces an arc to hypocrisy as much as justice? And couldn't the Russians think the West must be ironic to be so sanctimonious?

Although the Western elites can certainly roll their eyes—perhaps more effective than saying "bullshit"—I do find the liberal foreign policy establishment as bad at hearing irony as their domestic counterparts. When "populists" make outrageous statements, so much seems to be irony but gets parsed as the most serious of comments. Perhaps so also the Russian statements.

You also flag the way articulations vary with role—academy and practice, headquarters and field. That's another open field for investigation. One way in is to think of vulgates—as professional vocabularies expand their reach and user base, you get all these dialects and simplifications—in nongovernmental organization (NGO) advocacy as much as great power statecraft. It would be great to understand how that works, what is enabled and occluded by these internal differences—modes of elegance or professionalism.

And that bleeds into the diversity issue. Let's imagine Russia speaks a slightly different language exceedingly well—the language of *Kultur* against civilization, of organic history against cosmopolitan modernism. Those can certainly come across as outsider "bullshit," but they also have a long tradition within the common language of global legality. So I'm suspicious of the "they're not serious" allegation—a red flag that a part is asserting itself as the hegemonic whole.

Martti: Yes. They are certainly serious as efforts to change the genre and terrain of performance. We shall eventually see about their success.

David: We've talked about the way a distribution of capacities to participate in a hegemonic mode of engagement can make a difference. So, unsurprisingly, many smaller nations don't have enough diplomats to be in all the meetings, let alone to take notes and figure out what's going on in a complicated regulatory discussion at the global level, in which there's a person from Brussels, a person from Washington, DC, and forty-seven lobbyists from each place behind every door. No wonder you get different dialects. But the ever increasing "sophistication" of the lead players is also a dialect which often has exclusion as its raison d'être.

Before we leave this, another thing I think we don't understand that well is *uncertainty* in power. There's this new field, ignorance studies, examining the power of not knowing or asserting a lack of knowledge. Development practitioners have built a whole rule of law promotion industry around the central claim that the "rule of law" eludes definition. So there's a kind of empty core to be filled up with different power maneuvers—that seems like the tip of an "asserted ignorance" iceberg it would be worth exploring.

And then I think we've talked a lot about truth and the idea of speaking truth to power and why that's not really the right frame, but I don't think we have a good sense for *the power of inaccuracy,* the power of facts *that are visibly false,* ironic, or otherwise invented as alternatives to a dominant discourse of *truthiness,* as Jon Stewart used to say. So, I mean there are just a whole bunch of aspects of articulative power that escaped our grasp, up to now, but seem increasingly significant.

Martti: Well, articulative power still has a lot of purchase, so it's not just a turn back to geopolitics and E. H. Carr, but those, too, operate as forms of performance and articulation and have in that sense never really been away. The styles of diplomats and diplomat-lawyers change, just like styles of good advocacy at domestic courts or at the negotiation table. You in the United States have a much better developed sense of the strategic aspects of legal advocacy that is part of the law school training; with us in Europe, the gap between the law school—still often just rules and principles—and the strategic instruction that young lawyers receive in their first day job seems quite overwhelming.

David: That sounds right. Although people also learn the cultural forms in the academy of real life. My students do seem to come preloaded with the ideology of the establishment. I'm not sure where they got it, but they have it. And we're fine-tuning it, but we're not starting from scratch.

But let's go on to our fourth conversation, about differentiation and hegemony—and the hegemony of diversity in its many various forms.

One thing that strikes me is that we took this up in geographic terms—the hegemony of the North Atlantic or Europe or the United States in a world of territorial others. I'm less sure this is the best way to think about the "location" of hegemony or about the terrain of diversity. When we talked about a global elite with a shared technocratic, problem-solving, cosmopolitan sensibility splintered into "functional specializations," hegemony and diversity had a different face. The Hardt and Negri "empire" aimed at this. Arnulf Becker Lorca pressed hard against the idea of "the center" as territorial or North Atlantic rather than being a global production—and equally against "the South" as altogether different, let alone virtuous.

Martti: I hear you pointing to the experience that wherever one looks, the various entities and identities appear to be split among themselves, less homogeneous than we thought, more places of contestation than coherent programs of rulership. Hegemony used to be thought of as an ambiguous alignment of consent and coercion that in the international world was articulated in what Perry Anderson recently called the "political fictions of international law."[8] But I think this ultra-realist view ignores precisely the proliferation of legalities where the "international" no longer serves as a significant jurisdictional marker. My prior reference to "cyberlaw" would be an example. It will live alongside a huge number of other projects whose legal articulation manifests the pattern of consent and coercion typical of hegemony but whose extension is intellectual and epistemological instead of political or geographic.

It will be interesting to see new alliances being formulated between epistemic and geographic heterodoxies and maybe form new constellations, so to speak. This is where the science and technology studies you mentioned earlier have a lot to say—reminding me a little of the interest I had in the 1970s in the philosophy of science that opened such a promising way to critique mainstream social science. And governance may not always be what we may think first. A government at home may sometimes appear as a "domestic" actor with intensely national interests—but equally well as a group of representatives for wholly global interests and forms of knowledge, a kind of local negotiation between functional types of expertise who just happen to meet in some place where there are some resources.

David: And it can appear as a sectarian kleptocratic gang as well. But that reconfiguring of domestic rulers as representatives of a foreign/international agenda is certainly familiar. I do wish we had better paths to get beyond the image of "states"—and therefore national public leadership—as a hinge, even *the* hinge, between an inner and outer world, the waterline of sovereignty on the ship, so to speak. At a minimum it makes it harder to see so many others as that hinge—private powers, economic powers—and to see other hinges, along lines of race or wealth or cultural differentiation, for example.

It also gets in the way of our developing a good picture of how multiple legalities intersect with one another—all that interpenetration the "network" people urged us to see. We may need to push further with that, reconfiguring the multiple worldviews and cultures and legal realities around different axes. I do think global racial differentiation might be one: white supremacy as a line more critical than international/domestic. I think there's a lot of new work in human geography that might be useful; geographers and design people are struggling to picture and understand the arrangements of multiplicity. I bet we could learn something there. And probably from the folks who want to cross the human/everything else line in different ways.

Martti: There's also new work on jurisdiction which I think cuts across human geography and opens up new ways to trace the legal channeling of hegemony—the many ways private law allocates powers, for example. And then hegemony floats more of less invisibly from one type of institution and its associated governance structure to another; ideology does all kinds of work here—now it's Bretton Woods neoliberalism, now EU regulations, or China's Belt and Road, that are assumed to be where the world is "really" ruled. And yet, I would not give up the critical sense that what rules is a structure binding those purported "rulers" no less than everyone else. The seventeenth-century adage that "Princes rule people, but interest rules princes" remains valid; and the perception of "interest" if often conditioned by law.

David: The last point is key; "interest" is both a legal institution and an interpretive or articulative practice. The commentariat is always associating hegemony with a political geography—Britain, the United States, China, each getting a century, that kind of story. Posing questions like "Is the dollar's dominance at an end?" We have been trying to get away from that—the hegemony of law as a global professional grammar in the style of American legal thought might have a lot or very little to do with the "interests" of "the United States" if we even had a good way of figuring out what those were other than in the terms of that vocabulary.

But there's probably some relation—big powers do try to reconfigure the global institutional and legal infrastructure in their image, so all roads lead to Rome. For me, that's pretty unexplored terrain. What is "the dollar's dominance" as a legal institution—as a hegemony, detached from "the United States" if tethered to the Fed, Citibank, and a whole network of central bank reserves, trading practices, liquidity assessments, and so forth? And if what is hegemonic now lacks a geographical center, how to think about that, the powers and subordinations enabled, solidified.

What the disruptive powers are could also bear further study. For "international law" you can think about some classic cases—the Soviets, the Nazis, the anticolonial struggles. How do they become positions within the field? How much are they back-formations of the hegemony they oppose? Those dynamics are equally at play between the global technocracy of elite rule and all the forces that get labeled "populist." What other disruptive frameworks were launched? I'm thinking of Adom Getachew's terrific study of Pan-Africanism and Black nationalism.[9] "Outside" is less the appropriate metaphor than alternative, disruptive, resistant.

Martti: The outside might for example be defined as those who just "do not know," the people colloquially addressed as *populists,* the recent challengers of the cultural and professional elites. Here the politics of knowledge reveals itself as precisely such; but one can be "ignorant" in many different ways, including in appearing to possess a wrong kind of knowledge or by drawing, from shared knowledge, the wrong kinds of conclusions. I still think the political maneuver that stresses the corruption of the technological classes or the systems of knowledge production behind ruling elites tends to have this self-undermining quality. Once the "ignorant" outsiders pull themselves together and begin to rule, it does not take long before they are deradicalized and sucked into the cultural and epistemic systems.

David: *Populist* is a name hegemony gives its challengers, with all its associations, including the impossibility of it surviving as an alternative universalism or rulership capability. When it comes into power, it becomes a difference within—so, "authoritarianism" or "capitalism with Chinese characteristics." But it would be surprising if the "outside" were one thing, a kind of parallel coherence rather than a series of struggles over the question of whether there was a parallel coherence.

If we think about diversity as hegemony's current form, it would be great to know more about *which* diversity, structured as hegemony *in what way*? The pluralism of professional styles—each with a functional home, for example, contesting at the boundaries—is different from the pluralism of "equal" nation-states or "identities" like gender, race, or nationality. I have a sense for how this works in the United States. Are there parallels elsewhere, in China or Russia—or Europe, for that matter? Differences within hegemony? Alternative hegemonies waiting to be born?

Martti: What do you mean *parallel,* exactly, when you say that? How could it be parallel?

David: It might be that elites in China who deal with law in global affairs have a relationship with Chinese history, Chinese legal thought, and so forth, that is like the relation of American globalists to American legal thought, American history. Or maybe that's not how it is. Perhaps in China it's more German legal thought nailed onto various national political or historical traumas and preoccupations. Or perhaps the elite relationship to all this is less continuous with their professional identities than in our worlds; people seem to imagine Chinese international lawyers as part of a global "invisible college" more cosmopolitan than Chinese, distinct in a way no one would expect an American or European international lawyer to be. I don't know. Again, I'm thinking back on the discussions we've had about Becker Lorca's work on the situation of semiperipheral intellectuals. He draws them together as having a lot of parallels in their relationship to hegemonic thinking, and he also says they're situated in a national situation, and I wonder if that invocation of a common dynamic is enough to get a grip on the range of diverse positions that are out there.

Martti: This reminds me of Outi Korhonen's study of the cosmopolitan nationalism of late nineteenth-century Finnish lawyers as they were lobbying for Finland's independence, and especially the cultural and historical assumptions that made those two discourses—the international and the domestic—seem so utterly compatible.[10]

David: The other thing I would like to understand better is the way diversity is itself a hegemonic idea. I've been claiming that and I see it in contemporary American society certainly, where "diversity" is the ideology of the established powers, the "united colors of Benetton" as a translation of the national "e pluribus unum." So for U.S. elite consciousness, management of diversity is central—a particular diversity, managed in particular ways—and if you have trouble with this, you are outside in a way that is severely stigmatized. There seems to be an international parallel, not only in terms of "national identity" which everyone must have—see the preoccupation with statelessness—but probably also with other diversities, defined and managed in various ways.

In global terms, how do inequality and subordination disappear beneath diversity as a hegemonic managerial ideology? Or at least take a particular form—as the product, say, of malice/bias rather than structure/history, that kind of thing? So, cosmopolitanism has a particular form, insists upon itself in a particular way. I think we could get further figuring this out for global cosmopolitan practices.

Martti: I like your expression "hegemony of diversity"; people in that position do not usually think of themselves as hegemonic at all! But this raises the hard problem of how to deal with the dissonance—if that is what it is—between the simultaneous pursuits of diversity *and* equality. Law seems here quite central. As a system of "rules" it seeks equality. But its imposition over people in a situation of diversity creates inequality that then needs to be corrected casuistically—something that requires trust in the correcting institution. But trust cannot be taken for granted, as shown by the initial effort to govern by rules instead of just mandating ruling institutions to seek "good" solutions. Who decides when diverse treatment involves respect, and when inequality? If it is true, as we said earlier, that diversity is also a little bit in the eye of the beholder, then it becomes an even more contested terrain.

One person's diversity is surely another's chaos; where one feels completely capable of managing functional difference, another may feel utterly powerless and confused. Diversity may sometimes be performed as a gesture of liberal tolerance and generosity but experienced as hypocritical and paternalistic. It sometimes seems to me that this is the story of decolonization: as sovereignty traveled to the south, we celebrated the resulting diversity of UN membership—while at the same time making sure that acquired rights were protected by an investment regime those countries had to subscribe to. How diversity not only coexists with but produces exclusion is certainly worthy of another look.

But shall we move on?

David: We should. *Our fifth theme was history: legal history as criticism or critique in the international field.*

Lots of open questions here. You're more the historian, writing these comprehensive accounts, while I've been more a dabbler, telling bits of history to open questions rather than resolve them. But, either way, one could imagine a lot of new critical projects.

We talked a lot about the history of the present, so where does that start now? As you asked a moment ago, what has been the ideological background for today's arrangements? We also talked about *ruptures*—are we at one now? What does it mean now to assert that this is one? What's the power project there?

I've been thinking a lot about nostalgia for what people now call *the postwar order*—and the excitement that it might be back now that Russia has invaded Ukraine. It reminds me of the Cold War, which always seemed to be happening in another time. Even when I was in elementary school in the 1960s, the Cold War in the sense of the Cuban Missile Crisis or the Berlin Crisis was already over. And then it wasn't, and then it was, and so on. And now we look back and it was a consistent thing from the late 1940s until 1989—but *was* it over at that point? It doesn't seem Russian elites thought so—or they've come to think of what happened as an unfortunate continuation.

Martti: That international legal history may be told by producing different kinds of continuity or rupture highlights its performative nature. I mean, we in the North may think of the past seventy years in terms of the Cold War and what came thereafter, but I suppose from India or Algeria those years are seen differently, perhaps being about self-determination or incipient statehood, a realignment of politics with religion. In many recent histories the rise and fall of the New International Economic Order is presented as way more significant than situating Pershing missiles in West Germany. Europeans feel the war in Ukraine as a huge historical milestone—but countries representing over half of the world population abstained from critiquing Russia in the UN. What kind of history might join the war in Ukraine with the one in Ethiopia/Tigray?

Is present global hegemony a continuation of colonialism or something entirely different? Are capitalism or race appropriate categories to understand events in the recent past? I am very interested in the recent burst of new histories that ask such questions, or ones that focus on gendered framings of relations of political power, as in "the state body." But whose body is it?[11] But I also see that beyond those specific concerns, these histories still often operate with rather conventional concepts and periodizations; renewal of history writing is not in itself or necessarily a challenge to existing disciplines or their internal hegemonies.

As for the Cold War—that theme from the North Atlantic—I would say our experience in Europe was more concretely attached to everyday experience. Elites did feel constrained about what could be done; the iron curtain decisively framed the conversations over European integration and defense—both also intensely legal-institutional questions. But the Cold War also penetrated the political and cultural consciousness of people quite significantly, framing everything from tastes in music to friendships.

Cold War history also has an awkward relationship to *global* history, the kinds of things that took place within the UN or the trade and development worlds. Each of those tend to construct their history quite independently of the others, with different mileposts and continuities. The critical question, I think, is how some of these framings attain the status of a global vernacular while others remain the preserve of niche experts.

David: One question that I have. We have studied various historical figures somehow as organic Gramscian intellectuals of their class, of an international elite, whether professional or bureaucratic or cultural. Where would you start today to study the organic intellectuals of the global order? Who would you study?

Martti: From this present moment?

David: Now—or even from twenty years ago. I mean, I think it was reasonable to interpret your men of 1873 or my postwar legal policy people as being either representative of or participating in an elite consensus, for which they exhibited the legal form. If we were to do a history of the last twenty years, would it be a sociological study of corporate lawyers in London and, I don't know, government officials in Sydney, or targeting specialists in the air force? Or what? Certainly not International Court of Justice judges or international law professors.

Martti: In my lectures on the postwar era I have used Wolfgang Friedmann, and especially the contrast he made between the law of coexistence and law of cooperation, as an organic intellectual in the way you suggest, epitomizing the post–gentle civilizing generation.[12] And I have used our common friend, Tom Franck, as someone providing expression to the liberal institutionalism of the 1990s—his works *The Power of Legitimacy among Nations* and *The Empowered Self* are, I think, the most coherent expression on how the (leftist) liberal world saw the possibilities of the post–Cold War era.[13] Then there are Mohammed Bedjaoui and maybe Georges Abi-Saab, who may be cited as organic intellectuals on the side of the more activist part of the Global South. And who would epitomize the present moment—the moment of war, growing global inequality, and climate change? Hard to say.

David: Those were great choices for "postwar international law," and they thought they were in conversation with one another, thought they were "thought leaders" in today's terms, for a wider group with a place in established power. In this, they were like your men of 1873—I think of them as developing the wisdom of a particular tribe within a ruling class. For the "international law" field in the North Atlantic these were the guys, the reference points for others, the major positions and innovations.

One could extend the list in a variety of directions, but we know what it means to add Henkin or Crawford or Pellet—or Myres McDougal or some of his followers, even Richard Falk, with a quite different political orientation. I'm less sure Bedjaoui or Abi-Saab were "organic intellectuals" of "the South," although they often presented themselves that way—they were more the Tom Francks or René-Jean Dupuys of their world. More a subdivision of the global legal intelligentsia, don't you think?

If you started out today, however, I don't think you could identify the players that easily—nor, if you could, would they be that significant in the production of global legal thought. Students looking for a window on establishment thought are more readily drawn to the texts produced by leading bureaucracies—World Bank reports, say—or advocacy documents produced by leading NGOs. If you found those artifacts after a Vesuvius obliterated our world, you could puzzle something out about rulership, certainly.

Your "practicing lawyers" may be the thought leaders of the moment. Next month I'm giving the Lloyd Cutler Lecture at the American Academy in Berlin. Lloyd Cutler was a leading lawyer in the Washington legal establishment.

Martti: Never heard of him.

David: He advised presidents and had every possible public role, represented every major corporation—recognized as a "lion of the legal establishment." He wasn't an international lawyer, but I could imagine substituting someone like him for Wolfgang Friedmann if one had a sufficient archive of his thought and practice to work with.

While we're on history, it would be great to get a better sense for the history of the *ethical* as it has been woven in and out of legal thought and practice. I mean, you have described the historical warp and woof of utopian and realist thinking. I've written about the relationship between the ethical and the pragmatic in the human rights and other humanitarian fields. But I don't think we have a good sense of the ups and downs of ethical self-consciousness as a power dynamic. So when is it a powerful move to wear one's ethics on one's sleeve, and when does it just make you look ridiculous? How does that intersect with less ethically saturated styles?

Martti: In *Of War and Law* you demonstrate how ethical, strategic, religious, and policy vocabularies have at different times entered in and exited from the laws of armed conflict, or "humanitarian law."[14] The shifts in the very name of the field (laws of war/laws of armed conflict/humanitarian law) testify to historical changes in perspective and professional style. But I suppose it would be, above all, interesting to see how the different versions of the "ethical" might have assisted in the formation of competent legal performances. My hunch is that such a study would also demonstrate the fluidity of the boundary between ethics and "policy" and "economics."

I have been disappointed at how far the study of the role of the ethical in law has been monopolized by theorists of the analytical and Anglo variety and how constrained their analyses have been to iconic names such as Locke and Kant and Smith. The field has been dominated by normative studies on issues such as the contractual or noncontractual basis of the international society, it's cosmopolitan or noncosmopolitan character, and the endless pursuit of the "reflective equilibrium." Interesting as some of this work is, it contributes very little to understanding legal work or the transformations in the competence of the lawyer. Its frequent focus on minuscule nuances in iconic texts leaves little room for wider critical engagement.

David: I'm more interested in the history of ethics as authority rather than that inside-the-academy discussion of what ethics is/should be. Those guys may be "thought leaders" for the professional world of philosophy, but in American law, at least, the influence of "theories" developed in the hothouses of philosophical reflection is hard to find. I mean, the society is drenched in some version of Locke or Smith that people learned in high school, but that's also a different matter. People assert things in an ethical style—a style that ebbs and flows, has characteristic responses and reflexes. What is the intellectual history of that?

Martti: I am not thinking about the academy, either, but of the oscillation between the rhetoric of moral principle and Realpolitik, and other cognate idioms, as parts of competent lawyering. My sense is that what you call the "ethical style" in law would be rapidly mapped, at least for the twentieth century, and that the account you give of the emergence of an "ethical moment" in *Of War and Law* could be repeated in most other professional fields as well. I am sure it can be linked with the ebb and flow of formalist and antiformalist styles that again express variations in institutional cohesion and hegemonic strength. This might also involve studying the way it is sometimes the "ethical," sometimes the "political" or the "economic" style, that is used to assist or undermine legal performances. But as part of the practice of governance, I find the turn to the ethical in contemporary law unhelpful and question begging. Maybe it's just my bias against the analytical style, its overemphasis on a certain type of rationality that in practice often sounds a little platitudinous, a kind of testimony of poverty on the part of the lawyer.

David: There is saying "Rawls said this is the way to solve the trolley problem and so we should do *X*," which probably happens, but not that often. But then there is all the moral self-confidence—hubris, even—of Western talk of "war crimes" in Ukraine. I don't mean to invoke ethics as if it was some other domain, like "the political" that would save us from the simplifications of our tawdry legal speech, but rather that in the exercise of expert power and articulative authority there's the practice of ethically sodden legal assertions.

Perhaps what I have in mind is a contemporary parallel to your study of theology's rise and fall as a vocabulary of legal imagination. I don't think we have a good sense for the discursive role of ethical commitment in global legal activity.

But let's turn to our last conversation, which was about political economy and law in global affairs.

The "How did things become so unequal?" question has changed the appetite for critical engagements with global legality. As I recall our conversation, we were pretty tentative—more putting markers on the table for how inquiry might be undertaken than reporting what we'd found—although we used your recent book, I think, as a kind of template to begin with.

Martti: I agree, it's a research agenda more than a set of positions to take. I also find the notion of political economy quite obscure; surely there is no such thing as "economy" that would not be "political." That idea came up with the marginalists in the late nineteenth century, the Austrian school, and persists in what people now call neoliberalism—in other words, a series of anything but unpolitical propositions. In the same way, I argue in *To the Uttermost Parts of the Earth,* there is no economy that would also not be "legal." To the extent that one operates with contracts and property rights—with their countless derivations and permutations—one is moving in a world that is legal through and through. But I don't think we have a good history of economic thought that would possess this awareness; that political economy is also about ideas concerning the character and extent of ownership rights, the enforcement of different types of contracts, and the jurisdiction of public powers. I suppose I have occasionally been tempted by the proposition that, for most of the time, what passes as political economy is simply a particular style of operating with legal concepts and institutions, with some employment of mathematical techniques.

David: I agree with that. I do think taking apart economic notions to identify their legal foundations is a good way to begin. Things that economists take as facts, like credit, labor, and so forth, turn out to be legal institutions. Just putting law back in the story—as an intellectual frame, a nuts-and-bolts structure, a vocabulary through which economic activity is undertaken—would be important, given the way law disappears in the economic literature. I think we mentioned Chris Desan and Katherina Pistor's recent books along these lines.[15]

In order to get at *law in political economy* you have to do two things that are unusual. One is put property front and center—there's a "sovereignty gets all the credit, but property does all the work" problem to overcome. And then you have to break down the universalist impulse so predominant in thinking about law in global affairs to talk about winners and losers on the political and economic sides. So, trade as domination, not bargain; statehood as structured inequality rather than the reverse, and so on. You have to put hierarchies rather than ordered arrangements at the center of the story; that's a dramatic shift in how one thinks about law in global affairs.

So I think that's partly why we're really at the beginning: doing this kind of work requires more understanding of economics and the legal foundations of economics, more understanding of the significance of private law and property in the global situation. And a real resistance to the universalizing order-seeking missile that is legal thought.

Martti: Absolutely. One of my objectives in *To the Uttermost Parts of the Earth* was to bring to the surface the property relations that underlay—were actually often quite visible in—what lawyers have usually thought in terms of sovereignty, public law, diplomacy, and war. It is striking that the term *dominium* was once equally applicable to relations of power under arrangements we would now call private and public. There would be much more terrain to cover. For example, by far the largest part of what goes by the name of the history of the laws of war is actually about protecting particular types of property. Scratch the surface of sovereignty and you'll find a more or less complex network of contract and property relations that make sovereign rule possible and direct it toward specific objectives. And the other way around. Much of international policy is made possible by laws about taxation, but tax laws rarely find themselves in accounts of international legal history. It would be good to remember that the history of human rights is really a history of property—that is to say, of revolt against taxation.

David: Well, I guess—despite all our best efforts—the imaginative framing that we've been criticizing remains pretty powerful. You know, the world is organized around territorial nations with a global something on top; politics is a national thing and economics is a global thing, and politics is more or less a vertical thing and economics is more or less a horizontal thing. All these background ideas get in the way of understanding how law structures global political economy, so there's a long way to go.

Martti: Yes. And the world you just described, that description, is such a recent way to think about the world! Born in Germany in the nineteenth century. Where did other ideas go? I mean, for example, ideas such as a global commercial order to replace the British Atlantic empire, proposed in the late eighteenth century, or the idea of a global civil society situated between individual rights and statehood in the aftermath of the 1848 revolutions? It is very hard to see how the received legal toolbox could possibly deal with exorbitant global inequality, climate crisis, depletion of natural resources, and violence in its myriad forms. The tools we have are the ones that every day continue articulating that world into existence. The public diplomacy of states and the global enforcement of property claims—surely something cleverer is needed to think about the persistence of the human world.

David: We're reaching the end. I was right that it's hard to see what one doesn't see! We've, anyway, touched on things we are curious about. Probably we've missed more of what we've missed than we've seen—all those unknown unknowns. Nevertheless, one thing that has struck me in all these conversations is how uncertain and tentative our work has been—how many open questions there are and things that remain unclear. Not to mention that the terrain keeps shifting, so criticisms that may have hit their mark once might have less purchase now. Or more—one can always hope!

Martti: Yes. History shows that conventional frames, however steady they may have seemed, have collapsed, making new things visible. Knowing turns into ignorance, and some new performance, some new frame, will begin to impress. I think we've used just a fraction of law's resources, and critique will have to continue trying to open up that unused bit.

David: This has been a lot of fun. I'm going to miss these conversations—perhaps one day we'll have a few more and imagine another volume into being. One last coffee before we sign off?

Martti: Sure.

Notes

1. Karen Engle and Dan Danielsen (eds.), *After Identity: A Reader in Law and Culture* (New York: Routledge, 1995).

2. See Koskenniemi, "'Faith, Identity, and the Killing of the Innocent'"; and Kennedy, "The *Nuclear Weapons* Case."

3. Nathaniel Berman, "Legalizing Jerusalem, or, Of Law, Fantasy and Faith," 45 *Catholic University Law Review* 823 (1996); Nathaniel Berman, *Passion and Ambivalence: Colonialism, Nationalism, and International Law* (The Hague: Brill, 2011).

4. Koskenniemi, *To the Uttermost Parts of the Earth.*

5. Koskenniemi, "Enchanted by the Tools?"

6. Fuad Zarbiyev, "Of Bullshit, Lies and 'Demonstrably Rubbish' Justifications in International Law," *Völkerrechtsblog* (blog), March 18, 2022, https://voelkerrechtsblog.org/of-bullshit-lies-and-demonstrably-rubbish-justifications-in-international-law/.

7. Nathaniel Berman, "Power and Irony, or, International Law after the *Après-Guerre*," in *Le droit international vu par une generation de jurists* (Emmanuelle Jouannet, Hèléne Ruiz Fabri, and Jean-Marc Sorel, eds., Paris: UMR de Droit Comparé, 2007).

8. Perry Anderson, *The H-Word: The Peripateia of Hegemony* (London: Verso, 2017), 181.

9. Adom Getachew, *Worldmaking after Empire: The Rise and Fall of Self-Determination* (Princeton, NJ: Princeton University Press, 2019).

10. Outi Korhonen, *International Law Situated: An Analysis of the Lawyer's Stance towards History, Culture and Community* (The Hague: Kluwer Law International, 2000).

11. See Charlotte Epstein, *Birth of the State: The Place of the Body in Crafting Modern Politics* (Oxford: Oxford University Press, 2021).

12. Wolfgang Friedmann, *The Changing Structure of International Law* (London: Steven and Sons, 1964).

13. Thomas M. Franck, *The Power of Legitimacy among Nations* (New York: Oxford University Press, 1990); Thomas M. Franck, *The Empowered Self: Law and Society in an Age of Individualism* (New York: Oxford University Press, [1999] 2004).

14. Kennedy, *Of War and Law.*

15. Chris Desan, *Making Money: Coin, Currency, and the Coming of Capitalism* (Oxford: Oxford University Press, 2015); Katharina Pistor, *The Code of Capital: How the Law Creates Wealth and Inequality* (Princeton, NJ: Princeton University Press, 2020).

Authors' Works Cited

David Kennedy

"Autumn Weekends: An Essay on Law and Everyday Life." In *Law and Everyday Life* 191. Austin Sarat and Thomas R. Kearns, eds. Ann Arbor: University of Michigan Press, 1993.

Book review of Louis Henkin, *How Nations Behave*. 21 *Harvard International Law Journal* 301 (1980).

"The Context for Context: International Legal History in Struggle." In *History, Politics, Law: Thinking through the International* 69. Annabel Brett, Megan Donaldson, and Martti Koskenniemi, eds. Cambridge: Cambridge University Press, 2022.

"Critical Theory, Structuralism and Contemporary Legal Scholarship." 21 *New England Law Review* 209 (1986).

The Dark Sides of Virtue: Reassessing International Humanitarianism. Princeton, NJ: Princeton University Press, 2004.

"The Disciplines of International Law and Policy." 12 *Leiden Journal of International Law* 9 (1999).

"The International Human Rights Movement: Part of the Problem?" 3 *European Human Rights Law Review* 245 (2001).

International Legal Structures. Baden-Baden, Germany: Nomos, 1987.

"International Refugee Protection." 8 *Human Rights Quarterly* 1 (1986).

"The International Style in Postwar Law and Policy." 1 *Utah Law Review* 7 (1994).

"Law and the Political Economy of the World." 26 *Leiden Journal of International Law* 7 (2013).

"Law in Global Political Economy: Now You See It, Now You Don't." In *The Law of Political Economy: Transformation in Function of Law* 127. Poul F. Kjaer, ed. Cambridge: Cambridge University Press, 2020.

"The Methods and Politics of Comparative Law." In *Comparative Legal Studies: Traditions and Transitions* 345–433. Pierre Legrand and Roderick Munday, eds. Cambridge: Cambridge University Press 2003.

"The Move to Institutions." 8 *Cardozo Law Review* 841 (1987).

"New Approaches to Comparative Law: Comparativism and International Governance." 2 *Utah Law Review* 545 (1997).

"A New World Order: Yesterday, Today and Tomorrow." 4 *Transnational Law and Contemporary Problems* 330 (1994).

"The Nuclear Weapons Case." In *International Law, the International Court of Justice and Nuclear Weapons* 462. Laurence Boiusson de Chazournes and Philippe Sands, eds. Cambridge: Cambridge University Press, 1999.

Of War and Law. Princeton, NJ: Princeton University Press, 2006.

"One, Two, Three, Many Legal Orders: Legal Pluralism and the Cosmopolitan Dream." 31 *New York University Review of Law and Social Change* 641 (2007).

"Primitive Legal Scholarship." 27 *Harvard International Law Journal* 1 (1986).

"Receiving the International." 10 *Connecticut Journal of International Law* 1 (1994).

The Rights of Spring: A Memoir of Innocence Abroad. Princeton, NJ: Princeton University Press, 2009.

"The 'Rule of Law,' Political Choices, and Development Common Sense." In *The New Law and Economic Development: A Critical Appraisal* 96. David M. Trubek and Alvaro Santos, eds. New York: Cambridge University Press, 2006.

"Spring Break." 63 *Texas Law Review* 1337 (1985).

"Theses about International Law Discourse." 23 *German Yearbook of International Law* 353 (1980).

"Tom Franck and the Manhattan School." 35 *New York University Journal of International Law and Politics* 397 (2003).

"The Turn to Interpretation." 58 *Southern California Law Review* 251 (1985).

"Turning to Market Democracy: A Tale of Two Architectures." 32 *Harvard International Law Journal* 373 (1991).

"The Twentieth-Century Discipline of International Law in the United States." In *Looking Back at Law's Century* 386. Austin Sarat, Bryant Garth, and Robert A. Kagan, eds. Ithaca, NY: Cornell University Press, 2002.

"When Renewal Repeats: Thinking against the Box." 32 *New York University Journal of International Law and Politics* 335 (2000).

A World of Struggle: How Power, Law and Expertise Shape Global Political Economy. Princeton, NJ: Princeton University Press, (2016) 2018.

With William W. Fisher III (coeditors)

The Canon of American Legal Thought. Princeton, NJ: Princeton University Press, 2006.

Martti Koskenniemi

"Between Commitment and Cynicism: Outline for a Theory of International Law as Practice." In *Collection of Essays by Legal Advisers of States, Legal Advisers of International Organizations and Practitioners in the field of International Law* 495. New York: United Nations, 1999.

"Between Coordination and Constitution: International Law as a German Discipline." 15 *Redescriptions: Yearbook of Political Thought and Conceptual History and Feminist Theory* 45 (2011).

"Between Impunity and Show Trials." 6 *Max Planck Yearbook for United Nations Law* 1 (2002).

"Constitutionalism as Mindset: Reflections on Kantian Themes about International Law and Globalization." 8 *Theoretical Inquiries in Law* 9 (2007).

"Enchanted by the Tools? An Enlightenment Perspective; Twenty-First Annual Grotius Lecture, American Society of International Law." 35 *American University International Law Review* 397 (2020).

"'Faith, Identity, and the Killing of the Innocent': International Lawyers and Nuclear Weapons." 10 *Leiden Journal of International Law* 137 (1997).

From Apology to Utopia: The Structure of International Legal Argument. Cambridge: Cambridge University Press, (1989) 2005.

The Gentle Civilizer of Nations: The Rise and Fall of International Law, 1870–1960. Cambridge: Cambridge University Press, 2002.

"Hegemonic Regimes." In *Regime Interaction in International Law: Facing Fragmentation* 305. Margaret A. Young, ed. Cambridge: Cambridge University Press, 2011.

"A History of International Law Histories." In *The Oxford Handbook of the History of International Law* 943. Bardo Fassbender and Anne Peters, eds. Oxford: Oxford University Press, 2012.

International Law and the Far Right: Reflections of Law and Cynicism; Fourth Annual T. M. C. Asser Lecture. The Hague: T. M. C. Asser Press, 2019.

"Lauterpacht: The Victorian Tradition in International Law." 8 *European Journal of International Law* 215 (1997).

"Miserable Comforters: International Relations as a New Natural Law." 15 *European Journal of International Relations* 395 (2009).

The Politics of International Law. Oxford: Hart, 2011.

"Rights and the Bourgeois Revolution: The Rise of Political Economy." In *The Cambridge History of Rights.* Vol. 4, *The Eighteenth and Nineteenth Centuries.* Jennifer Pitts and Dan Edelstein, eds. Cambridge: Cambridge University Press, forthcoming.

To the Uttermost Parts of the Earth: Legal Imagination and International Power 1300–1870. Cambridge: Cambridge University Press, 2021.

What Use for Sovereignty Today?" 1 *Asian Journal of International Law* 61 (2011).

"The Wonderful Artificiality of States." 88 *Proceedings of the American Society of International Law* 22 (1994).

With Ville Kari

"A More Elevated Patriotism: The Emergence of International and Comparative Law (Nineteenth Century)." In *The Oxford Handbook of European Legal History* 975. Heikki Pihlajamäki, Markus Dubber, and Mark Godfrey, eds.. Oxford: Oxford University Press, 2018.